MASTERPIECES

MUSEUM OF FINE ARTS BUDAPEST

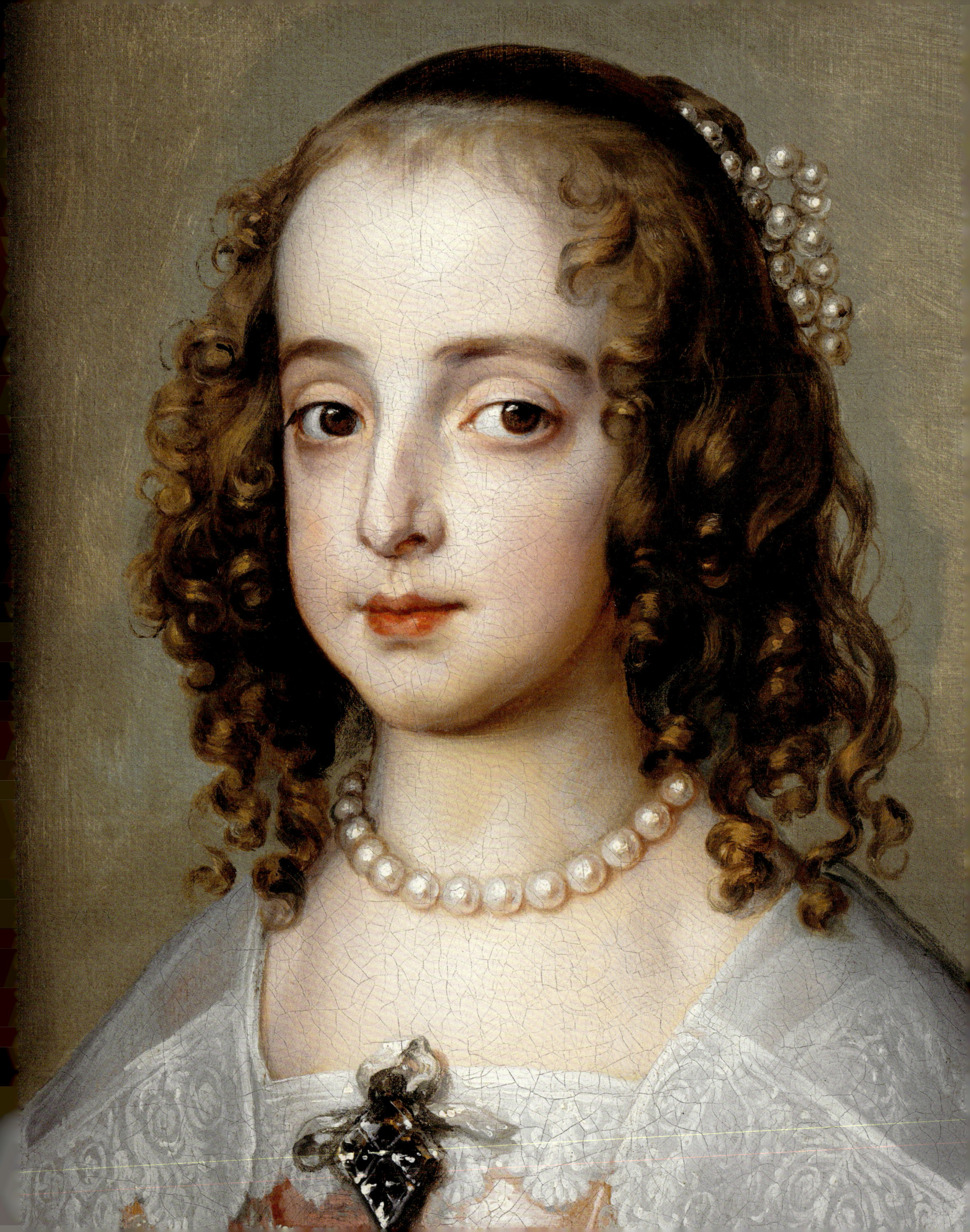

MASTERPIECES

MUSEUM OF FINE ARTS BUDAPEST

Museum of Fine Arts Budapest
2019

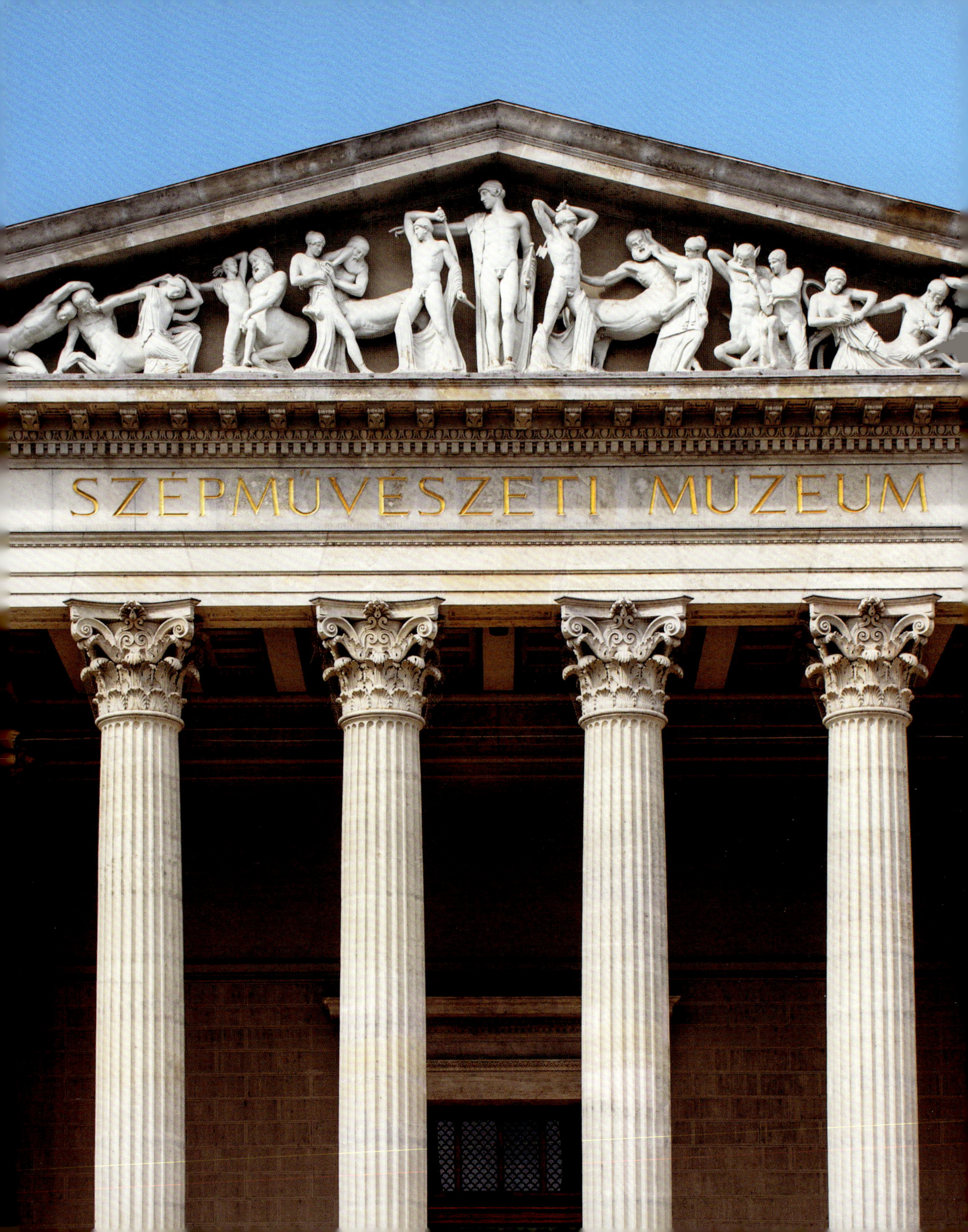
SZÉPMŰVÉSZETI MÚZEUM

The building of the Museum of Fine Arts is one of the prime jewels in Heroes' Square, the magnificent square that crowns Budapest's great avenue: this prominent location also serves to indicate the imposing role it has played in Hungary's cultural life. Its creation in 1896 was one of the most significant of the major investments aimed to demonstrate the dynamic development of the country which, on the millennium of its foundation as a state, had moved from being a dominion of Austria to being a partner state of equal rank. The purpose of the new museum was to provide a comprehensive view of the history of the visual arts, thereby also fostering the development of art in Hungary.

What the museum preserves is apparently unchanging, indeed, ideally it should be eternally settled, because the treasures entrusted to us must be passed down without loss from generation to generation. But the very reason we guard the masterpieces so jealously is just because they are not merely the documents of a bygone age. It is our belief that the pinnacles of the history of artistic achievement preserved in the museum convey novel messages to each generation, with relevance to the present day. And as the world changes and always sees something different in the masterpieces, we too have the task of reinterpreting them over and again, of exploring the messages they convey for today.

The small album you are holding gives a taste of the finest pieces in the collections of the Budapest Museum of Fine Arts. From the ocean we have scooped up a few drops of water in which something of the whole is reflected. This volume is a kind of souvenir, and no substitute for perusing the rooms of the museum in person, yet it can help us, later at home, to recollect this world, which (we believe) is immensely rich. It captures the impression of a moment, and inspires us to return at a different moment, with different eyes, discovering new aspects.

DR. LÁSZLÓ BAÁN
DIRECTOR-GENERAL

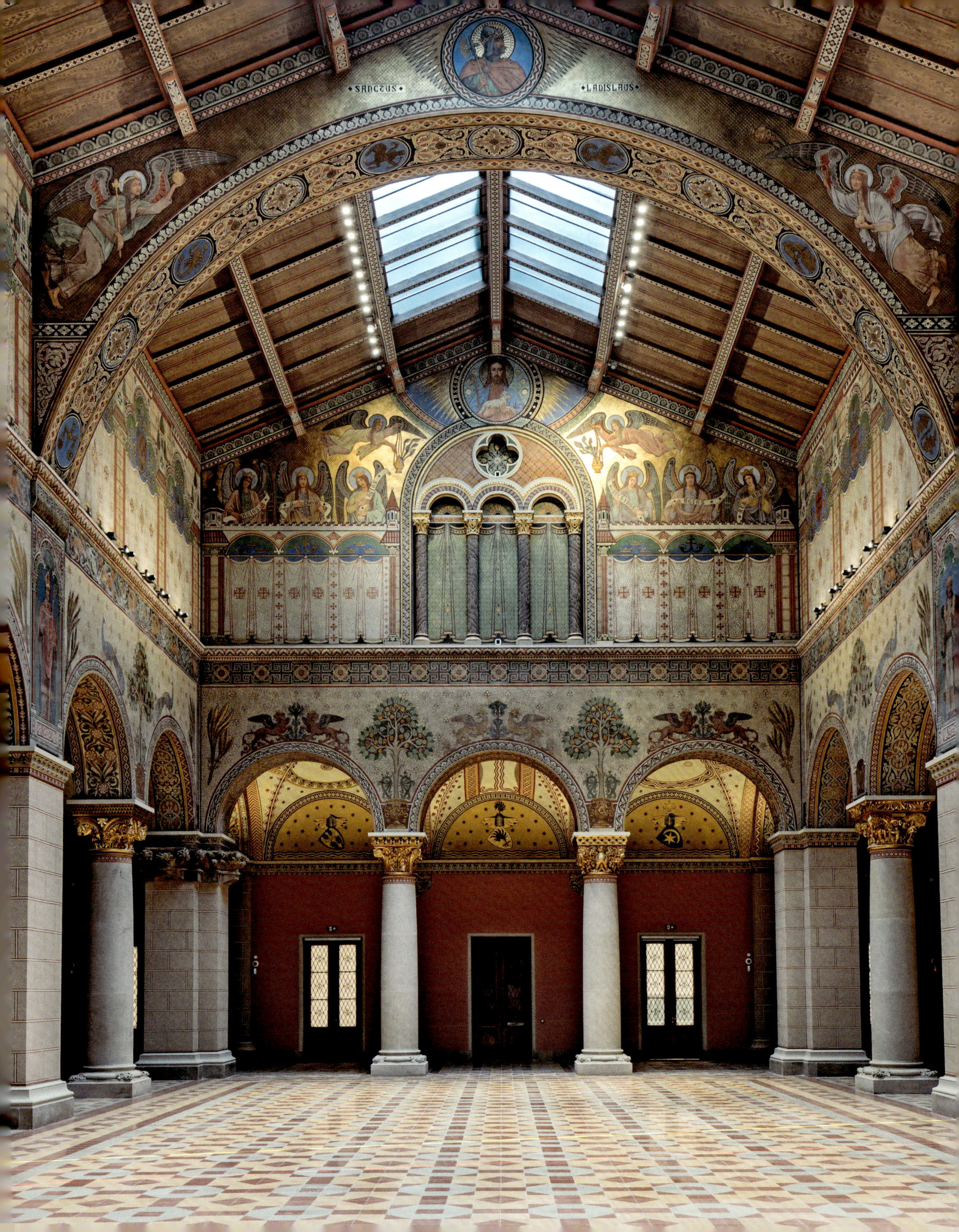

•SANCTUS•
•LADISLAUS•

The museum as an institution is a characteristic product of nineteenth-century Europe. It is begotten of the idea that the world can and should be perceived, and the path to this cognition is to explore every pebble, every atom of which it is made, to describe them and classify them each. Once we have classified and arranged the trees, from them emerges the forest: from the great map of their similarities and differences in minute details, their relation to one another, unfolds the general order of the world. The reasons and causes of processes and changes, and ulti- mately the driving forces of the universe, manifest themselves. And once we know and understand the world, then in possession of this knowledge we can shape it in our own image. This was an age that desired to construct the new and modern, not by repealing the past, but as an organic continuation of historical development, as a synthesis of the most excellent of past achievements. Consequently there was a general belief that the key to the creation of great works was the study and understanding of the works of their predecessors – in other words, the museum. And yet there are few large museums in the world that reflect this approach as clearly as the Budapest Museum of Fine Arts. The majority of important public art collections grew out of private collections. And private collectors usually have very different criteria to museums. A private collector has every right to be biased, to purchase pieces that are close to his personal character and taste, that move him.

The basis for many large national collections in the world is given by the treas- ures of the country's ruling dynasty. Such collections, though not quite as subjective in nature as a private collection, are also born from quite a different motivation to that of a museum. For centuries their function was official representation, in other words to proclaim the greatness, the refined erudition, and wealth of the owners.

Neither private nor dynastic collections were inspired primarily by the thirst for learning, for encyclopaedic knowledge, but rather by the desire to take delight and entertain. But the genesis of the Museum of Fine Arts was different, and this is precisely what gives it its remarkable character. The brief yet fortuitous meeting of an extraordinary moment in history and an extraordinary personality fashioned this cornerstone of Hungarian national culture, and defines its image to this day.

The Museum of Fine Arts is the work of Károly Pulszky (1853–1899). His fa- ther Ferenc Pulszky (later director of the Hungarian National Museum) was forced to emigrate after the failed War of Independence of 1848–49. His son was born and brought up in London, where he saw how the museums became the supreme symbols of Britain's status as a world power and the leaven of national pride. In Pulszky's character a first-class scholar was combined with the boundless ambi- tion of a builder and developer of the nation, who (just like his famed predecessor

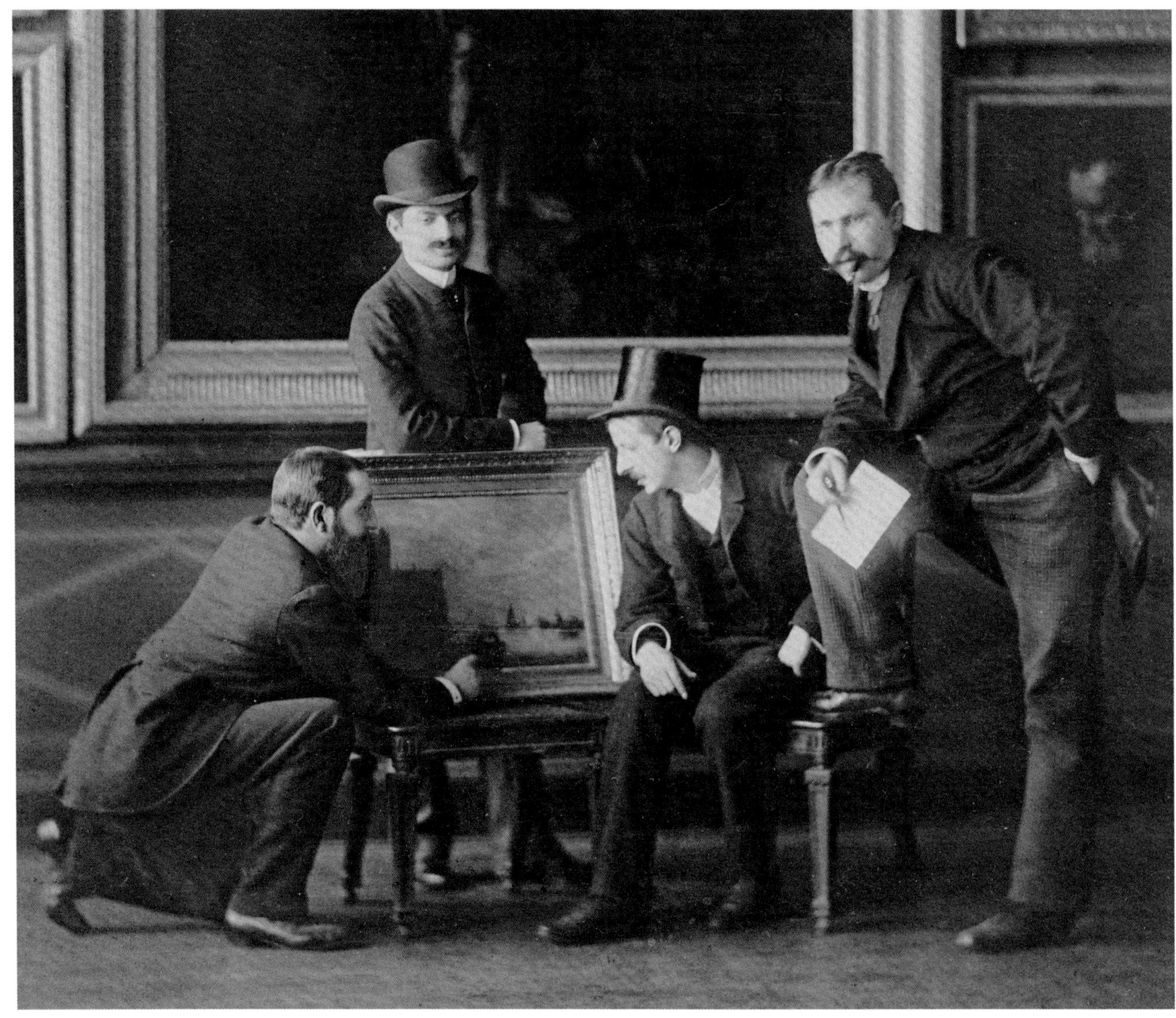

Istvàn Széchenyi with the founding of the Academy of Sciences and other institutions) wanted to raise Hungary to be level with England, the flagship of the modern world. Through thick and thin, relentlessly, he strove to create the perfect museum, which would provide a complete encyclopaedia of the history of the arts, and in which all the branches of art of every era of human civilization could be studied from high quality examples. All this was not merely an end in itself, but in the thinking of the time was a prerequisite for the development of world-class contemporary Hungarian art.

In an exceptionally felicitous moment in Hungarian history, Pulszky's passionate ambition met with political sympathy and generous financial resources. Hungary perhaps never experienced such an unfettered economic boom and optimistic

Károly Pulszky inspecting a painting, 1890s
Hungarian National Museum, Historical Photographic Collection

mood as between 1867 and 1914; and very rarely have politicians recognised the power of culture and the arts in national development as they did then. Thus in 1894 the Hungarian government agreed to Pulszky's plan for the creation of the Museum of Fine Arts, and set aside a vast sum, 3.6 million forints (more than the contemporary value of over two metric tons of gold) to realise it. This included 1.5 million forints earmarked for the construction costs of the new museum building, and 2.1 million forints for acquisitions for the collections. Pulszky's opus was not conjured out of thin air. It rested on two pillars: one robust and strong, the other a little awkward, and yet indispensible. The first was the gallery of Hungary's most powerful, richest aristocratic dynasty, the princely Esterházy family, which the Hungarian state purchased in 1871. This collection was monarchic in nature, with a great many splendid masterpieces from the giants of the sixteenth and seventeenth centuries. But the gallery almost completely bypassed the "primitive" art of the centuries before 1500, the excessively frivolous French rococo, and even the unsettling masters that strayed so far from the mainstream, like El Greco.

It is customary to characterise the Esterházy collection as being Goethean in taste, and indeed, it came into being when the entire continent hung on the words of that stern German dictator of taste: the turn of the eighteenth and nineteenth centuries. It was created by Prince Miklós Esterházy II (1765–1833), the most powerful nobleman in Hungary, a highly cultured and immensely rich aristocrat, for whom the gallery was not only a passion, a labour of love, but also an instrument of propaganda to raise awareness of the rank and prestige of his family. Accordingly, from 1814 the collection was open to the public in Vienna, the capital of the empire,

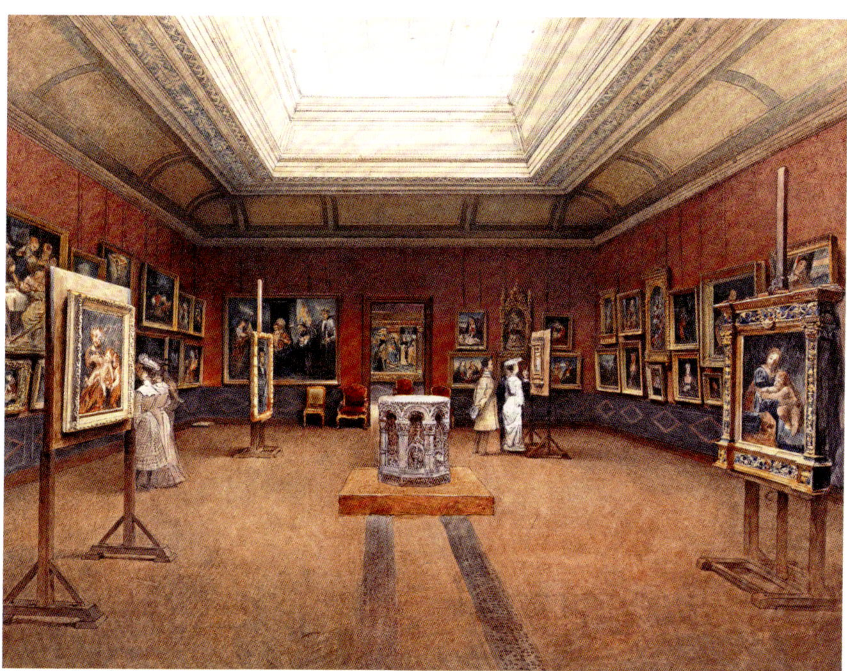

The Italian Renaissance Room of the National Picture Gallery in the building of the Hungarian Academy of Sciences, 1871
(Watercolour by Gyula Háry)
Museum of Fine Arts, Budapest

rivalling with two other illustrious Vienna galleries: the collections of the imperial house and the Liechtenstein family. Almost from the moment it opened, the Hungarian public urged over and again that the gallery move to the Hungarian capital, yet the princely family long resisted. The transfer was finally effected in 1865, and six years later the gallery became the property of the Hungarian state. The purchased works consisted of 637 paintings, 3,500 drawings and 51,000 prints: this profuse collection would hold its ground even today as an independent museum.

The Esterházy gallery was soon conflated with the other pillar of today's collection, the art collection of the Hungarian National Museum which, although it contained a few first-rate masterpieces, had a somewhat awkward character due to the circumstances of its creation. The only section of it to be in any way coherent was the contemporary Hungarian collection, which was enriched by regular purchases. European art in general was represented by the sumptuous collection donated to the museum by János László Pyrker, archbishop of Eger (1772–1847) in

Joseph Fischer, curator of the Esterházy gallery, in his atelier, 1808
(Engraving by Joseph Fischer)
Museum of Fine Arts, Budapest

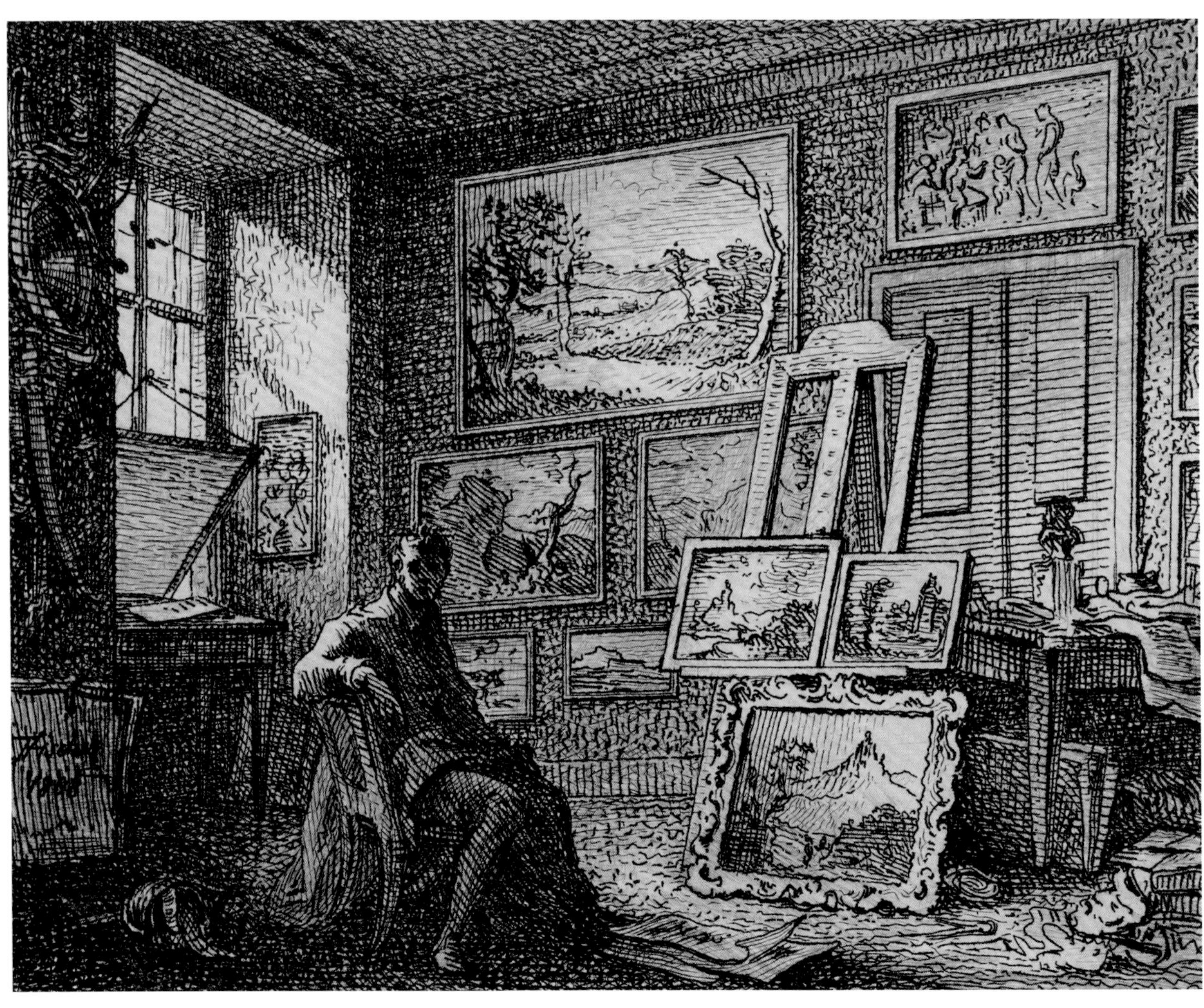

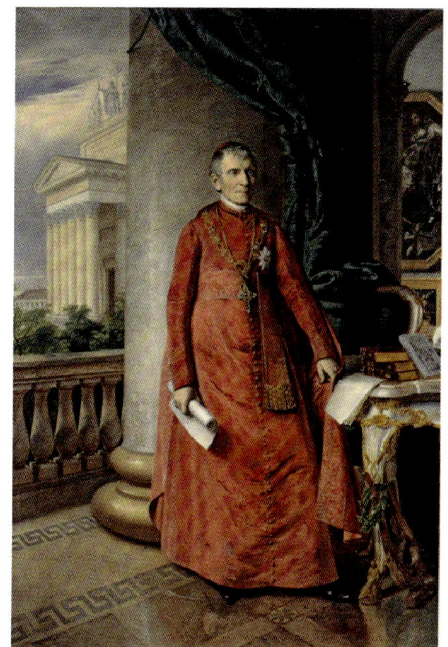

**Portrait of Archbishop
János László Pyrker,** 1842
(Painting by Miklós Barabás)
István Dobó Castle Museum, Eger

1836. This outstanding scholar, writer and prelate acquired most of the 194 paint-ings in 1820–1827, when he held the seat of the patriarch of Venice. Accordingly, the majority of the works are from Venetian painting; this rich art is embraced at a splendid level of quality. The Pyrker donation thus became a milestone on the path to forming the Museum of Fine Arts: the museum gallery no longer played the role of being a collection of works of local interest, but staked a claim to being a repository of general culture. It is thus no exaggeration that Pyrker's contemporar-ies feted him as the creator of the "National Gallery".

A third significant group, which passed to the ownership of the new gallery after the Esterházy collection was purchased, was a further step on the path towards general universality. A donation of sixty-two paintings from Arnold Ipolyi, bishop of Nagyvárad (1823–1886) of a series of outstanding works filled perhaps the most conspicuous gap in the collection: the then rediscovered "untainted, sincere" world of fourteenth- and fifteenth-century painting.

Károly Pulszky was made director of the gallery in 1884. The ambitious plan en-visaging the Museum of Fine Arts included both the construction of a new suitably spacious building, and a far-reaching acquisitions policy. In the proposal priority was given to the development of the sculpture collection (mostly through plaster casts); from early painting the key fields mentioned for the redressing of short-comings were fourteenth- and fifteenth-century Tuscan monumental painting, and the seventeenth-century Dutch masters. Seen with modern eyes, Pulszky's plan appears to be castles in the air, but in this era of optimism it actually became reality. The ceremonial founding of the Museum of Fine Arts took place in 1896, but Pulszky was able to start the large-scale purchases in 1893. Over the follow-ing two years he purchased 297 paintings, 142 sculptures, 50 drawings, and 600 engravings, most of them excellent works. His acquisitions went from medieval wellheads and Cretan icons to the paintings of Greuze, though they were prepon-derantly Italian Renaissance works.

This album works features only one or two pieces purchased by Pulszky. Yet it is no exaggeration to say, as intimated above, that the Museum of Fine Arts is his opus. The unique character of the museum is after all given not by the highlights, the peaks that everybody knows well, but the contour of the plateaus surrounding the high points. Those excellent pieces which locate the peaks in interpretative, il-luminating company, and thus reveal their true significance. Masterpieces almost never come into being as solitary cedars in the desert, but they grow even taller than the others in a rich, inspiring nutritional soil, in the midst of luxuriant vegeta-tion. The unusual virtue of the Museum of Fine Arts lies in the fact that its rooms present a complete panorama of a given era.

Pulszky's fundamental principle of a general comprehensive collection re-mained the basic ideal of development in later decades too. Successors attempt-ed to go further down this path, and make the museum even more universal. In 1906, on behalf of the Hungarian state, Bishop Péter Vay purchased in loco many hundreds of Japanese paintings, sculptures and woodcuts. Two years later, with

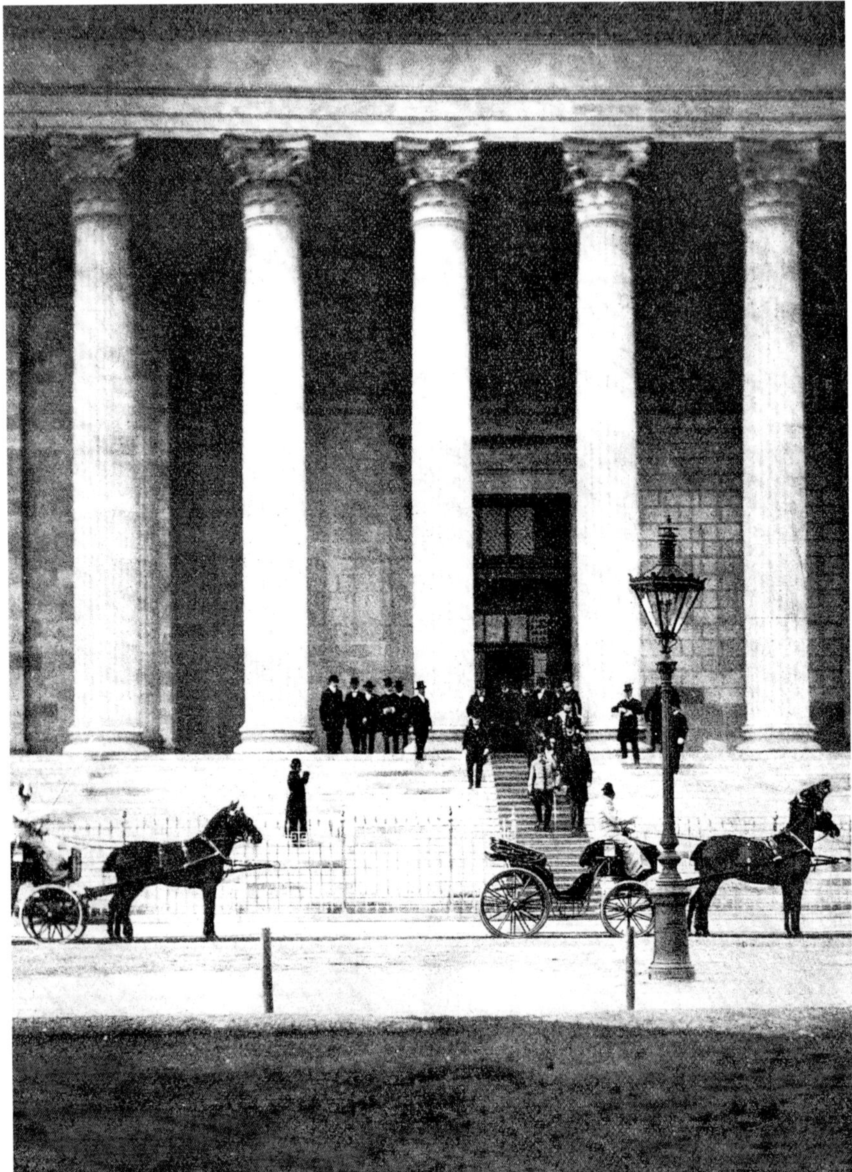

the purchase of 135 marble objets from German archaeologist Paul Arndt, a new chapter opened in the museum's collecting of ancient Greco-Roman art, which from this point on concentrated not on plaster casts of famous masterpieces of antique sculpture, but on the acquisition of original pieces. Meanwhile the collecting of Hungarian and global contemporary art continued in full swing, with large-scale lavish state purchases.

Hungary's exceptional economic and cultural development was arrested by War World I, which had tragic repercussions for the country. With this the spectacular extension of the Museum of Fine Arts came to an end, and settled down into dedicated everyday work. Even after this the collection was of course enriched with important works from year to year, but no new trails were beaten out. The heroic era, formational for the basis of the collection's character, had come to an end. In the following decades two changes of great importance took place, though both meant only the reorganising of the existing collections. The first was the Museums Act of 1934, pursuant to which the ancient Egyptian art treasures of the National Museum and the Ethnographic Museum would go to form the Egyptian collection of the Museum of Fine Arts; this would later develop into a comprehensive, world-class collection through the large excavations conducted by the museum's experts. At the same time the Ferenc Hopp Museum of East Asian Art, which until this time had been a branch of the Museum of Fine Arts, was given over to the Museum of Applied Arts.

The furthest-reaching event of the twentieth century, and also the most disorientating, is that as a solution to the permanent and increasingly acute lack of space the works of Hungarian art were removed in two phases and organised into an independent museum. First, nineteenth- and twentieth-century Hungarian artworks were moved to the newly founded Hungarian National Gallery in 1957, then in 1974 Hungarian art from the Middle Ages to 1800 was also transferred there. The life of the museum took a new turn in 2012, when the collection, previously separated into Hungarian art and international art, was reunified. Now, visitors can enjoy

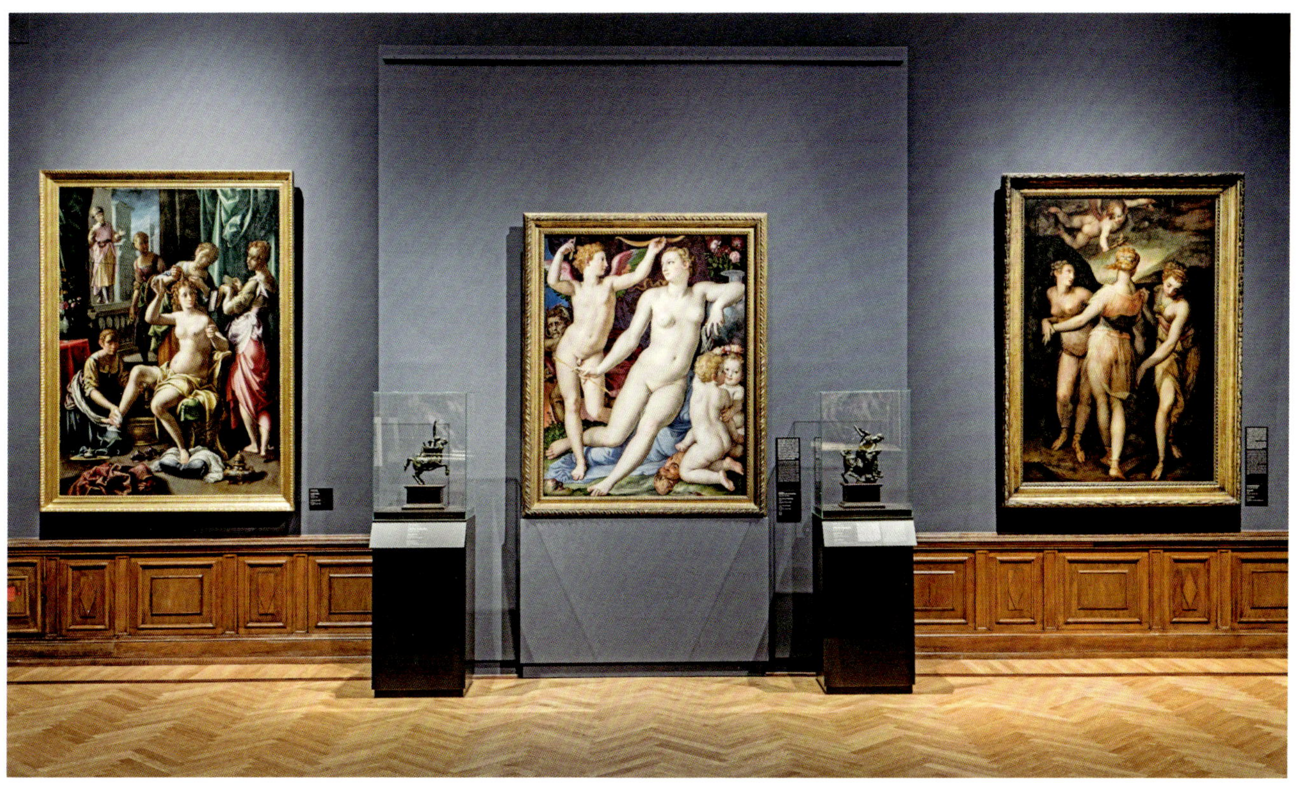

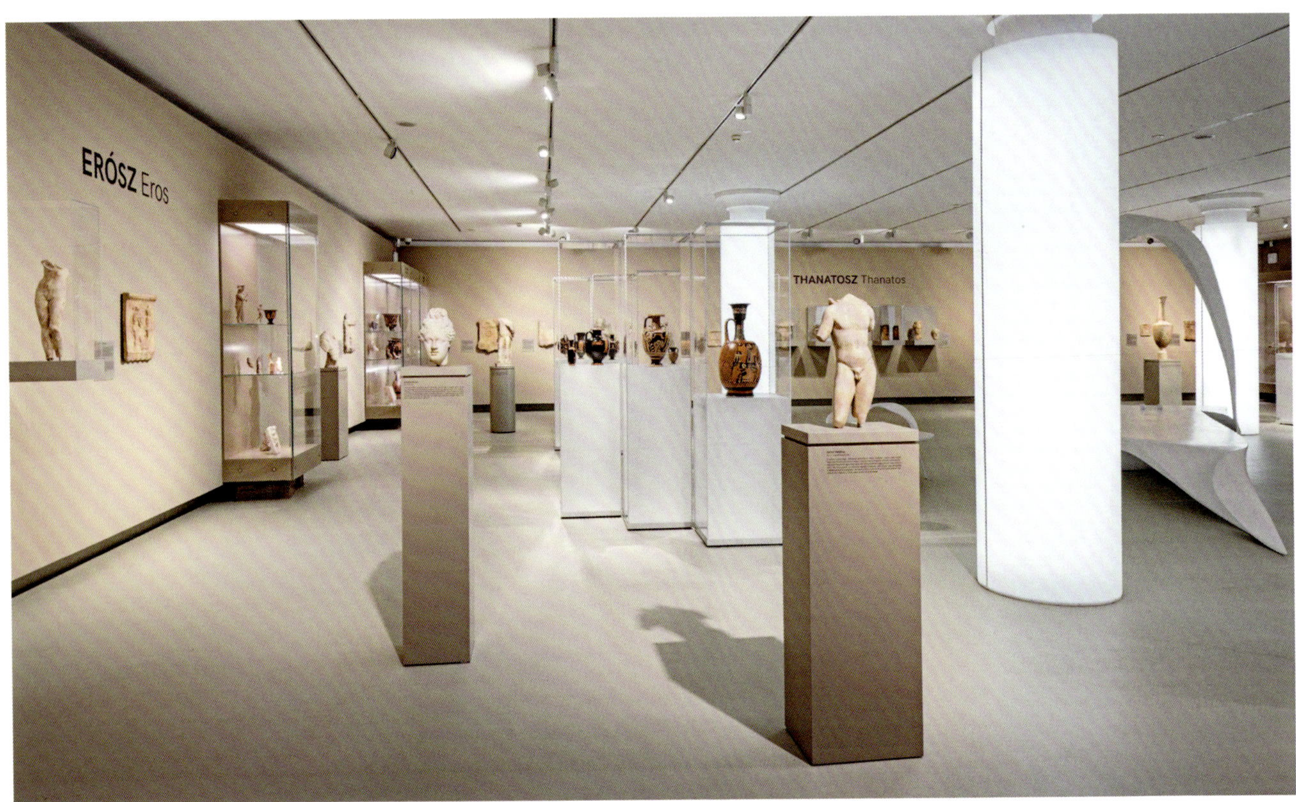

"classical" art, dating from Antiquity until the end of the eighteenth century, in the building on Heroes' Square, while modern and contemporary works are housed in Buda Castle.

Today the situation is uncertain, but it seems that in some form the two collection will perhaps soon be unified once more. Nowadays, the Budapest Museum of Fine Arts, like the other museums of the world, faces grave challenges. The world has changed radically. The traditional forms, paths, and purposes of education and culture are undergoing a transformation. A museum can no longer be a temple dominated by reverence; it shall become a forum where every individual visitor seeks out his own personal interpretation of one work or another, and engages with it in dialogue, or even debate. In recent decades the relationship between visual culture and the book culture dominant for centuries, had been turned on its head: the museum, as the traditional guardian and expounder of visual culture, cannot allow itself to ignore this change of tide, nor indeed to fail to be the vanguard of the shift. The museum has a key role in the public's mastering of the grammar of visual communication, of their learning to understand and use pictures to express their own ideas. The collections of the Museum of Fine Arts make it uniquely suitable for this task due to their wide range and variety.

AXEL VÉCSEY

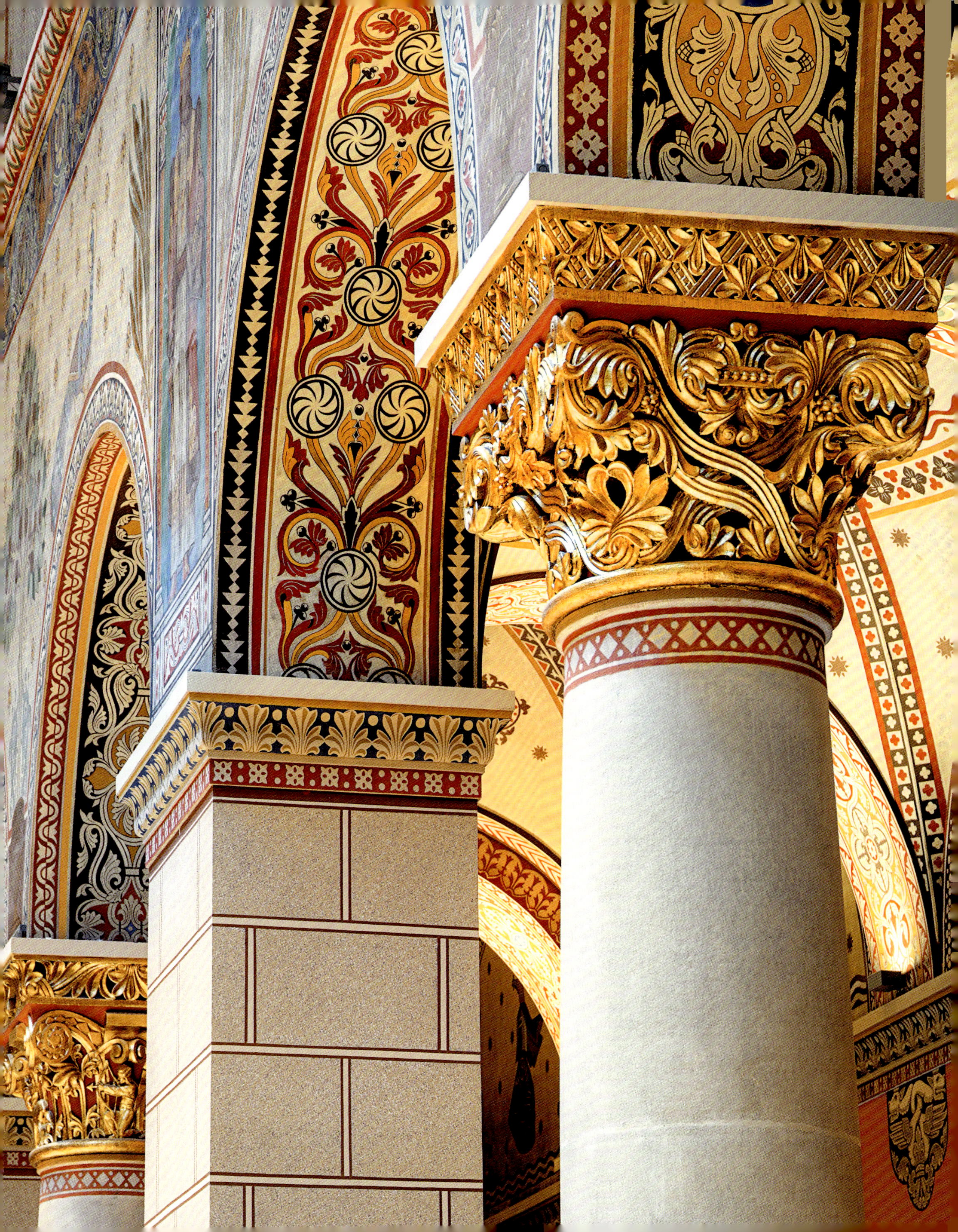

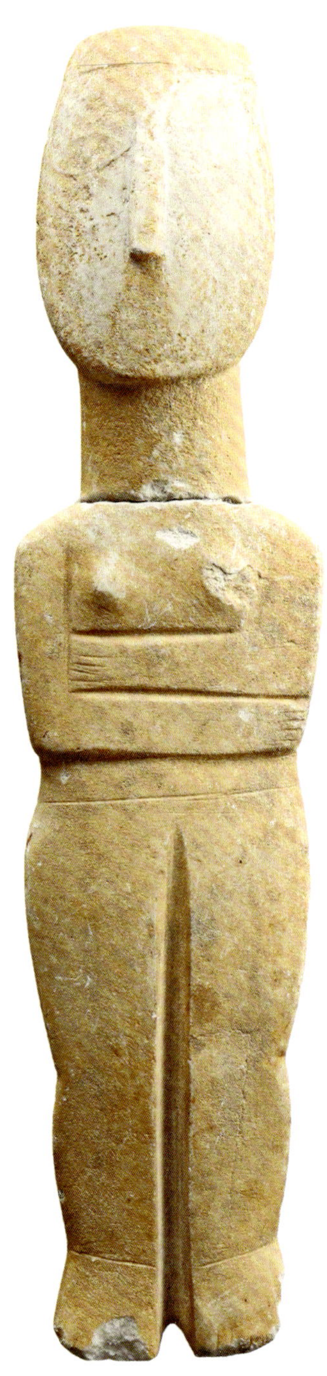

Cycladic civilization

Idol

ca. 2700–2400 BC
Marble, height: 61 cm
Purchase from the Paul Arndt collection, 1908
Inv. no. 4708

Lying to the east of the Greek mainland, in the isles of the Cyclades which are rich in marble (Naxos, Paros, Syros and Amorgos) the most striking works of early Bronze Age art are the marble idols. Most often they represent naked female figures with folded arms and their feet fixed down. The majority of the figurines were found in tombs, laid next to the deceased, but their precise function has not been identified. The Cycladic representation of the human body, radically different from classical art and with an emphasis on pure elements of form, also inspired several twentieth-century artists. On the face of most idols the nose is the only detail defined, but the white surface was once brightly painted. On the Budapest piece to the right of the nose we can clearly see the formerly painted arc of the almond-shaped eye protruding from the surface. Above the right eye we can faintly see yet another eye, similar in size and shape: the idol was thus originally painted with four eyes. The ridge on the brow, also originally painted, may have been a hairband or a diadem.

The particular features of this statue are its large size and the richness of its painted decoration. Most Cycladic figurines are 20–40 cm high; an idol larger than 60 cm is rather rare. Of its painted attributes, the two pairs of eyes may have invested the statue with the ability to see all, and the diadem with power, so it perhaps depicts not a simple mortal, but some being with supernatural powers.

SZILVIA LAKATOS

Stele of Noferhaut

1479–1425 BC

Red standstone, 98 × 52 × 32 cm

Transferred from the Hungarian National Museum, 1934

Inv. no. 51.2143

This stele was purchased by Count Waldstein in Luxor. Its original owner, Noferhaut, an officer of pharaoh Thutmosis III, set up the stele as a votive gift to the god Amun-Re. Noferhaut was chief of the medjai-troops (a type of desert police) and overseer of the foreign lands.

In the upper section of the stele an offering scene is depicted: Thutmosis III, Noferhaut's lord, is shown offering papyrus and lotus flowers to the god Amun-Re, king of the gods, whose figure appears seated on a throne in front of an altar. In the lower section, the text of a hymn can be read. The hymn is addressed to Amun by Noferhaut, who is shown in front of the text with his arms lifted in adoration, and with various animals (fowl, gazelles, and fish) hanging from a stick over his shoulders. The depicted animals are offerings to the god, and represent the entire cosmos (sky, earth, and water) under the authority of Amun, and are also symbols of localities (marshland, desert, and water) which were regarded by the Egyptians as homes for the forces of chaos. By presenting these symbolic animals to Amun, Noferhaut affirms that he has fulfilled the task entrusted to him by the king, and seen to it that the desert and foreign regions are integrated into the ordered world ruled by Thutmosis III.

KATALIN KÓTHAY

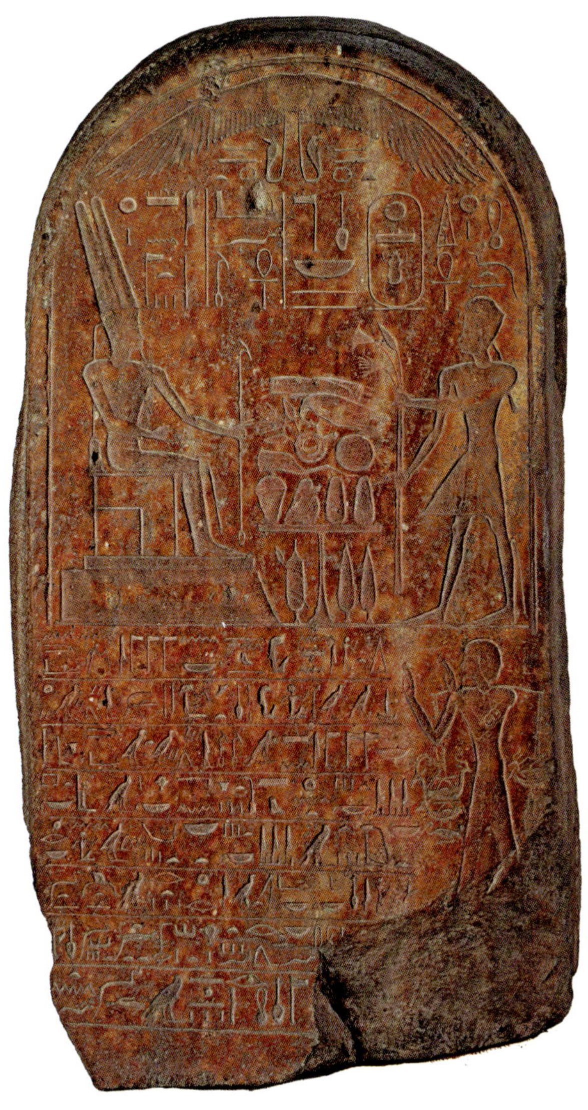

Egypt, New Kingdom (1580–1085 BC)

Head of a Man

ca. 1350–1290 BC
Limestone, height: 22 cm
Transferred from the Hungarian National Museum, 1934
Inv. no. 51.2262

Towards the end of the Eighteenth Dynasty, in the Amarna period (ca. 1353–1333 BC), profound changes occurred in Egyptian religious and artistic thinking. The new subjects and the somewhat naturalistic trend in art was a dramatic departure from the traditional, timeless Egyptian style. Very soon, however, in the subsequent post-Amarna period, artists returned to old subjects and methods. Yet some of the innovations persisted and influenced later art.

This statue head, exhibiting traits of both traditional and Amarna art, was probably produced in the post-Amarna period. Consistent with the traditional style, the idealised face – though it represents a young man – does not actually reflect the age of its owner, nor his personality, or emotions. Yet the naturalistic rendering of the eyes and lips, as well as the form of the pierced earlobes, is reminiscent of Amarna art. The superbly carved head may come from a seated or kneeling statue representing a man of high status. His titles and name were probably inscribed on the back pillar, the remaining small part of which preserves only a few signs of a two-column hieroglyphic inscription. Originally the head was painted, and it is documented that traces of red ochre were still visible on the face in the 1930s, when it was transferred to the Museum of Fine Arts from the Hungarian National Museum.

K A T A L I N   K Ó T H A Y

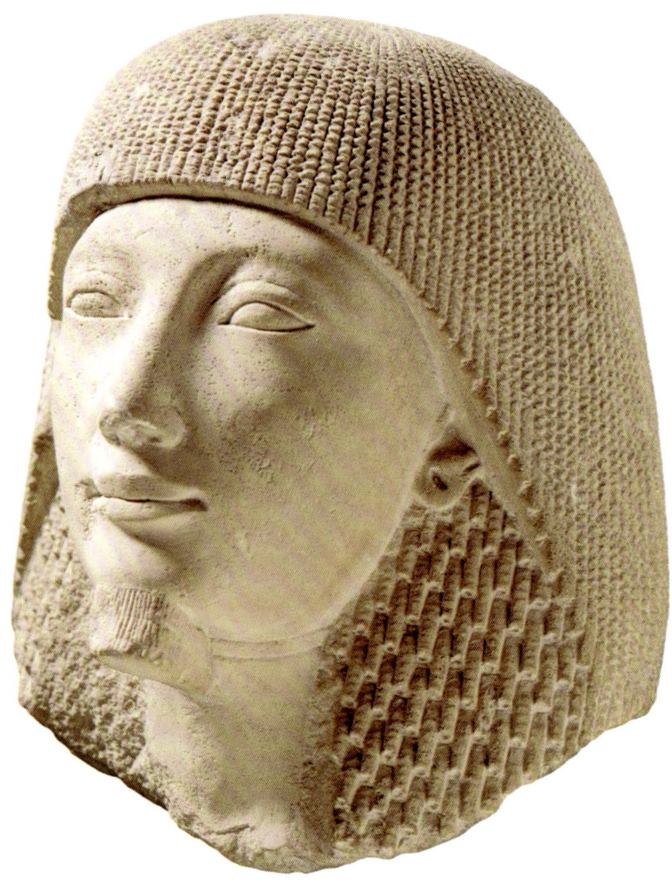

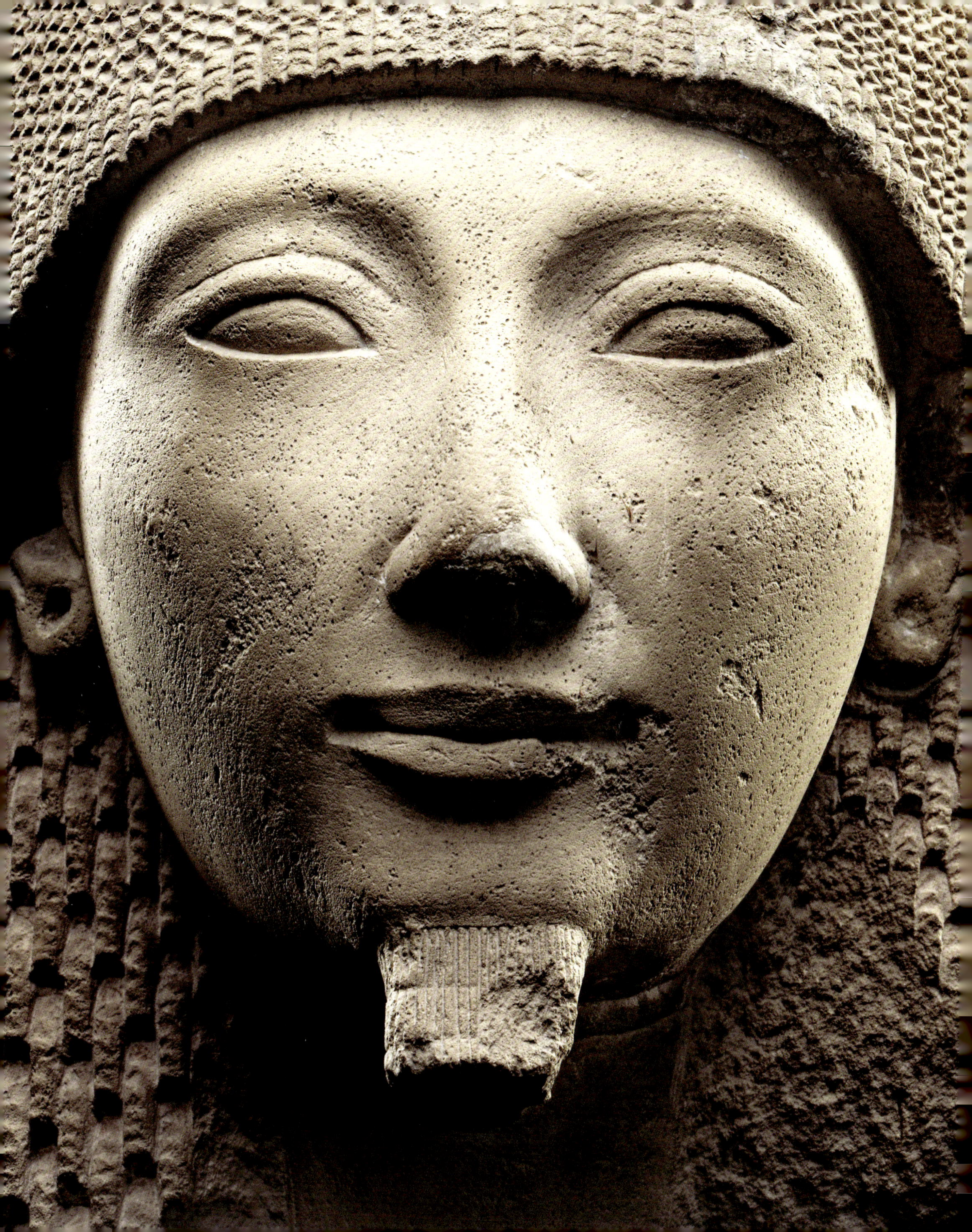

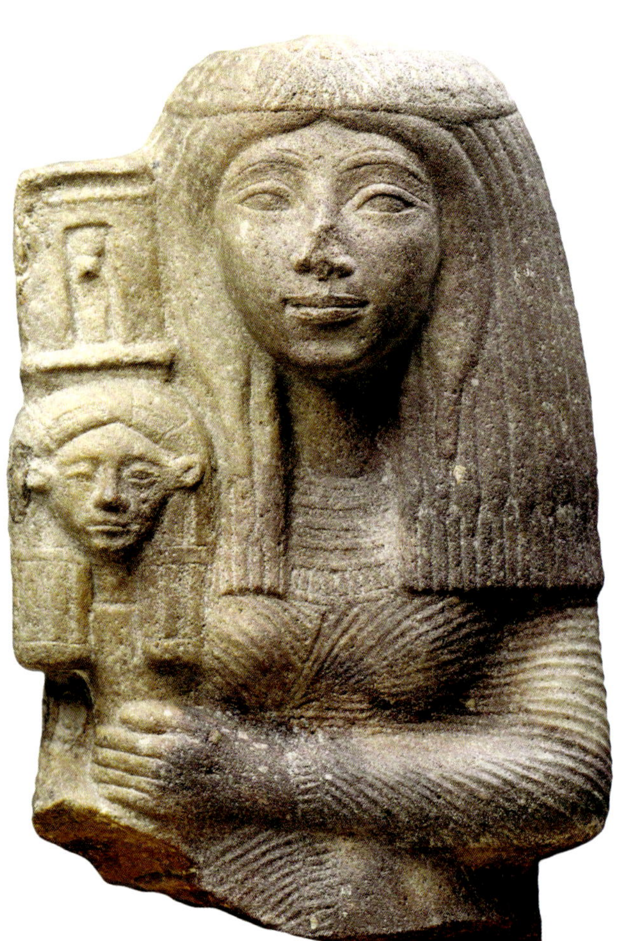

Egypt, Ramesside Period (13th century BC)

Young Lady with the Standard of the Goddess Hathor

Crystal sandstone, 35 cm
Transferred from the Hungarian National Museum, 1934
Inv. no. 51.2048

The statue fragment depicts a young woman. Her head is covered with a braided wig, the top of which is ornamented with a bunch of lotus flowers. She wears a decorative necklace and a gently pleated dress. She holds a divine attribute fastened upon a handle or a pole at her right shoulder, supported by her left hand. The attribute shows the human head of Hathor *en-face* with the ears of a cow. Her head is surmounted by a chapel façade, with the figure of a cobra rearing up (another representation of Hathor) in its entrance.

Hathor was one of the most important divinities of the Egyptian pantheon. Among her manifold appearances the most frequently represented is the cow, referring to her as universal divine mother who gives birth to the sun god and the pharaoh. When represented in human form, she is most frequently attributed with horns or ears of a cow, alluding to her divine maternal and regenerative power.

The design of the divine emblem recalls those of votive sistra, ritual rattle instruments, which were one of the Hathoric symbols used by her priestesses during religious celebrations held in the temples of the goddess. In these rituals music and dance with erotic associations played an important role, and were believed to have regenerating power. During the New Kingdom female members of the royal family and court were closely linked with Hathoric rituals. It is thus highly probable that the owner of the statue was of noble origin and served as a priestess of Hathor during her life.

ÉVA LIPTAY

Egypt, 21st Dynasty (1069–945 BC)

Funerary papyrus

Papyrus, painted, 100 × 10 cm
Purchased in 1935
Inv. no. 51.2547

The purpose of funerary papyri was to equip the deceased with all kinds of necessary information during his or her perilous journey to the netherworld which, it was hoped, would end with rebirth in divine form. Two deities played a particularly important role in these conceptions of the afterlife: the sun-god Re and Osiris, the ruler of the netherworld. The papyrus contains no texts. Nevertheless, the strong semantic link among the four separate scene panels is as cohesive as the grammar of a verbal text. The artist was inspired by the Netherworld Books of the tombs in the Valley of the Kings at Thebes which depict the nocturnal journey of the sun-god.

In the first scene, the knives in the head of the serpent clearly show that the being depicted is Apophis, the defeated enemy of the sun-god Re. The serpents of the second and third scenes, however, are benevolent, and assist in the rebirth of the sun-god and the deceased. In the third scene the bird-shaped spiritual aspect (*ba*) of the deceased appears presenting an offering to the sun-god who is depicted in the solar barque (in the form of a *wedjat*-eye encircled by the sun-disc). The closing scene shows two scarabs and an ithyphallic divine figure. The location is the mountain of the eastern horizon; at the moment before sunrise. The artist masterfully represented the last "productive moment" full of tension, condensing all regenerative and creative energies into one point.

ÉVA LIPTAY

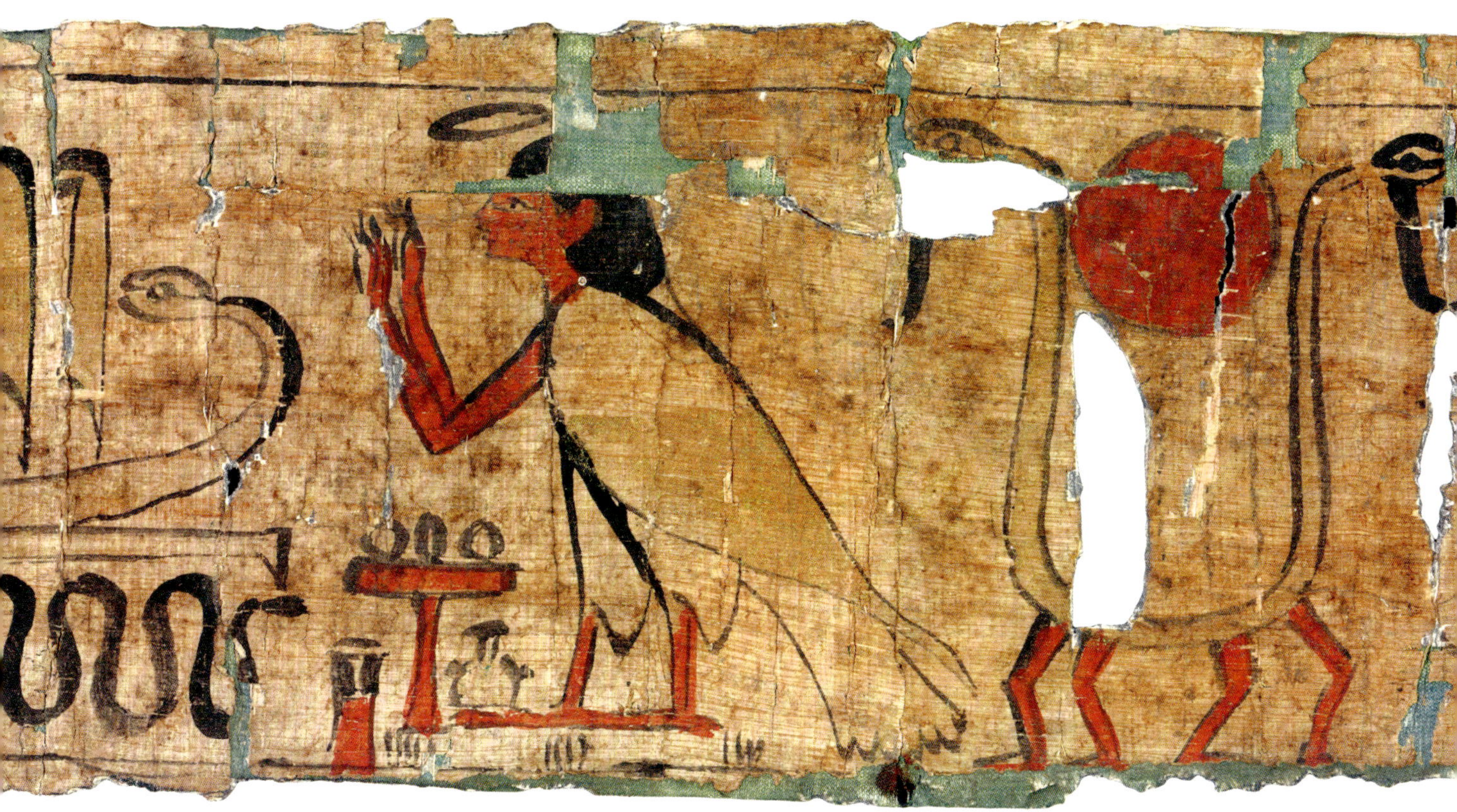

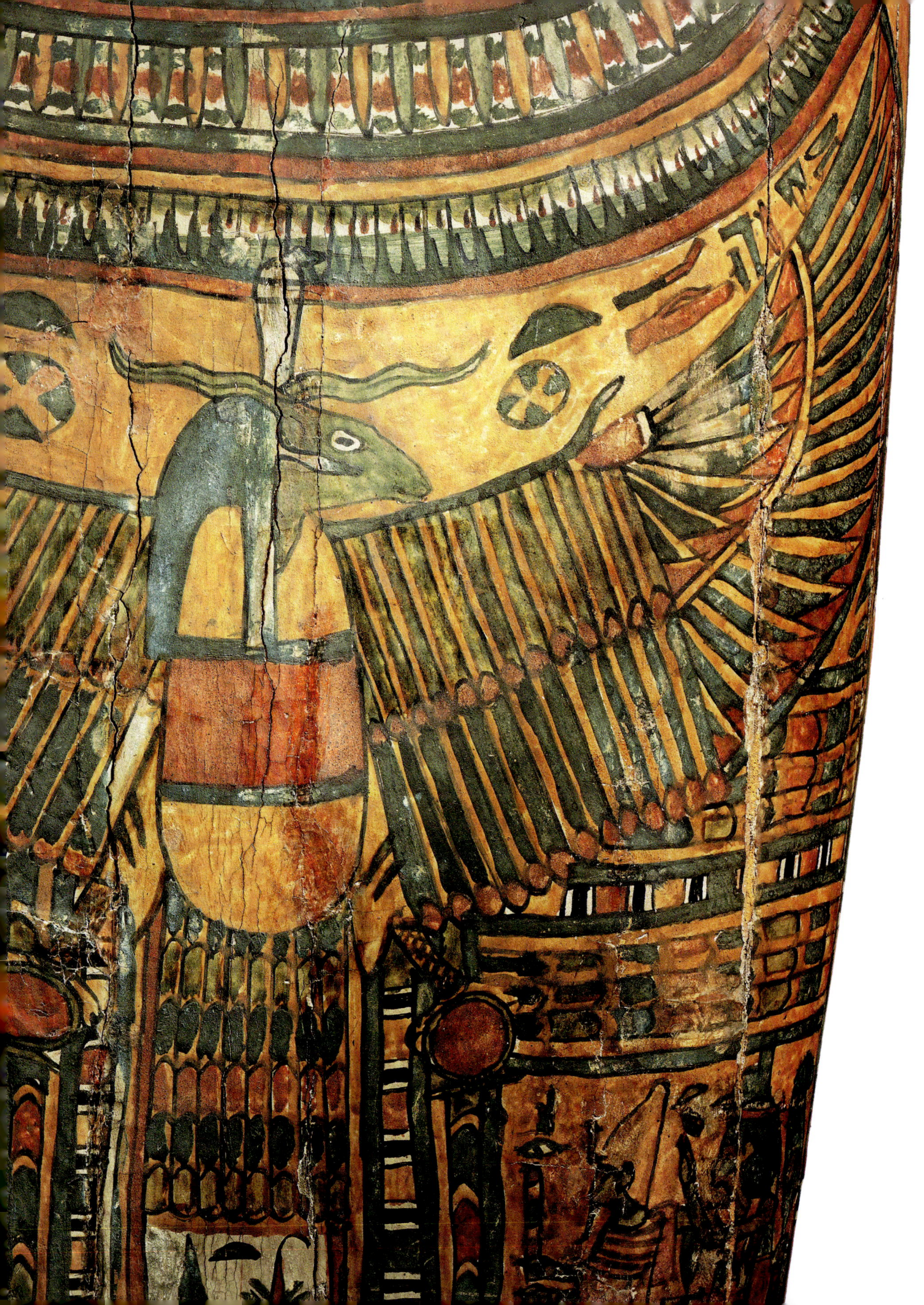

Egypt, 22nd Dynasty (945–715 BC)

Anthropoid coffin of Dihoriaut

ca. 750 BC
Gesso and linen on wood, 179 × 48 cm
Transferred from the Archiepiscopal Museum, Eger, 1950
Inv. no. 51.1995/1–2

In the Egyptian concept of the afterlife, the soul left the body on death in the form of a bird (called *ba*), and joined the cyclical path of the sun god. In order to be reborn after death, it was essential for *ba* to periodically find its way back to the mummy lying in the burial chamber, and unite with it. Thus the coffin had to resemble as far as possible the deified state of the deceased, so as to be recognisable to the returning *ba*. During the era of Libyan pharaohs (from the tenth century BC) the attitude toward death had become more passive. The fate of the deceased became more dependent on divine intervention than on the living, and, as a result, temples (and funerary statues within) gained a greater role in the funerary cult. Consequently, from the second half of the eighth century BC coffins were designed to emphasise their statue-like character with low pedestals under the feet, and back-pillars for the base.

The central figure of the lid is the ram-headed, bird-bodied deity, the afterlife aspect of the sun god, protectively stretching out his wings over the deceased. The tail of the bird continues in a column of polychrome hieroglyphic inscription consisting of a short offering formula which divides the surface of the lid under the waist into two symmetrical halves. On each lateral zone run three scenes panels with the figures of Osiris and protective funerary deities (the four Sons of Horus), and down below winged sun-discs provide magical protection and rebirth for the deceased.

ÉVA LIPTAY

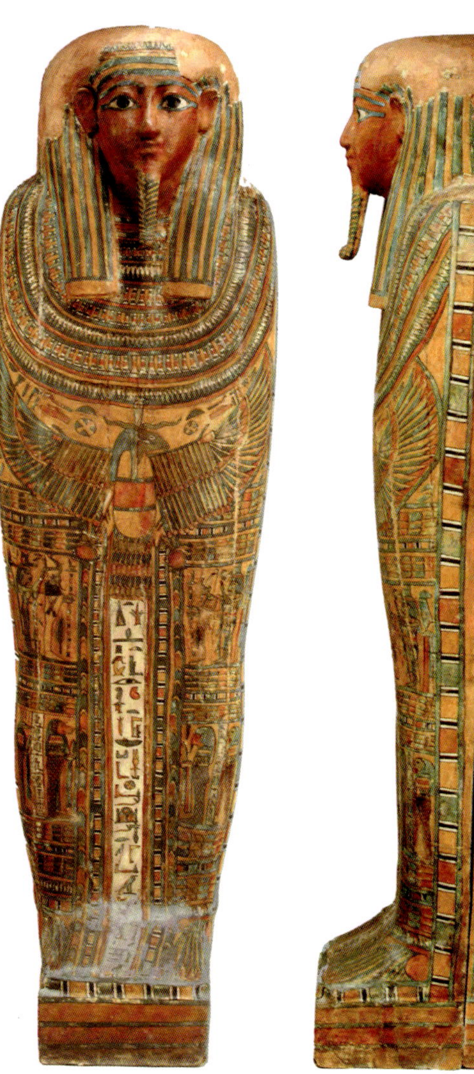

Statuette of a cat

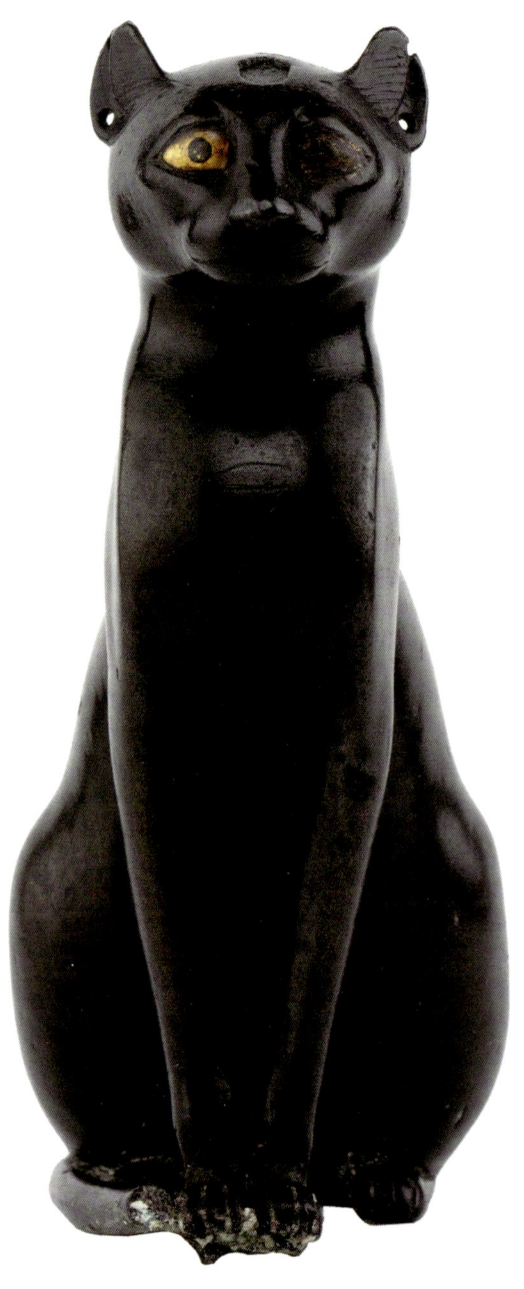

7th–6th century BC
Bronze, height: 15 cm
Transferred from the Ráth György Museum, 1950
Inv. no. 51.2356

According to ancient Egyptian belief, the gods could express either their destructive or their benevolent side to mortals. The ferality and playfulness typical of felines was expressed on the one hand by the unbridled ferocity and bloodthirstiness of the lioness (Sakhmet/Tefnut), and on the other by the benevolent effect of the cat goddess Bastet, placing emphasis on her domesticated and supple nature.

Both aspects of the goddess are closely linked to the sun-god and solar concepts. According to the *Myth of the Solar Eye* she is the daughter of the god, (actually personifying the divine Solar Eye) who according to myth in a fit of anger transformed herself into the shape of a lioness (or a wild cat), and strayed into the remote South. The sun-god dispatched the baboon-shaped Thot in pursuit of her and he managed to bring her back in a domesticated and pacified cat form. The head of this statuette is carved with a scarab beetle (the rising form of the sun-god), referring to the animal's link with the sun-god. The eyes are inlaid in gold. One of the rock crystal pupils decorating the eyes has been lost.

During the first millennium BC the main religious centre of the goddess Bastet venerated in cat form was the town of Bubastis in the Eastern Delta. Herodotus gives a vivid account of the fertility ceremonies performed there. Hundreds of statuettes like this, obviously intended to represent the cult image of the temple, were presented as votive offerings to the goddess.

É V A   L I P T A Y

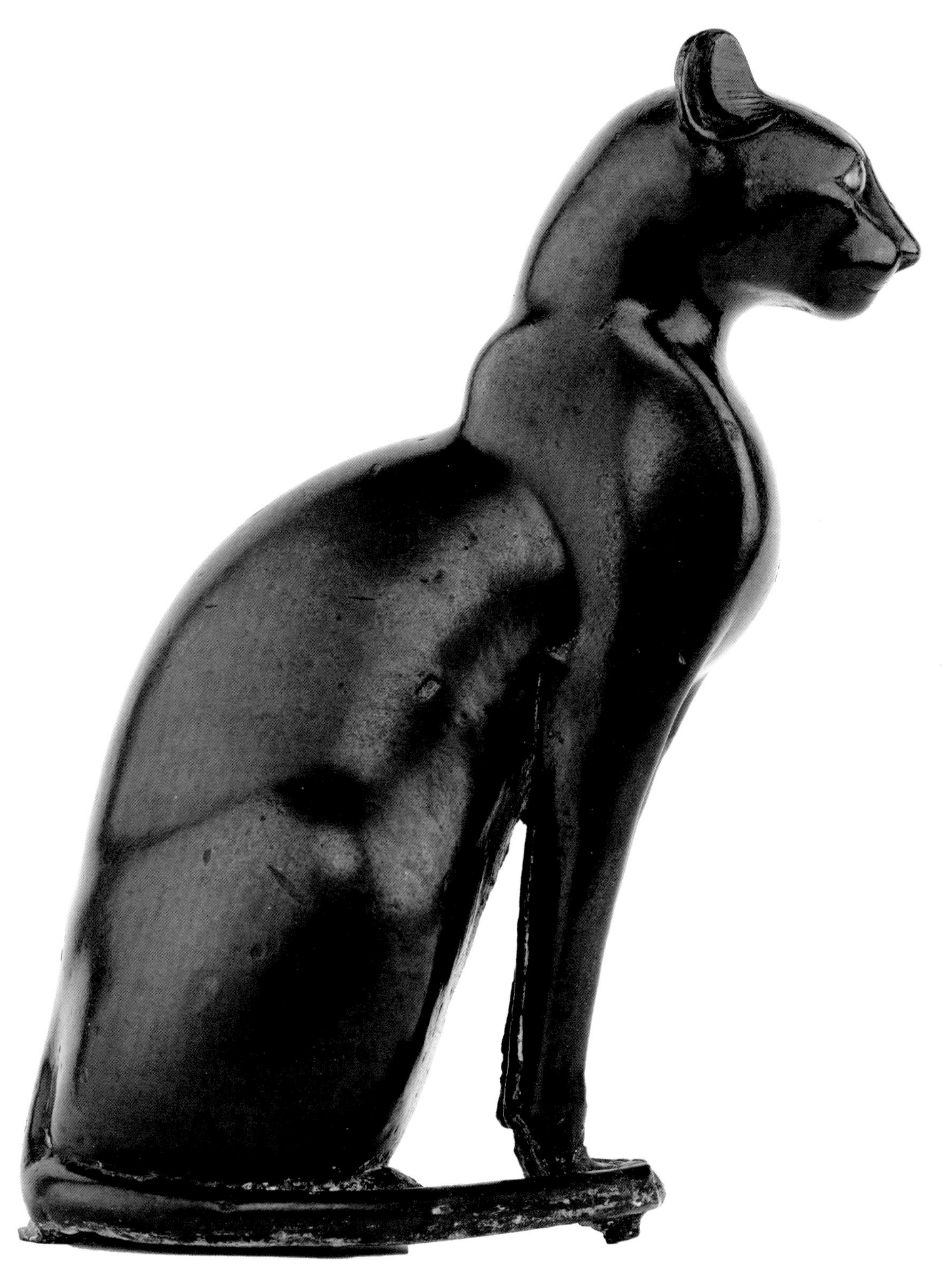

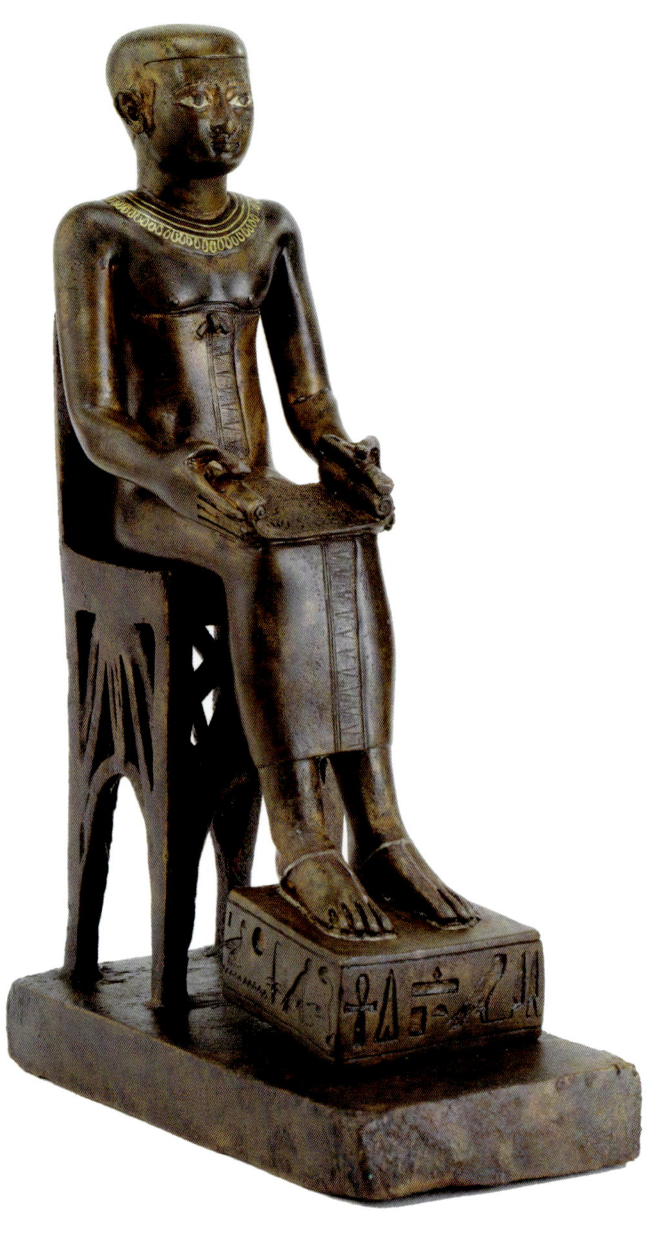

Egypt, 26th Dynasty (764–525 BC)

Statue of Imhotep

7th century BC
Bronze, with precious metal inlays, height: 17.6 cm
Transferred from the Ráth György Museum, 1950
Inv. no. 51.2313

Imhotep lived during the Third Dynasty (ca. 2686–2613 BC) of the Old Kingdom and was high priest of Heliopolis and architect of King Djoser's Step Pyramid complex, which was built at Saqqara. In later times he was regarded as a man of wisdom and the author of admonitions. From the Twenty-Sixth Dynasty, the so-called Saite Period (664–525 BC), onward he was revered as a god with his own cult and temple. His worship was most widespread in the country during the Ptolemaic period (305–30 BC), when he was equated with Asklepios, the Greek god of medicine. Many votive statues were dedicated to Imhotep to ask for his help and intercession in sickness and infertility, and in rebirth in the afterlife. The Budapest Imhotep, a splendidly executed bronze with fine inlays of gold, electrum, and silver, is an early and top-quality example of these votive statues. According to the inscription written on its plinth, the statue was dedicated to Imhotep for the benefit of a man called Kham-Khonsu. Imhotep is represented seated on a chair with a papyrus scroll on his lap. The hieroglyphic inscription engraved on the papyrus asks for Imhotep's intercession with the god Ta-tenen, the personification of the afterlife.

The statue formed part of the Fejérváry–Pulszky collection as early as in 1842. By 1873 it came into the collection of György Ráth, whose widow presented the whole collection to the Hungarian state after Ráth's death.

K A T A L I N   K Ó T H A Y

Andokides Painter (active ca. 530–515 BC)

Red-figure kylix

ca. 520 BC
Terracotta, diameter: 21.5 cm
From the collection of Antal Haan, 1950
Inv. no. 51.28

In Athenian vase painting around 525 BC red-figure decoration appeared alongside the already customary black-figure style. The so-called Andokides Painter was among the pioneers of red-figure pottery, though he was trained in the black-figure tradition. The large amphoras for storing wine were his favourite vase type, and he decorated one side in the old technique, and the other with the new. He only made a few kylixes, which were used as drinking cups at banquets.

The anonymous artist was named after Andokides, the potter who made and signed some of the vases decorated by him. He himself never signed his works, so they can be identified only by a thorough examination. The Budapest kylix is undoubtedly by the Andokides Painter: the characteristic profiles with a slightly protruding and sometimes downward-turning lower lip, the peculiar bulging shapes of the heads, the elbows and ankles are all features typical of him.

The Budapest kylix is markedly different from his other cups decorated in red-figure, as it is much smaller to those. Its size is usual for black-figure kylixes, as is the Gorgon's head on the inside of the cup. Decorating the outside with eyes also customary with black-figure kylixes, whereas on red-figure pieces alongside the eyes the palmette was an indispensible element. The Andokides Painter thus straddled two eras: he used the forms and part of the decorative system of black-figure pottery combined with the red-figure technique.

SZILVIA LAKATOS

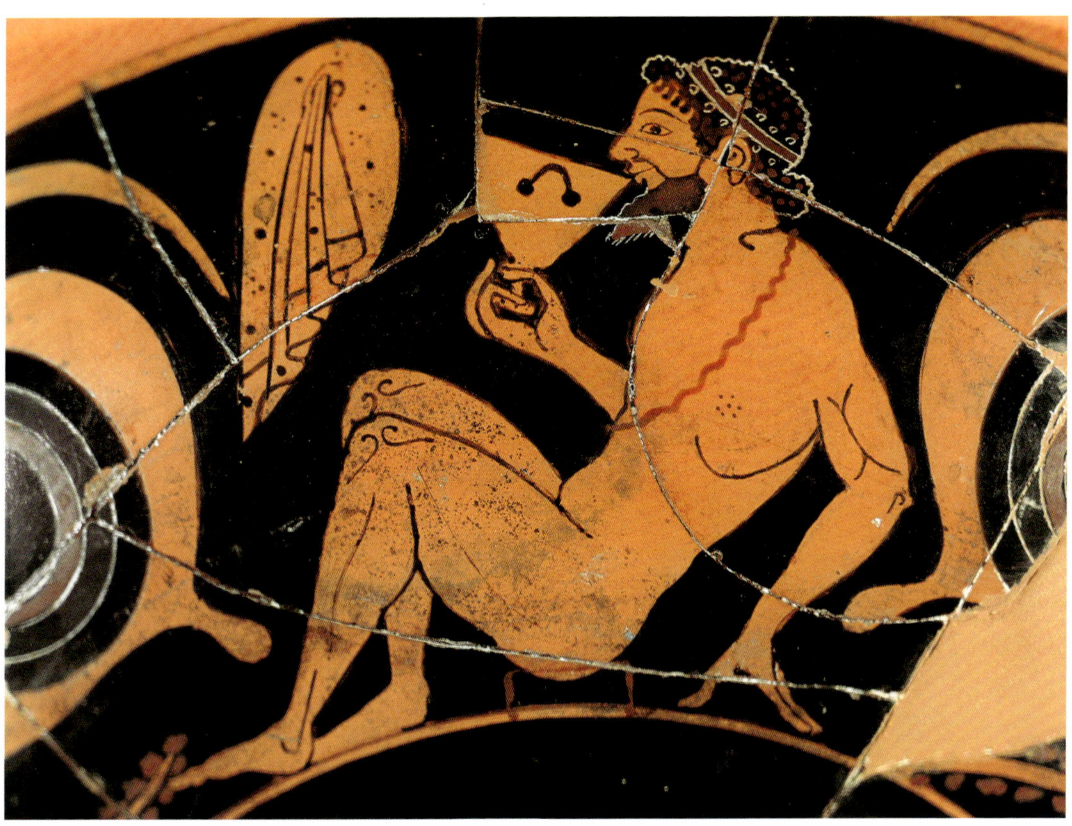

Cippus base

5th century BC
Pietra fetida, height: 29.5 cm
Purchased in 2006
Inv. no. 2006.2.A

In the sixth century BC Chiusi was one of the largest Etruscan artistic centers, and its stone carving workshops had their own special way of preparing tombs. The urns, sarcophagi, and the characteristic multipart funerary columns (called cippuses) were carved from the local limestone (which has a rather offensive smell, hence its name: "fetid stone") and were decorated with scenes related to burial ceremonies.

This cippus base is carved on all four sides with excellently preserved reliefs showing scenes from funeral games. The sports are clearly recognisable: competitors in chariot and running races, wrestling, boxing, and athletes throwing the discus and javelin. Each competition is watched over by umpires holding the sign of their office, the fasces, consisting of a long rod and three branches; clerks write up the results. The games are accompanied by music, and to complete the show is a troupe of acrobats and masked Phersu figures (beings between the worlds of men and gods, who often appear in Etruscan feasts). Competitions held in honour of the dead were also customary in ancient Greece: in the 23rd canto of the *Iliad,* Achilles holds the games and offers the prizes himself in memory of his deceased friend, Patroclus. The scenes depicted on this base appear in almost exactly the same form in artworks from other large Etruscan centres of the 6th and 5th centuries (tomb frescoes, vase decorations), so this may have been the customary programme for funeral games in Etruria.

S Z I L V I A   L A K A T O S

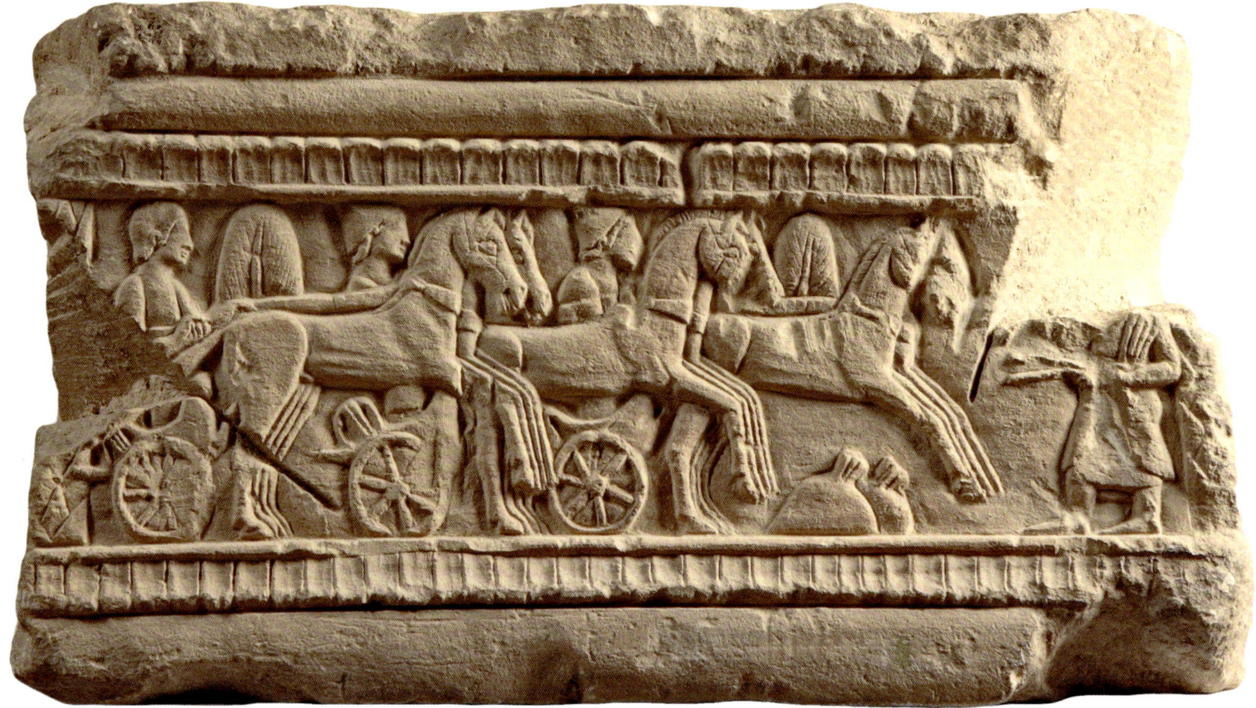

Grimani jug

ca. 450 BC
Bronze, height: 31.2 cm
Transferred from the Museum of Applied Arts, 1949
Inv. no. 56.11.A

Gábor Fejérváry, with his nephew Ferenc Pulszky, created Hungary's most important private collection of ancient art. He bought this bronze jug, dating from the classical period of Greek art, from the collection of the Grimani family of Venice in 1833. Judging by the shape, the Grimani jug was used at banquets for decanting wine. The body of bronze vessels had formerly been cast, but by the fifth century BC they were hammered from sheet metal, and thus in spite of the use of common decorative motifs each piece was individual.

    The tongue pattern running around the foot, the pearl-string-like ribbing following the arc of the handle and the palmette which closes it merely complement the two figures intended as the main adornments of this graceful jug. On the edge of the lip sits a bearded figure with pointed ears, holding drinking horns. This is Silenos, a companion to Dionysos, god of wine. Behind him, at the base of the handle, is a siren with wings spread. The ancient Greeks believed these woman-headed birds awaited those entering the underworld, that with their enticing song they might soften the bitterness of death. The linking of wild revelry and death may seem odd, but it was not alien to Greek thought. They believed they would have parties in the beyond too, so the necessary vessels were often placed next to the dead. The Grimani jug, which is completely intact, was probably placed in the depths of a tomb shortly after it was made, to accompany its owner on his or her journey to the realm of Hades.

SZILVIA LAKATOS

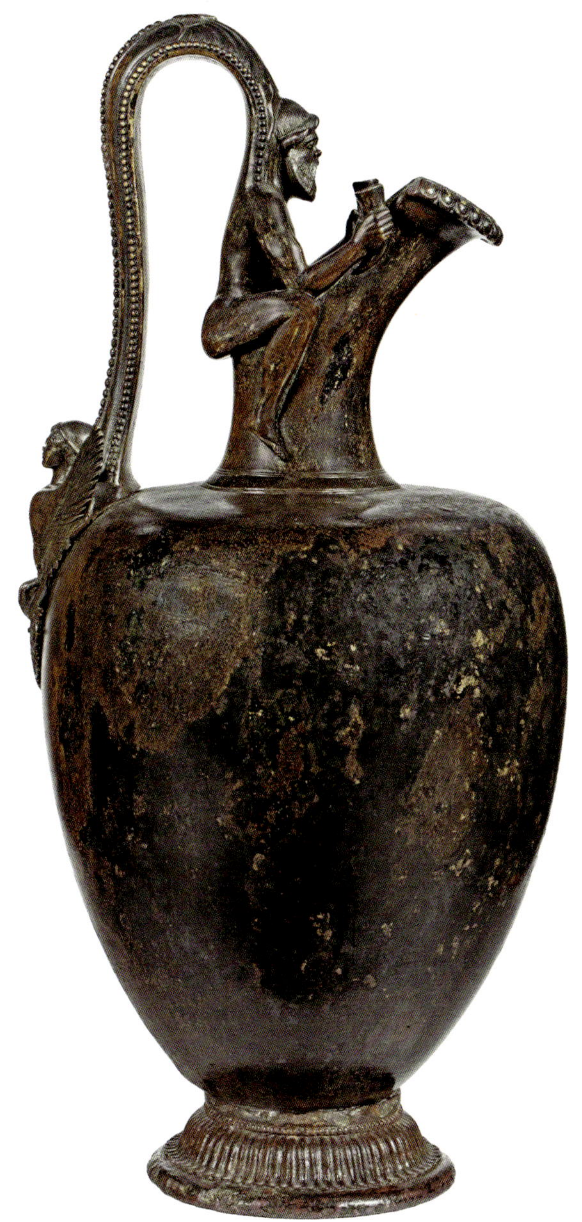

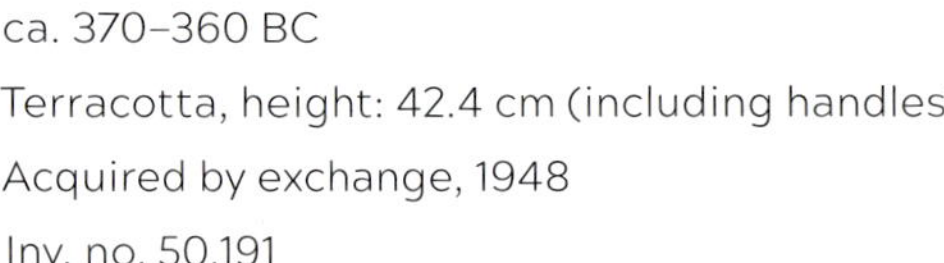

Brooklyn–Budapest Painter (active ca. 380–360 BC)

Lucanian red-figure nestoris

ca. 370–360 BC
Terracotta, height: 42.4 cm (including handles)
Acquired by exchange, 1948
Inv. no. 50.191

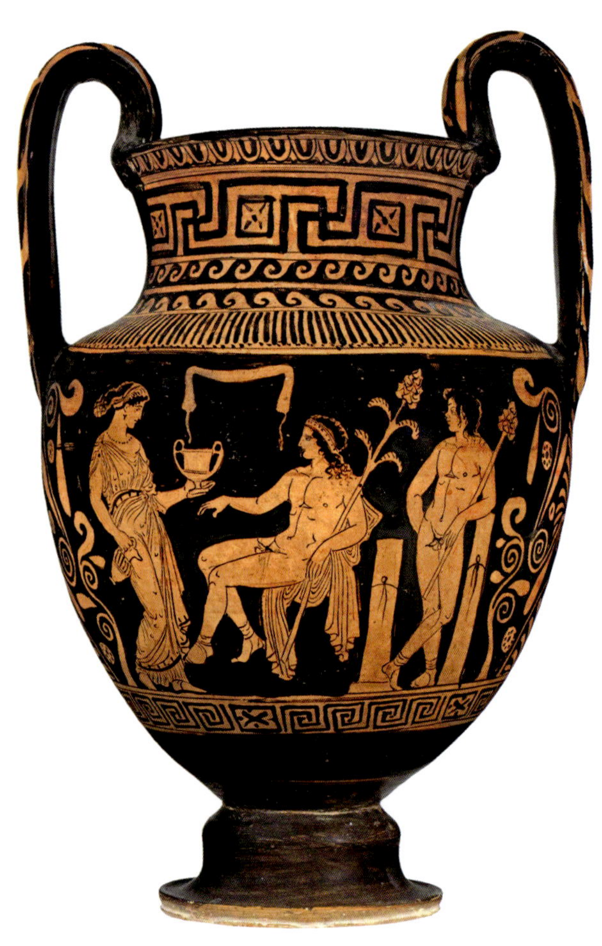

Red-figure vase painting developed in Athens about 525 BC. For the following century the masters of Athens pursued the technique with almost no competition. From about 430 BC, vase painters and potters moved from Athens (entangled in a severe war with Sparta) to southern Italy, where Metapontion in Lucania became one of the Greek centres of vase-painting.

In spite of its Greek name, the nestoris is not Greek in origin. It was named in the nineteenth century after Nestor, whose goblet resembled this form as it was described in Homer's *Iliad*. However, it is actually a variation of a vase type of the Messapii, the inhabitants of the peninsula of Salento, in the southeastern corner of Italy. The Greek potters were thus in contact with the local populace, and learnt from them, adapting to their needs. Though the form of the vase is of local origin, it is decorated with a typically Greek scene. In the middle sits the young god Dionysos, holding the thyrsus, a staff adorned with ivy leaves. On the left a female figure offers him a cup of wine. At the right edge of the scene a satyr leaning on a column serves to emphases the Dionysian mood. Yet the ribbon encircling the two columns suggests that the scene is set before a tomb, in a burial ground. In this case the image may depict the welcoming of the deceased into Dionysos's entourage, a religious belief popular in southern Italy. The vase may originally have been intended as a grave good, perhaps for the very female figure in the design.

SZILVIA LAKATOS

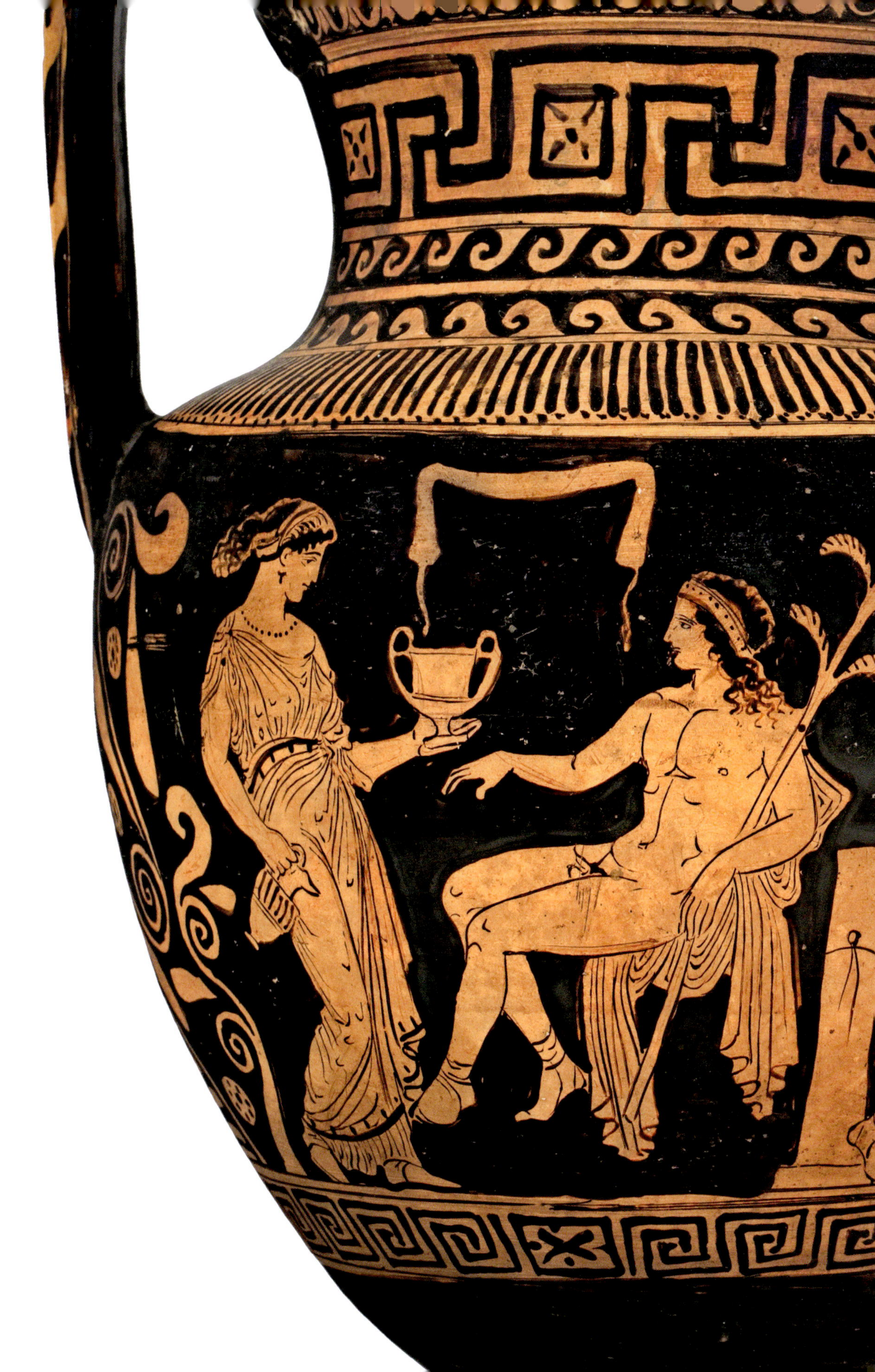

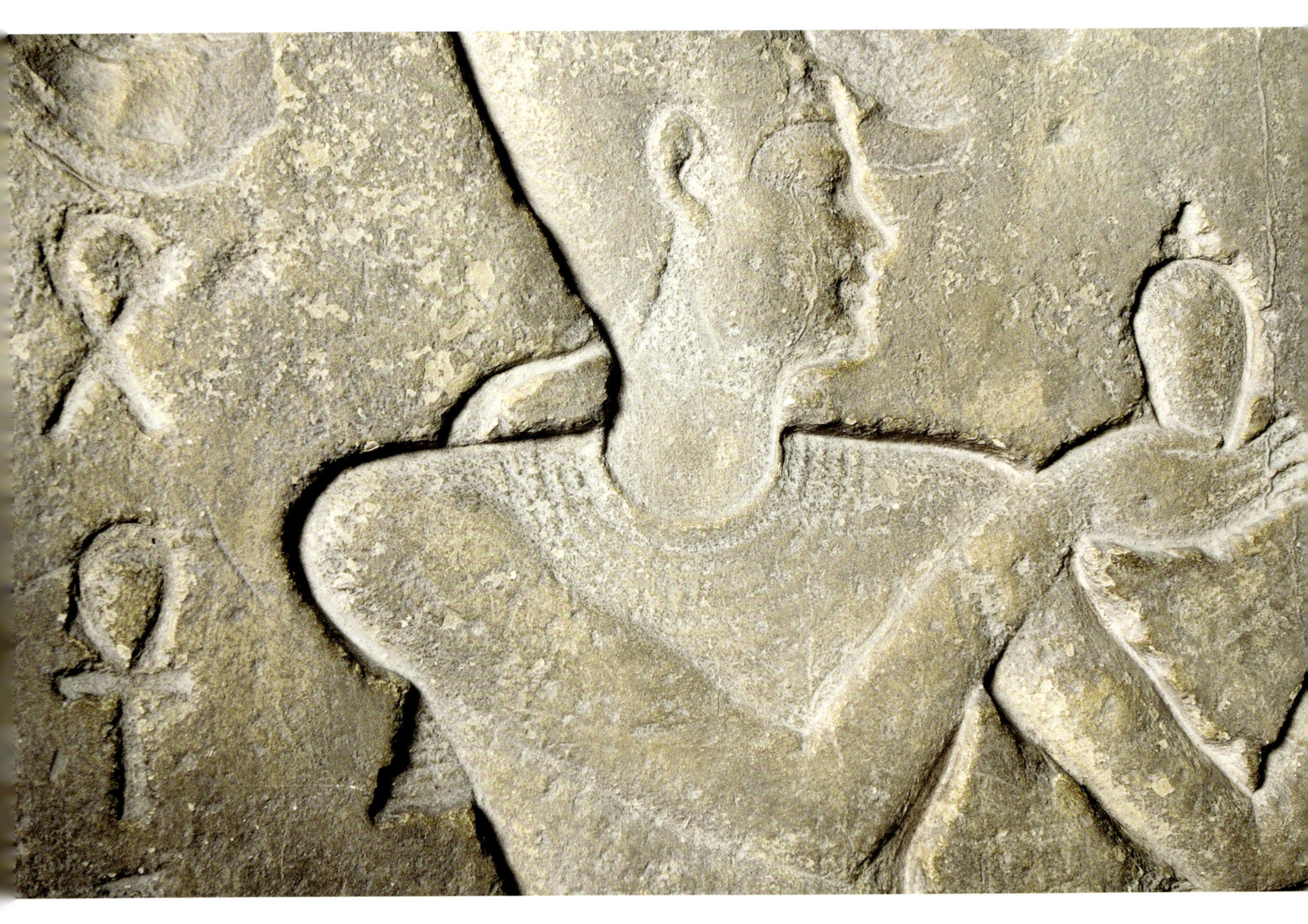

Relief fragments from a Ptolemaic temple

ca. 305–285 BC
Limestone, height: 31 cm, width: 96–142 cm
From the excavation at Kom el-Akhmar, 1907
Inv. no. 51.2156–60

The relief fragments once decorated the walls of a temple built at the beginning of the Ptolemaic Period at Kom el-Akhmar, near Sharuna in Middle Egypt. The Budapest fragments, together with other similar pieces now in Vienna and Cracow, were found in 1907 by an Austro-Hungarian expedition sponsored by Fülöp Back, a Hungarian merchant living in Egypt. The reliefs depict and name the founder of the temple, Ptolemy Soter I, as well as gods and goddesses. The Ptolemies, who ruled over Egypt following the death of Alexander the Great, made it a conscious part of their religious policy to maintain the ancient religious institutions. By renewing and enlarging old temples or building new ones, they ensured the continuity of the cults of major Egyptian gods. The decorations of these temples show these rulers of foreign origin represented with traditional pharaonic attributes and insignia. Ptolemy I Soter and his son and successor, Ptolemy II Philadelphos (who probably also built at Kom el-Akhmar) provided funds for temple constructions at several major traditional cult centres all over Egypt. The building of the temple at Kom el-Akhmar, an important administrative and religious centre already from the third millennium BC, can be seen as part of these religious policies. In earlier times the town was a centre of the cult of the god Nemty, venerated in the form of a dual falcon, while its Ptolemaic temple was dedicated to the local form of the cult of the falcon god Horus.

KATALIN KÓTHAY

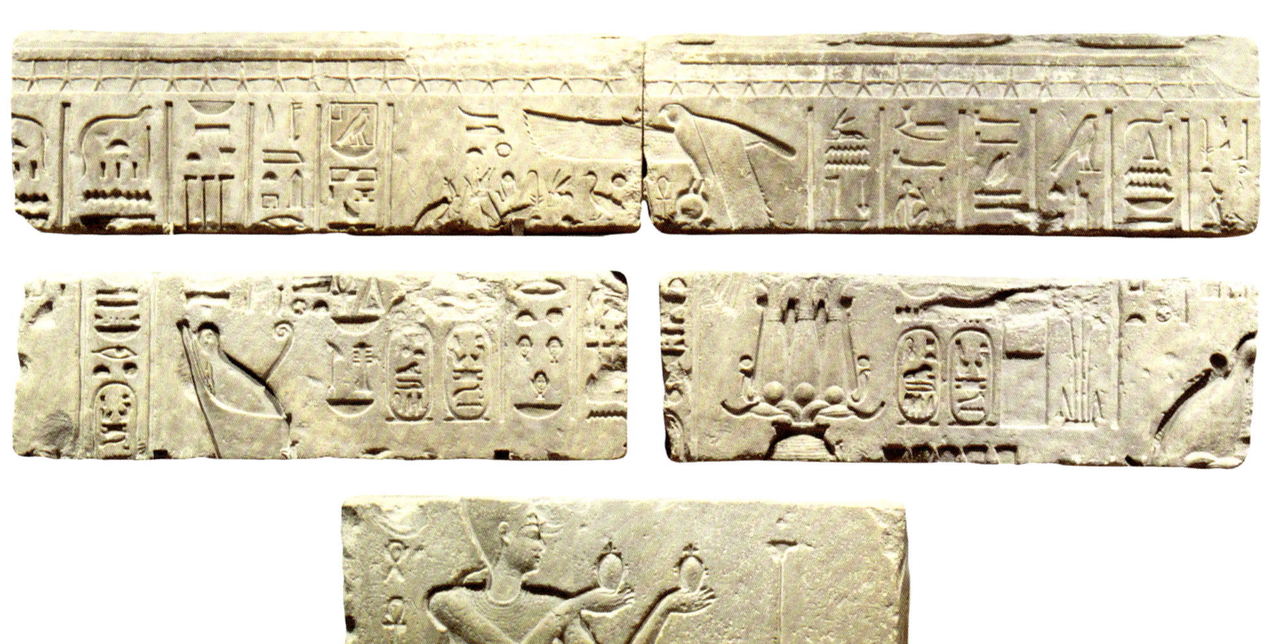

"Budapest Dancer"

ca. 150–100 BC
Parian marble, height: 62 cm
Purchase from the Paul Arndt collection, 1908
Inv. no. 4759

The statue known as the *Budapest Dancer* is one of the Museum of Fine Arts' most famous classical antiquities. It portrays a young girl as she pulls her cloak to one side and, leaning forward, looks before her feet. Its fame is due to its being one of the finest specimens of early Hellenistic (third century BC) sculpture. One of the main innovations of the period was the exploration of the artistic possibilities of the "multi-view" compositions. In contrast to earlier sculptures designed for one single main viewpoint, the girl's movements can only be understood by revolving around the statue.

In the Hellenistic era it became common in public buildings and homes of the wealthy to erect statues with a merely ornamental function; the *Budapest Dancer* was probably made for such a purpose. Since the carving on the back of the statue is much rougher, it was clearly not intended for an all-round view, but before some background, for instance in a niche. The subject of the statue is uncertain, as is the question of whether the girl is a mythological character or a mortal. She is traditionally considered to be a dancer, but her movements do not correspond to any of the known classical ways of imaging dance. On the basis of her forward-leaning motion she could be interpreted as a decorative figure for a fountain or pool, the portrait of a girl looking at herself reflected in the water. Equally, it may be one of the new genre scenes of the Hellenistic era, the girl gathering her clothes.

SZILVIA LAKATOS

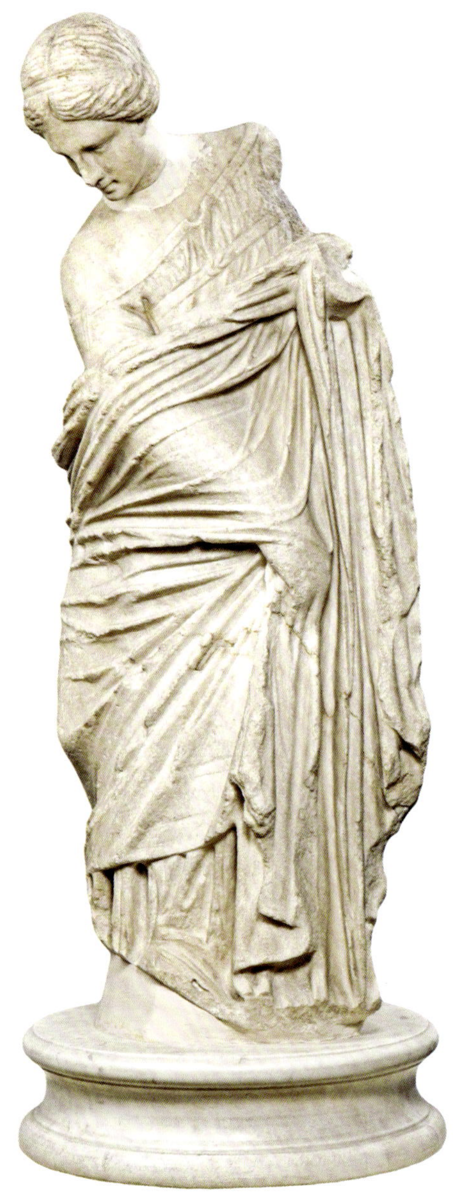

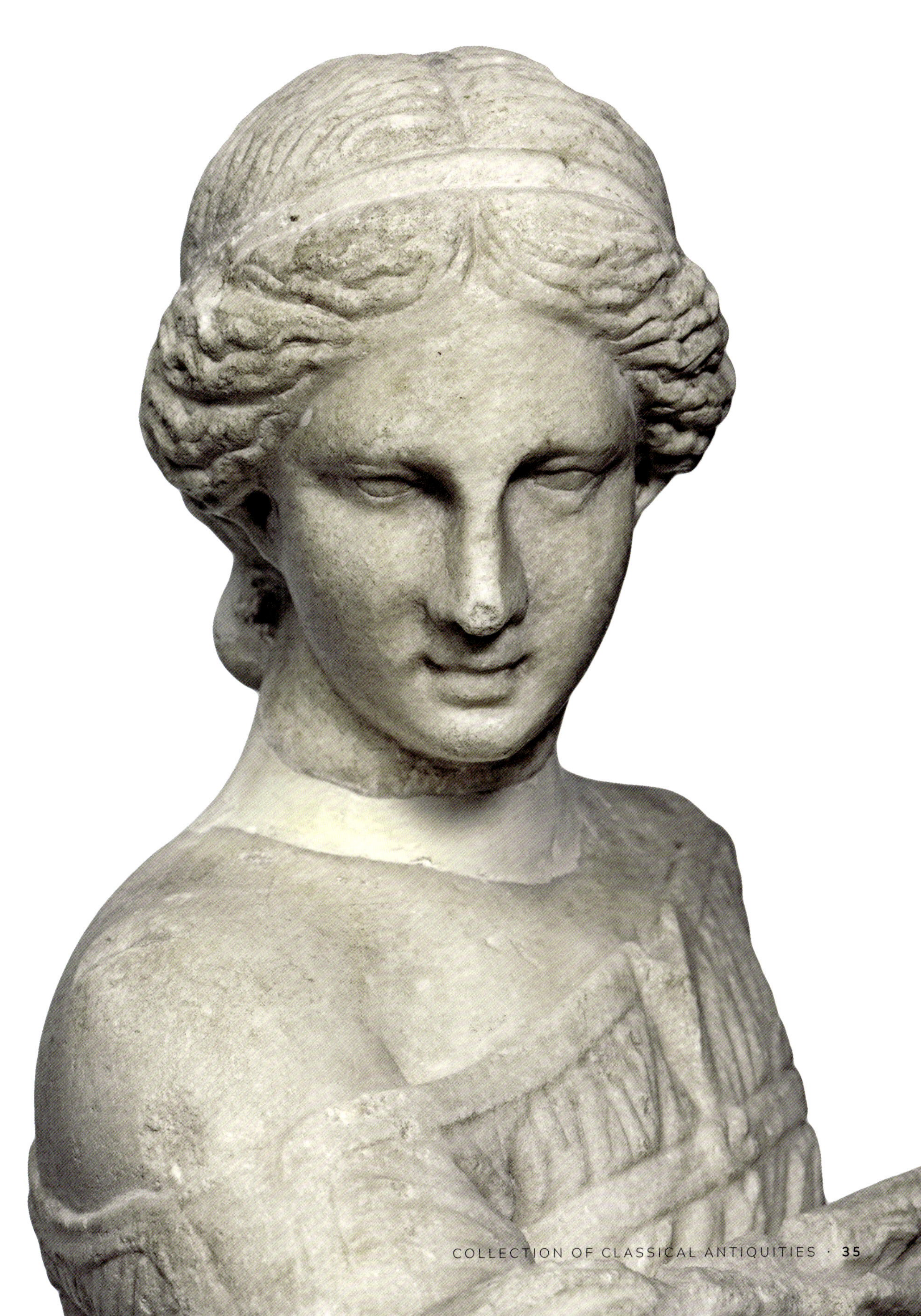

Fragment of a ceremonial procession

Second quarter of the 1st century AD
Luna (Carrara) marble, height: 107 cm
Purchased in 2000
Inv. no. 2000.24.A

At the end of a decades-long civil war, Octavianus, later to become Emperor Augustus, took power. He maintained the semblance of a republic, but with the help of a powerful propaganda machine, which made the mythical story of his family the origin myth of the entire Roman people, he created an autocracy. It is no coincidence then that the ceremonial chariots shown in the relief, used for transporting sacred objects of the state gods, are decorated with scenes that had been made the key points of Rome's ancient history. On one side of the chariot Aeneas, son of the goddess Venus, rescues his father and son from the fire devouring Troy, in order to set out on his journey that would lead to his new home, Italy. On the other side we see Romulus, the founder of Rome, with the weapons confiscated from the defeated enemy warlord. To position Aeneas, Augustus's mythical ancestor, alongside Romulus, venerated by Romans as the founder of Rome, and to make him his equal, was a contemporary political statement: it was intended to legitimise the rule of Augustus, who also proclaimed himself the scion of Venus.

The relief is part of a larger cycle intended for a memorial of Augustus's victory at Actium in 31 BC, which put an end to the civil war. Part of the series depicted the battle at sea, and the other panels the subsequent celebrations. After Augustus's death he was venerated as a god, and temples were erected to him. The reliefs may have adorned just such a shrine serving for the cult of the emperor.

SZILVIA LAKATOS

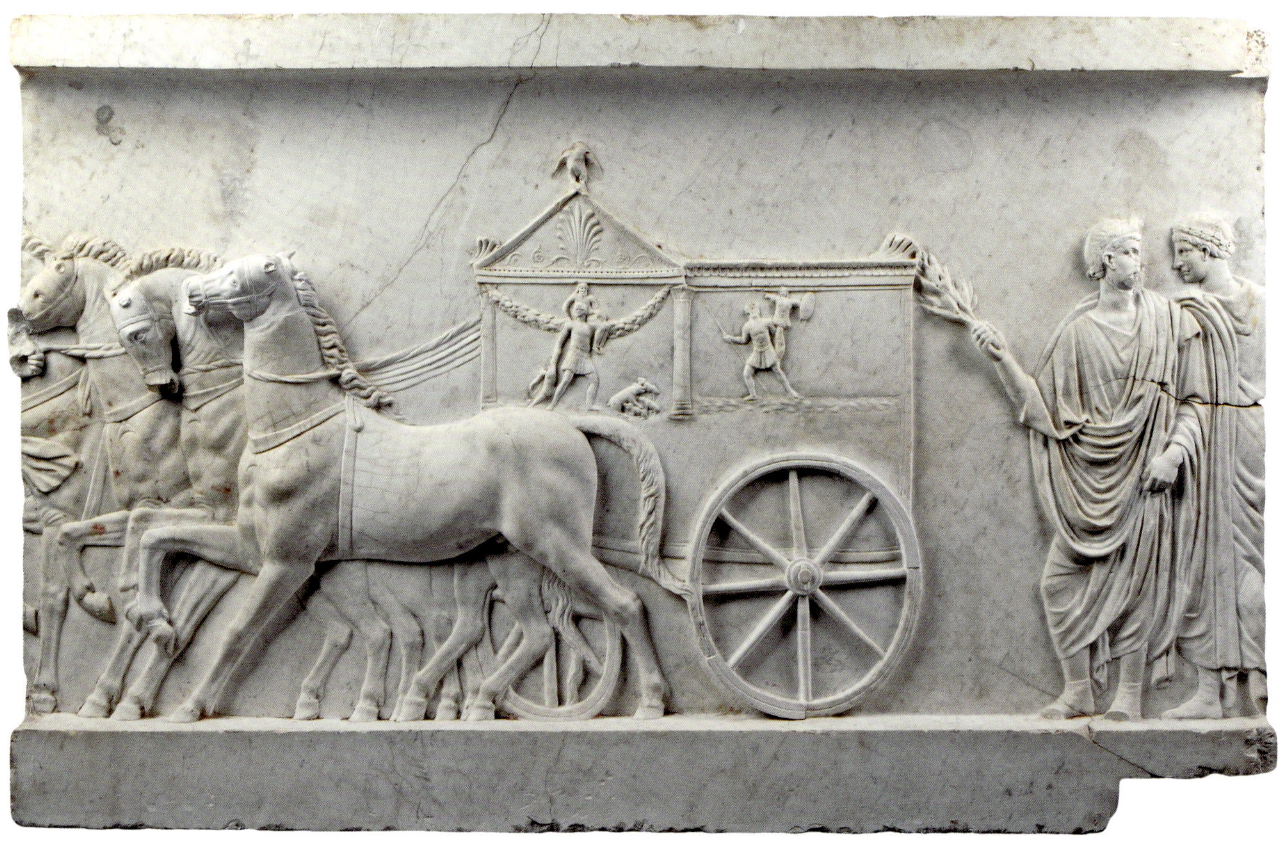

Orpheus

3rd century AD
Mosaic, height: 97 cm
Purchased in 2004
Inv. no. 2005.7.A

After the destruction of Carthage (146 BC) the central part of Northern Africa became the Roman province called Africa. Agricultural production in the large local estates played a crucial role in supplying the empire, so Africa became one of the richest regions. In terms of art, the area was closely linked to the classical culture of the Greco-Roman world. For instance, the floors of wealthy villas were adorned with vast mosaics depicting stories from mythology.

Orpheus was the most famous songster in Greek mythology. His singing and playing the lyre charmed even the gods of the underworld, who restored to him his dead wife, Eurydice. His music even subdued wild animals – this scene was a popular subject for Roman mosaics, with Orpheus in the centre, and round about the animals turning to face him. This mosaic may also have been the central part of such a large-scale composition.

Orpheus became especially popular from the beginning of the third century, in the late imperial period which faced the crisis of the empire and classical culture. By then the figure of the singer had been enriched with novel elements: for instance, he was thought to be the originator of a Greek religious belief which aimed to secure the soul's prosperity in the afterlife. The image of the divine singer thus offered countless possibilities of interpretation, which varied according to era, region and intellectual persuasion. In fact, his figure was adopted unchanged by Early Christian art as one possible form of representation of Christ.

SZILVIA LAKATOS

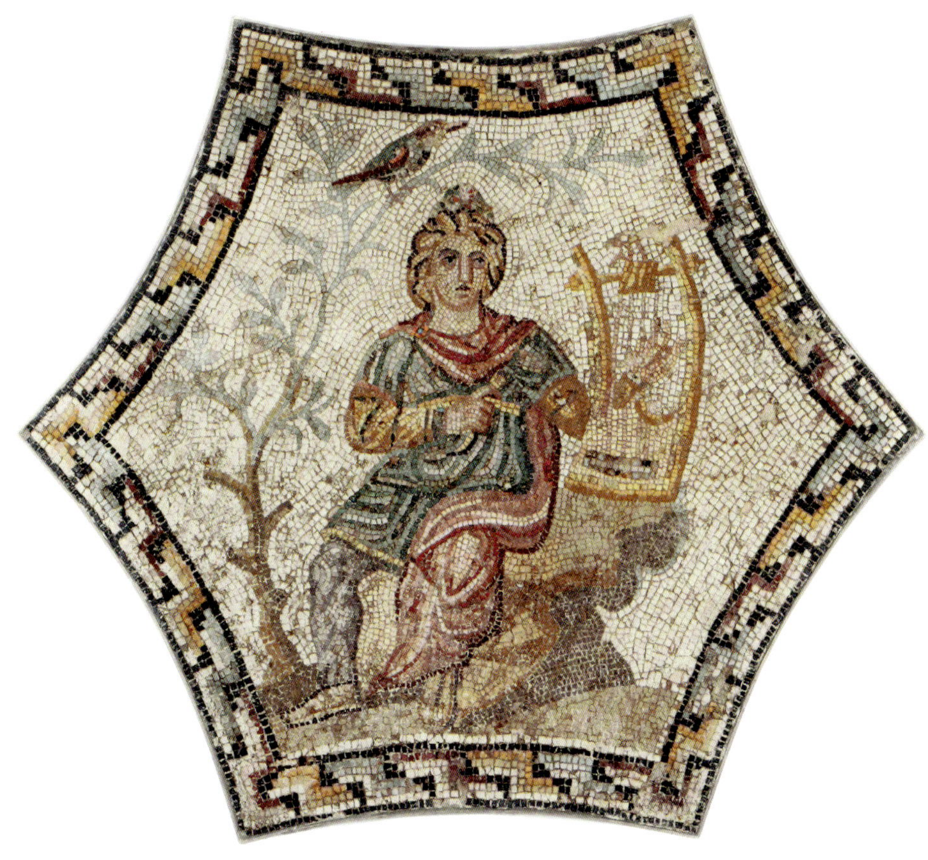

Head of a King

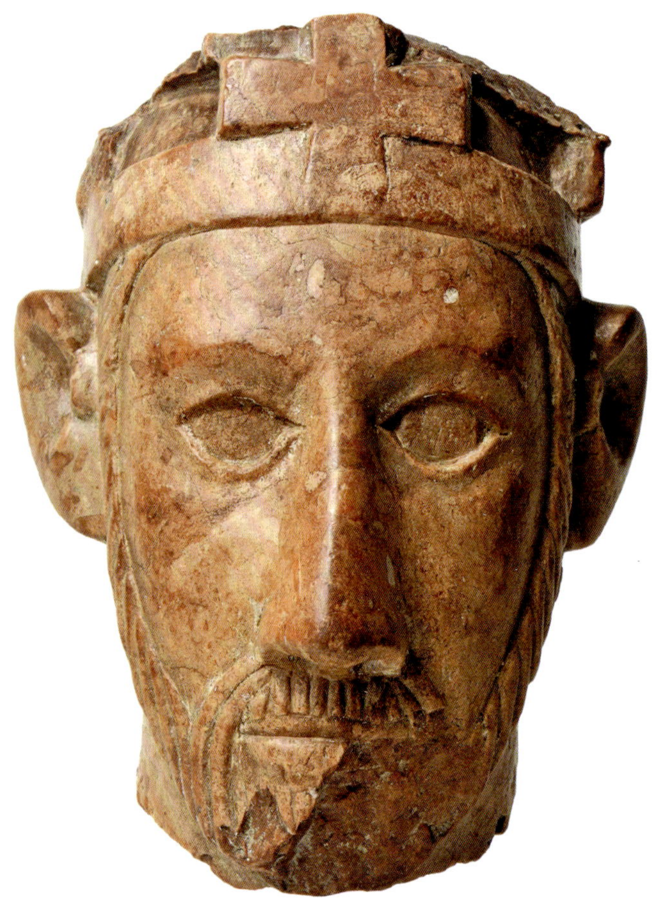

From Kalocsa, ca. 1200–1230
Red limestone, 17 × 13.5 × 12 cm
Transferred from the Hungarian National Museum, 1936
Inv. no. 53.364

The Hungarian National Museum, Hungary's first public museum, owes much of its early history to those noblemen and church leaders who contributed to the museum's development, either by donating money or by offering their own personal collections to the nation. Lajos Haynald (1816–1891), for example, the highly cultured and scholarly Archbishop of Kalocsa, gave the museum his entire library as well as his botanical collection, comprising over a hundred thousand plant specimens. Haynald's interests also stretched to Hungarian history and art, and he organised the first archaeological excavations of the medieval parts of Kalocsa Cathedral, which he followed attentively all the way through. The most important church in Kalocsa had been rebuilt at the start of the thirteenth century in the spirit of the new French style, the Gothic, but due to the Mongol invasions and later reconstruction work, hardly anything remained of it. The excavations uncovered numerous Gothic stone carvings, and thanks to the archbishop's generosity, they ended up in the National Museum. Among them is this small statue of a head wearing a crown.

Despite some claims that the statue depicts King Saint Stephen I, it is more likely that it was part of a relief of Christ the King. Like many of the prominent decorative elements of medieval buildings in Hungary, the head was carved from red limestone, which resembles the noble appearance of red marble. This suggests that the relief may originally have adorned one of the entrances to Kalocsa Cathedral.

ORSOLYA VERESS

The Expectant Virgin (Maria Gravida)

Fragment of a panel painting, 1409 ?
Tempera and gold on pine, 89 × 78 cm
Inv. no. 52.656

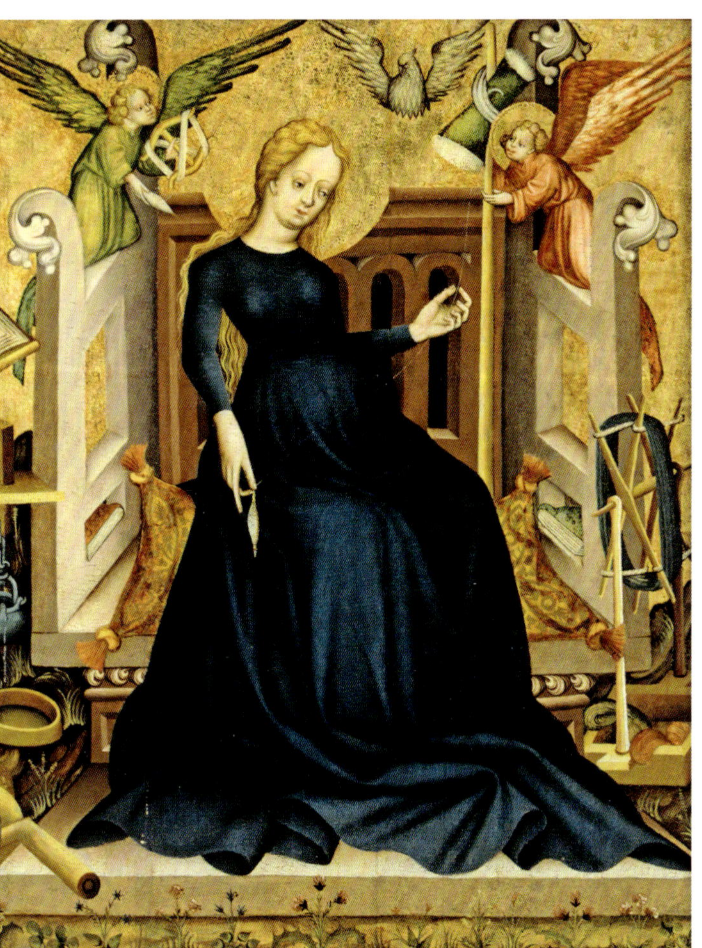

The main purpose of this fragmentary painting is to inspire awe in the Virgin, who is depicted pregnant with the Saviour. The dove of the Holy Spirit hovers above Mary's head. The spindle, reel and thread allude to spinning, evidence of her diligence, while the basin, the water bowl and the towel, as well as the colourful flowers in the foreground, are symbols of cleanliness. According to the brush drawing discovered on the ground layer of the picture, which was not included in the finished version, on Mary's belly, the artist originally planned to depict the unborn Jesus in the foetal position, ringed with a halo and carrying the cross of his Crucifixion on his right shoulder. At the same time, near the left edge of the painting, the straw hat, the staff and the small barrel indicate that Mary's betrothed, Saint Joseph, was originally present in the picture: the green wing belonged to the angel Joseph saw in his dream, who dispelled his doubts about the chastity of the Holy Virgin. With its complexity of allusions, all of which would have been familiar to contemporary viewers, the painting served as an aid to personal religious contemplation. It may have been a self-contained work, erected in a church setting, or it could have been the central element of an altarpiece. According to some observers, this, the earliest painting of outstanding quality in the collection of the Museum of Fine Arts, may be the oldest surviving exemplar of medieval Viennese panel painting. The artist may be regarded as the first specific individual of a major workshop in Vienna that was widely active in the second decade of the fifteenth century.

GYÖRGYI POSZLER

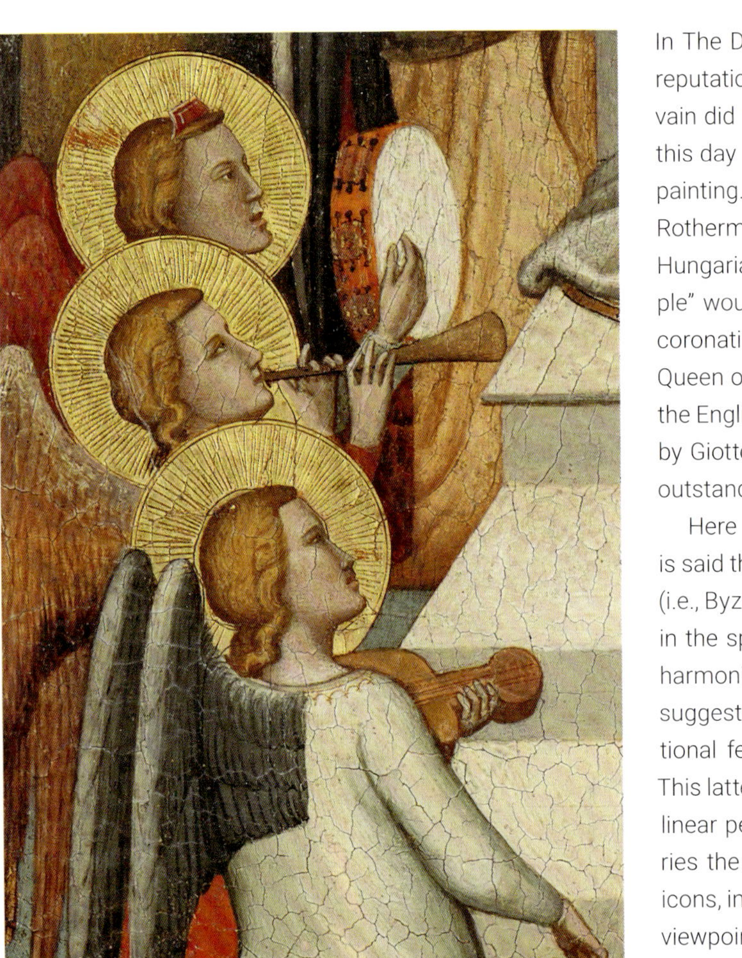

Maso di Banco

(active in Florence, in the 2nd quarter of the 14th century)

The Coronation of the Virgin

ca. 1328–1330

Tempera and gold on poplar, 51.2 × 51.7 cm

Gift of Lord Rothermere (London), 1940

Inv. no. 7793

In The Divine Comedy Dante predicted that Giotto's brilliant reputation would be but a fleeting glory. He was wrong: in vain did new more eloquent or passionate masters come; to this day Giotto is venerated as the father of modern Western painting. It is no wonder that the British press magnate Lord Rothermere, who was put forward as a possible heir to the Hungarian royal throne, felt that a fitting donation to "his people" would be a fine, characteristic Giotto, which depicted a coronation scene: the inauguration of the Virgin Mary as Queen of Heaven. And though the crown did not finally go to the Englishman, and the picture is no longer considered to be by Giotto but by his most excellent pupil Maso di Banco, its outstanding value has indubitably remained.

Here we see the essence of Giotto's stylistic revolution. It is said that he translated the language of painting from Greek (i.e., Byzantine) to Latin, and his rational style is indeed rooted in the spirit of classical antiquity. The ultimate theme is the harmonious order which reigns in the created world: this is suggested by both the calm mood free of pathos or emotional fervour, and the clear, rational geometrical structure. This latter is unified by the new method of representing space, linear perspective, the system which would define for centuries the way Western artists saw the world. Unlike with the icons, in this system the scene is seen from a single, personal viewpoint, making the beholder the very centre of the picture's microcosm.

A X E L   V É C S E Y

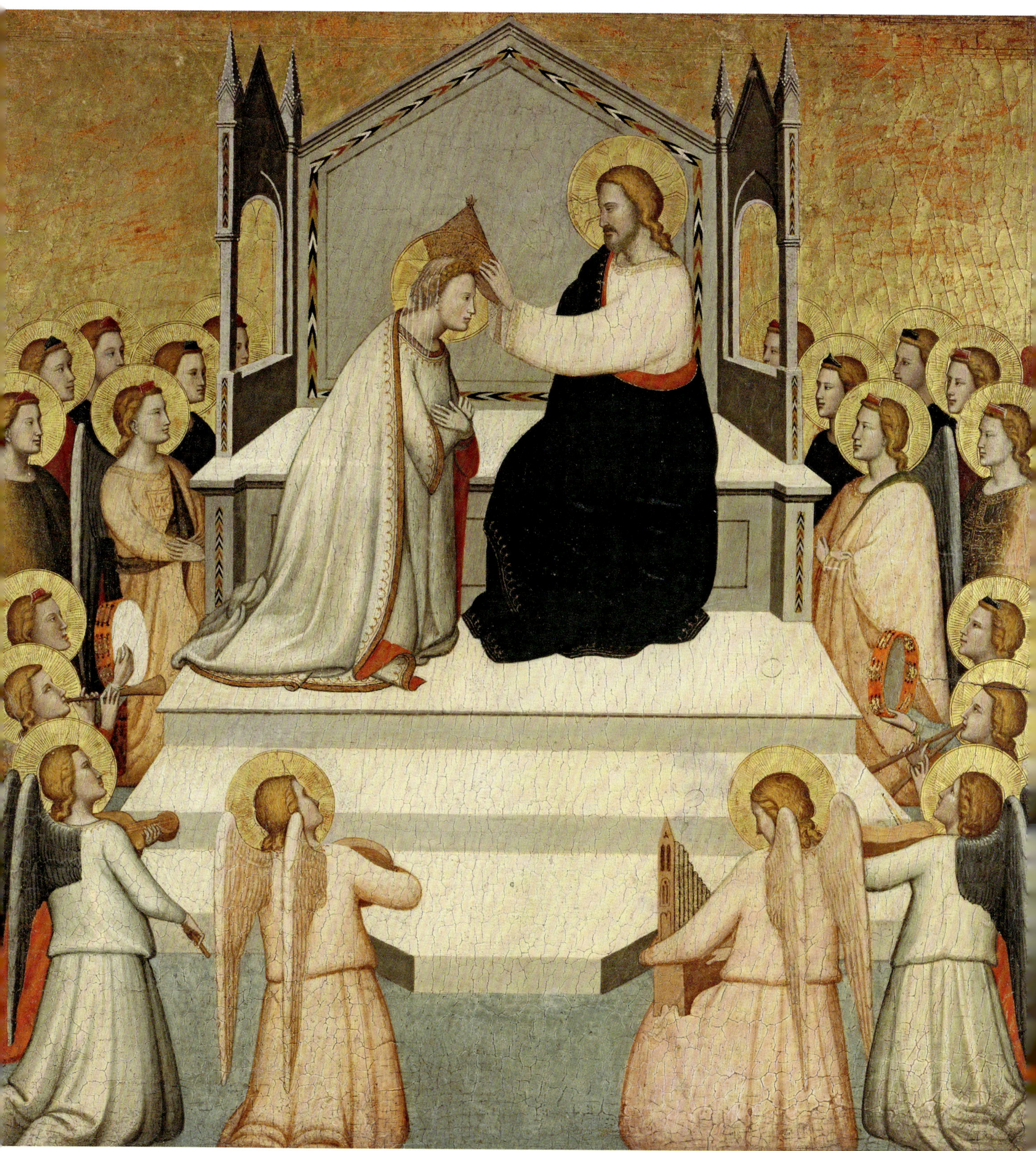

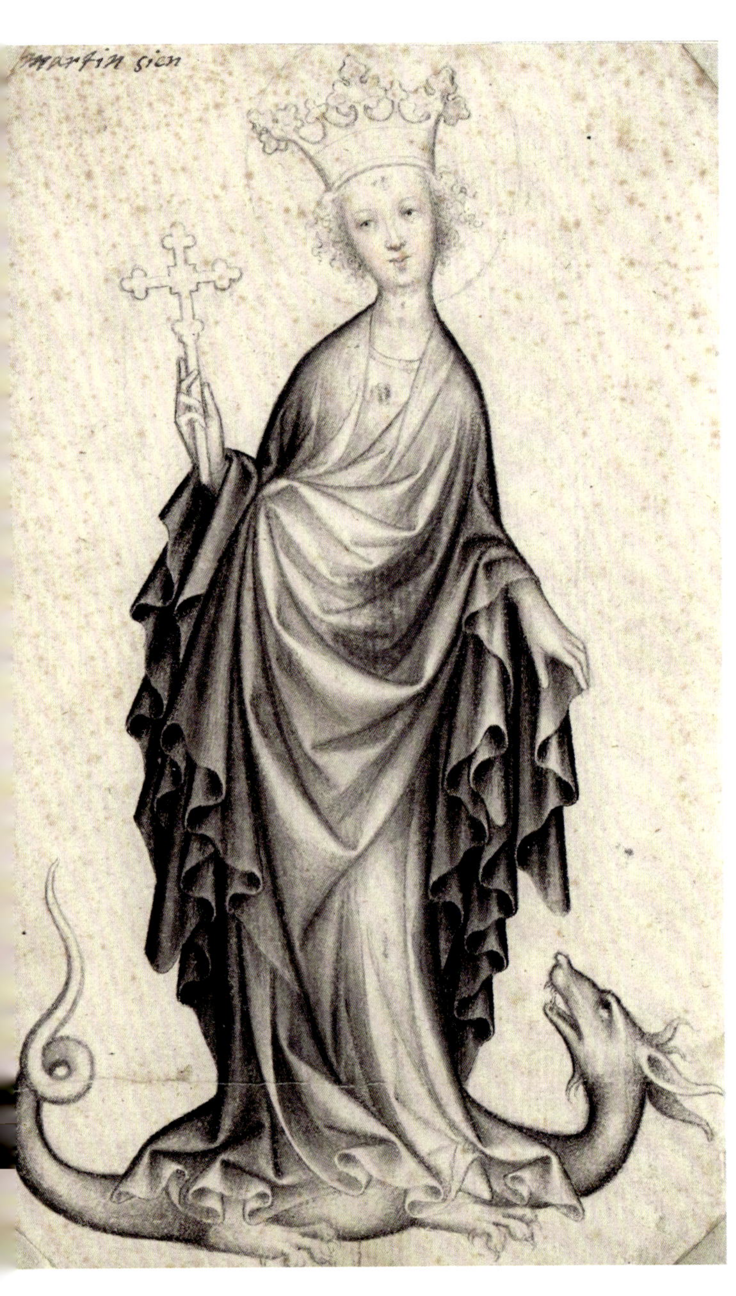

Czech artist

Saint Margaret

ca. 1410–1415
Brush, black ink, black and red chalk and grey wash on paper,
214 × 140 mm
Esterházy collection, purchased in 1871
Inv. no. 1

In the chaotic time of the political and ideological decline of the late Middle Ages a wealth of art sprang forth. The art of around 1400, international Gothic, conquered all the important ruling centres of Europe simultaneously: courts of kings, dukes and nobles. Prague, the new imperial residence of the Holy Roman Emperor, was then at its zenith. Late Czech Gothic infiltrated not only nearby towns, but made its influence felt in the whole of Central European art.

The Budapest *Saint Margaret*, drawn with soft lines in the elegant pose of the "Beautiful Madonnas", popular in international Gothic art, is probably the work of a Czech master. Madonnas and saints curved in a gentle S-shape, radiating tenderness and calm, often appear on panel pictures, as book illustrations and as statues. This Saint Margaret, her mantle falling in deep folds and shaded with a high degree of plasticity, may have been intended as a model for a sculpture.

Medieval masters did not generally work directly from nature, but gleaned inspiration from earlier works of art. The pattern sheets which preserved popular motifs were greatly respected in the workshops, and jealously guarded. However, very few drawings from this period are known. The Budapest *Saint Margaret*, which is in surprisingly good condition, and is unusually large for the era, is a rare, fine work of Gothic art.

ZOLTÁN KÁRPÁTI

German or Prague sculptor

Beautiful Madonna

ca. 1430
Painted limestone, 124.5 × 43 × 32 cm
Purchased in Frankfurt, 1916
Inv. no. 4967

European art around 1400 took on a uniform decorative style which swept away the differences between the various artistic centres. This style, which appeared simultaneously in many important centres in Europe and affected all branches of art, is now known as international Gothic. The lyrical, soft, and elegant style of late Gothic is perhaps most strikingly embodied in the Madonna statues, which were known as *Beautiful Madonnas* on account of their main characteristic, the idealised charm suggestive of supernatural beauty. This outstanding statue is one of the best known of the Beautiful Madonnas. Typically for this type, the Virgin is shown with a conspicuously young face, a tall crown, and her markedly emphasized S-bend body is covered by a softly draped ample cloak carved into tubular pleats.

Identifying the place where the Beautiful Madonnas were made, in the uniform style that infused all of European art, is usually a very tall order. In the case of the Budapest sculpture, bought on the Frankfurt art market, even the provenance is doubtful. Thus it has been associated with almost every important artistic centre of the time: it has been considered a Rheinish, Silesian, or Salzburg work, but most likely seems an origin in the Prague region. Equally debatable is the time it was sculpted. While it was initially compared to early Madonnas produced around 1390, it is now held to be rather a work from the close of the period, at about 1430.

MIRIAM SZŐCS

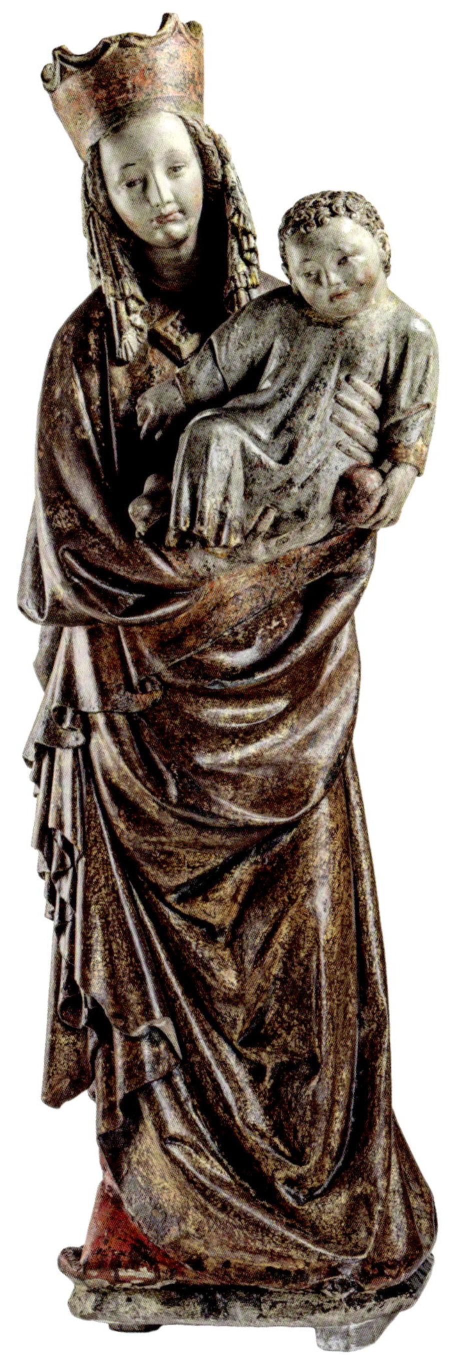

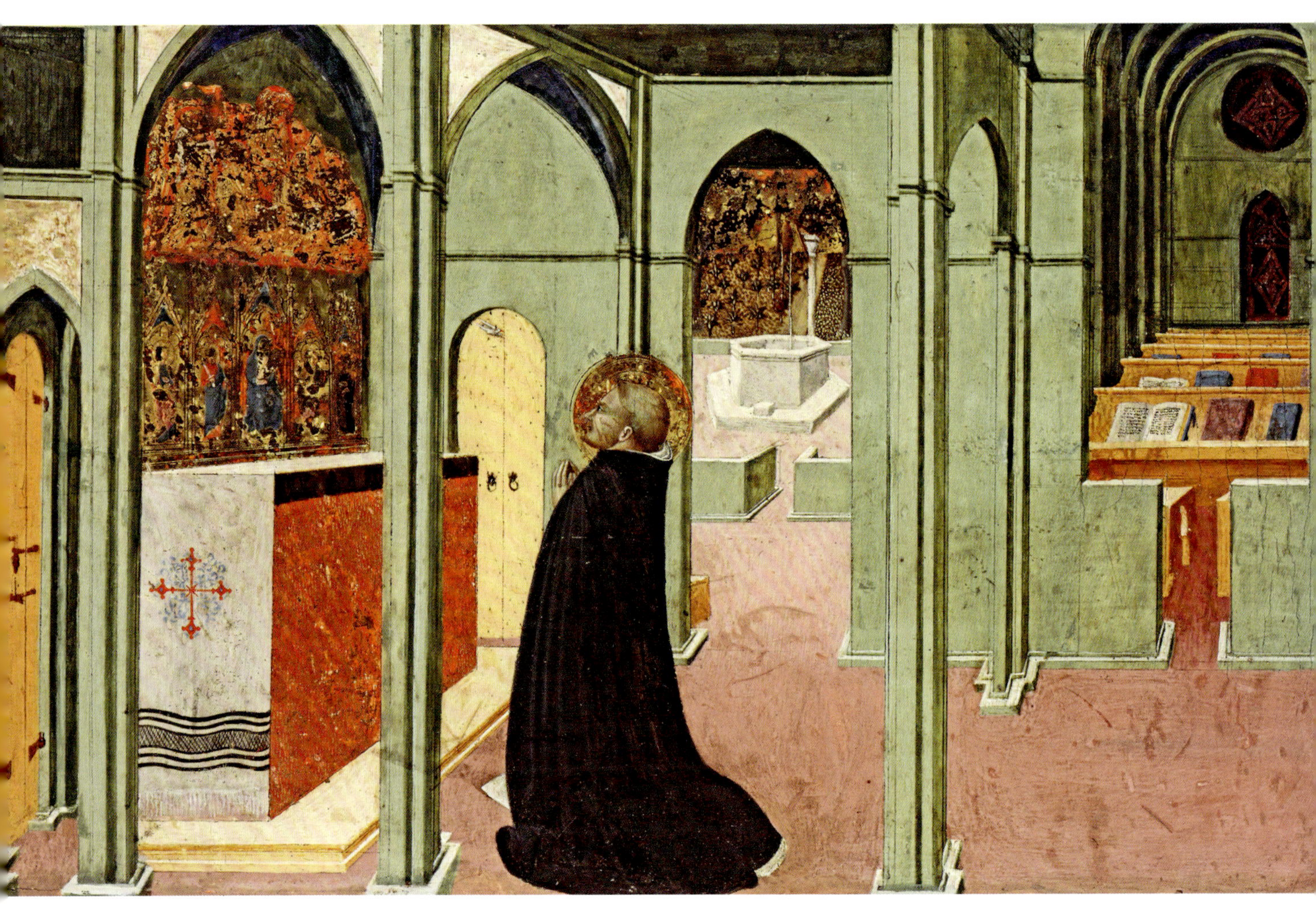

Sassetta (Stefano di Giovanni)
(ca. 1400–1450)

Saint Thomas Aquinas in Prayer

ca. 1423–1425
Tempera and gold on wood, 23.6 × 39 cm
Gift of Arnold Ipolyi, 1872
Inv. no. 32

"You have written well of me, Thomas" said the vision of Christ, according to the legend, to Saint Thomas of Aquinas, when he prayed for a sign of whether what he had written was true. The last great painter of the lyrical Sienese Gothic school, Sassetta's brush brings to life with a kind of "magic realism" the enchanting world where the believer engages in intimate discourse with the divine sphere day by day. The saint now pleads for inspiration in front of a household altar, and his prayer is answered: Christ embodies in golden light and sends to him the dove of the Holy Spirit. The miracle takes place in the interior of a monastery, brought to life with many familiar details. The codices left open on the desks remind us the friars who used to fill the library with life. In the background a view opens onto a garden and within it a fountain, the centre of everyday life in the monastery. This tiny masterpiece comes from a polyptych's predella, the horizontal base supporting the larger pictures. The altarpiece was commissioned by the Sienese guild of wool merchants, and was kept locked in a cupboard in the guild's headquarters. Each year on the feast of Corpus Christi it was erected in front of the building, and an open-air mass was celebrated before it to the participants of the procession. The tradition lasted until the sixteenth century, when the altarpiece was moved into a church. Finally it met the fate of so many medieval polyptychs: it was sawn into pieces and sold to art collectors.

A X E L   V É C S E Y

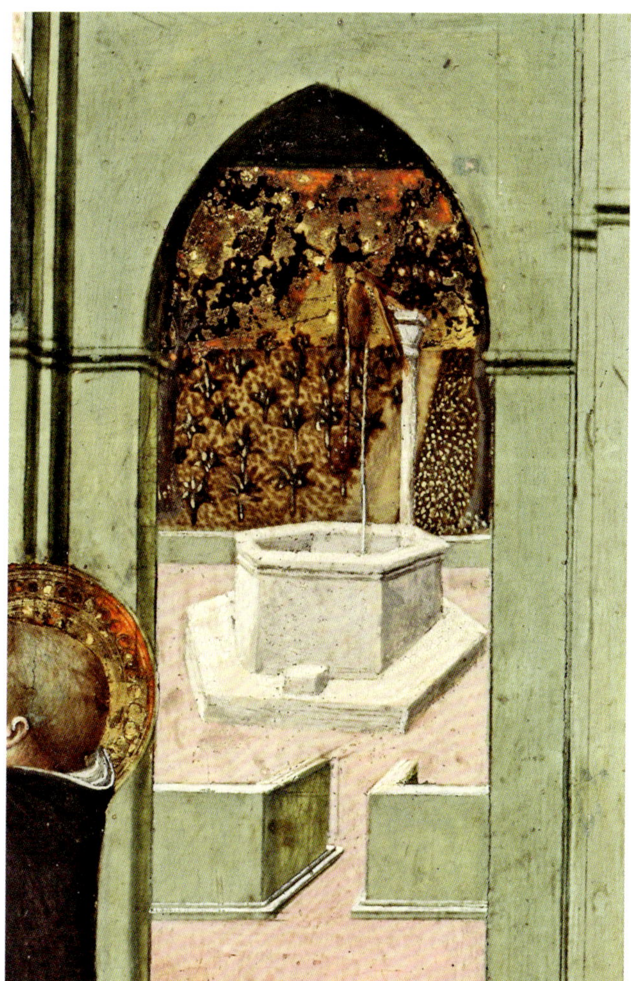

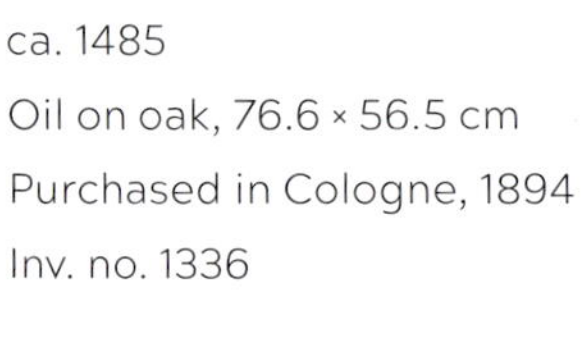

Gerard David (ca. 1460–1523)

The Adoration of the Shepherds

ca. 1485
Oil on oak, 76.6 × 56.5 cm
Purchased in Cologne, 1894
Inv. no. 1336

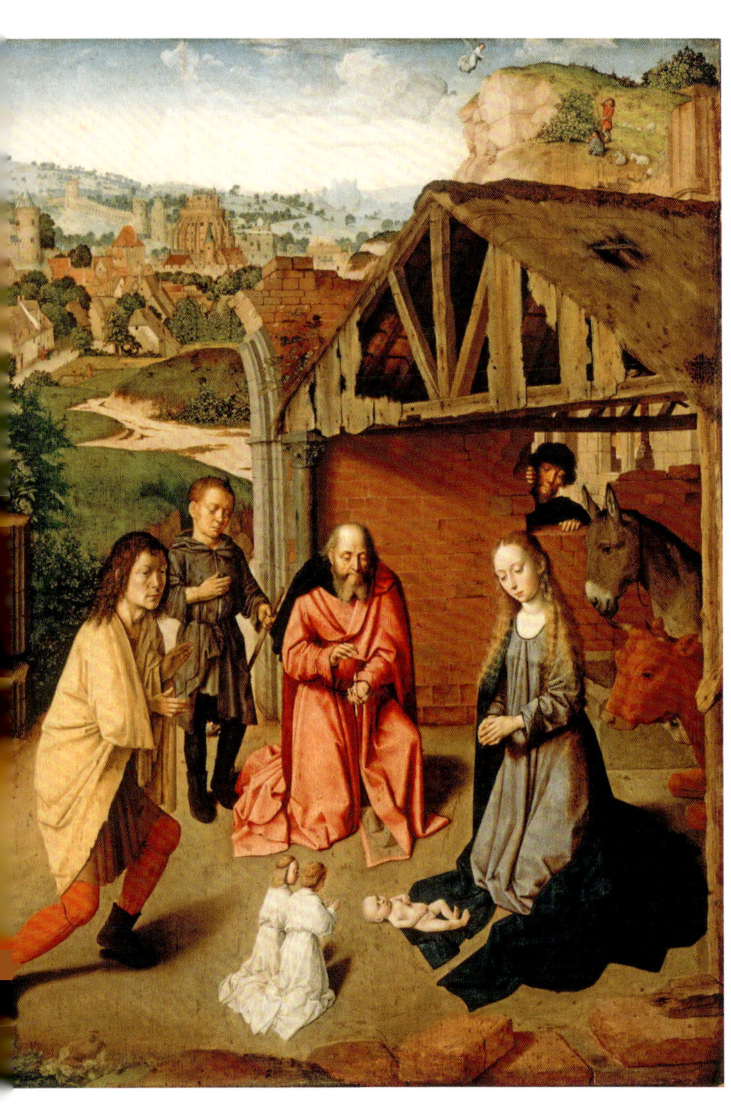

Gerard David was the last great master to practise the stylistic tradition of Early Netherlandish painting that originated with Jan van Eyck. This is a curious art, with a radically different approach to that of Italian contemporaries, who incidentally were enthusiastic admirers of Northern paintings; indeed, it was from these that they picked up the knack of painting with oils. But this technical innovation, which charmed onto the surface a vitreous shine like a transparent precious stone, is only one of countless means with which these pictures enchant the receptive viewer. The aesthetics of "small is beautiful", the meticulous and affectionate execution of every minute detail of the depicted world, is what makes this refined style so vivid.

The jewelbox-like town of Bruges, where David settled as a young man, looks as if it were the essence of this tradition. Here worked the most eminent painter of the time, Hans Memling, whose elegant, courtly style exercised a decisive influence on the youth. As the cityscape visible in the background is enlivened with all manner of small details, so the story is enriched with all kinds of episodes, in order to bring the miracle closer to the viewer, that it be more directly experienced. For instance, the candle in Joseph's hand reminds us that actually it is night, though the light radiating from the newborn shines bright as day over the landscape. The young shepherd in a yellow cape bears the painter's own features.

A X E L   V É C S E Y

Petrus Christus (ca. 1415–1475/1476)

Virgin and Child

ca. 1450–1455
Oil on oak, 55.8 × 31.8 cm
From the estate of Count János Pálffy, 1912
Inv. no. 4324

Long before the radical movements of the twentieth century, artists already abstracted from visible reality in a number of different ways. Early Netherlandish painting, which began with Jan van Eyck, showed us the hairs on our heads and the leaves on the trees as though we were looking at them through a magnifying glass, with countless details recreated with immaculate precision. This, in itself, is the first abstraction, for this is not our natural way of seeing things: we tend to focus on certain details and ignore others, not to make a full inventory of everything in sight. The execution of the details is also untrue to life, for it idealises the spectacle, as though every object and body were made of some impeccable material, with the surface polished to a perfect sheen. This is not the mundane world, but a celestial replica, bathed in a heavenly glow. The third abstraction involves the careful selection of motifs, which is an intrinsic part of devotional paintings. In this diminutive picture by Petrus Christus, the Bruges master who inherited the tradition of Van Eyck, the Virgin Mary, holding the Infant Jesus, is seen through an arched gateway, standing on a terrace that ends in an ornate seat, overlooking a landscape – these elements are there for a reason, as visualisations of the liturgical metaphors used in honour of Mary. She is the "Gate of Heaven" and the "Seat of Wisdom", while her Son redeems the world from Original Sin, alluded to by the gilt bronze statues placed in the frame of the archway. Jesus is still a babe in arms, but his right hand is raised in blessing, while in his left he holds the globe, a symbol of redemption.

VILMOS TÁTRAI

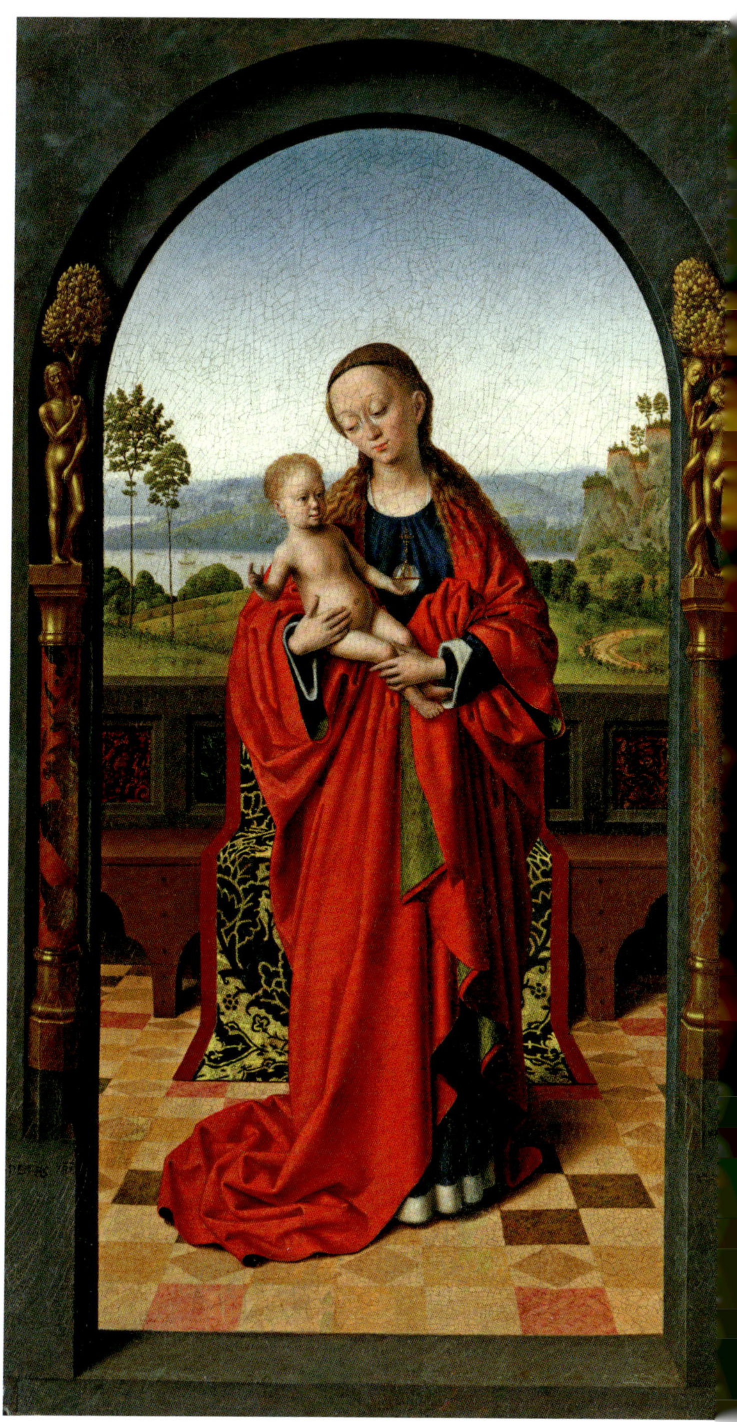

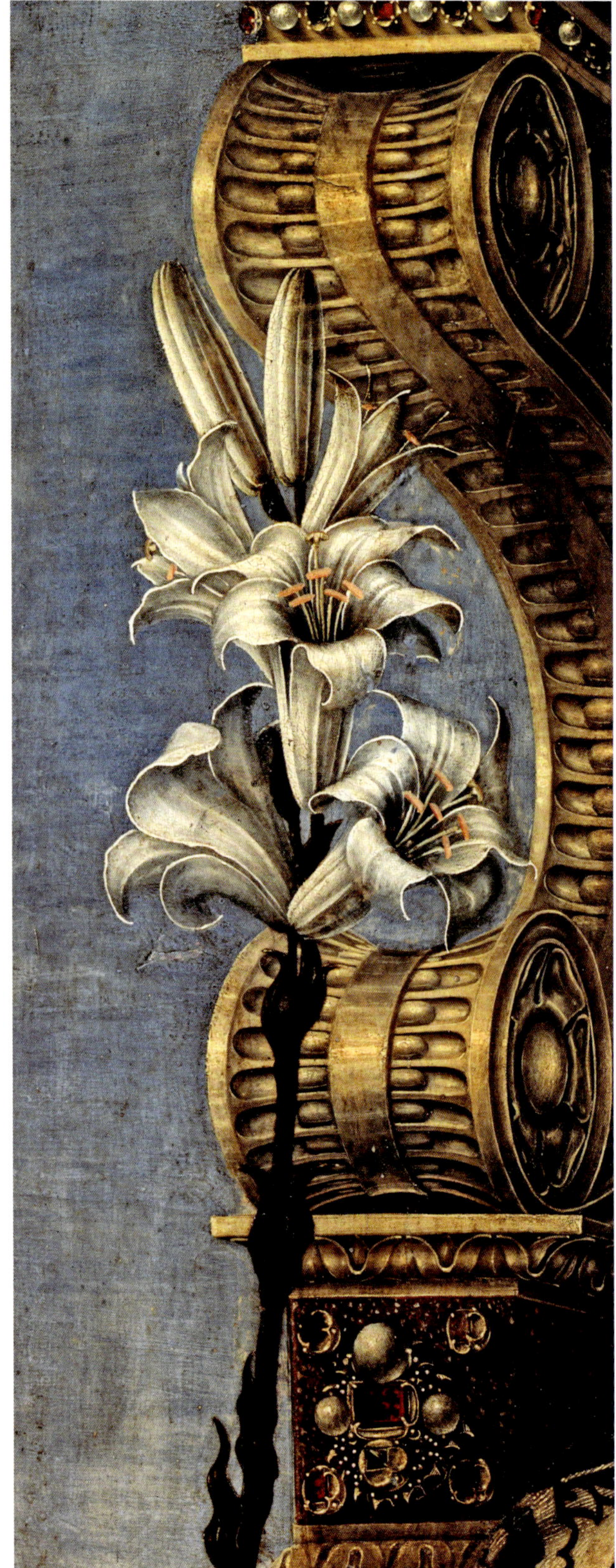

Michele Pannonio (ca. 1400–1464)

The Muse Thalia

ca. 1456–1457
Tempera and oil on poplar, 136.5 × 82 cm
Gift of Arnold Ipolyi, 1880
Inv. no. 44

The wealthy urban bourgeoisie of Renaissance Italy liked to take refuge from the summer heat or epidemics in their countryside villas. As Boccaccio recounts in the *Decameron*, here they would relax, with instructive and amusing stories, music, dance, and witty conversation – in other words, they paid tribute to the muses. It was no coincidence, then, that they often adorned the walls with pictures of the muses. This was the case in what was perhaps one of the most famous summer retreats, the dukes of Ferrara's villa Belfiore ('beautiful flower'), where this picture comes from.

Michele Pannonio's name suggests that he was from Hungary (Pannonia). He may have been a friend of another famous Hungarian in the court at Ferrara, the poet Janus Pannonius, whose master Guarino da Verona devised the concept for the muses at Belfiore. The surviving text reveals that here we see Thalia, who is shown in the role of the muse of agriculture rather than the patroness of comedy. This is indicated by the motto at the bottom of the picture ("I taught man to plant"), and also the mature ears of wheat surrounding Thalia's head, the bunch of grapes in her hand, and the luxuriant fruit surrounding her throne. Her pregnant state, unusual for the muses, further reinforces the idea of fertility.

The willowy form of Thalia's body, her graceful curves and soft contours recall late Gothic taste. The lilies and swags of fruit, painted with robust naturalism, are more modern in style: they may have been painted by the gifted rival of Pannonio, Cosmè Tura.

AXEL VÉCSEY

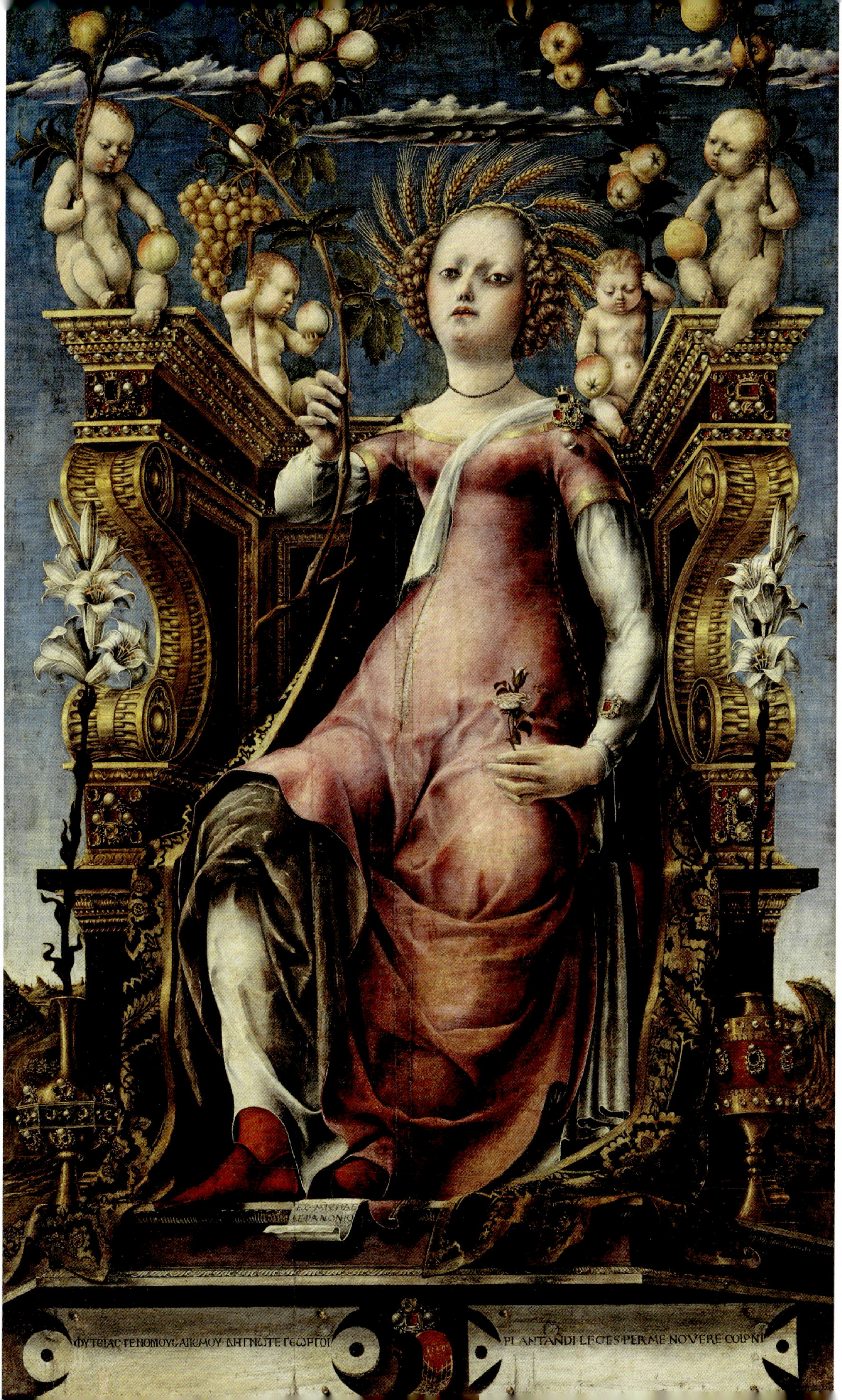

ΦΥΤΕΙΑΣ ΤΕ ΝΟΜΟΥΣ ΑΠ ΕΜΟΥ ΔΗ ΓΝΩΤΕ ΓΕΩΡΓΟΙ
PLANTANDI LEGES PER ME NOVERE COLONI

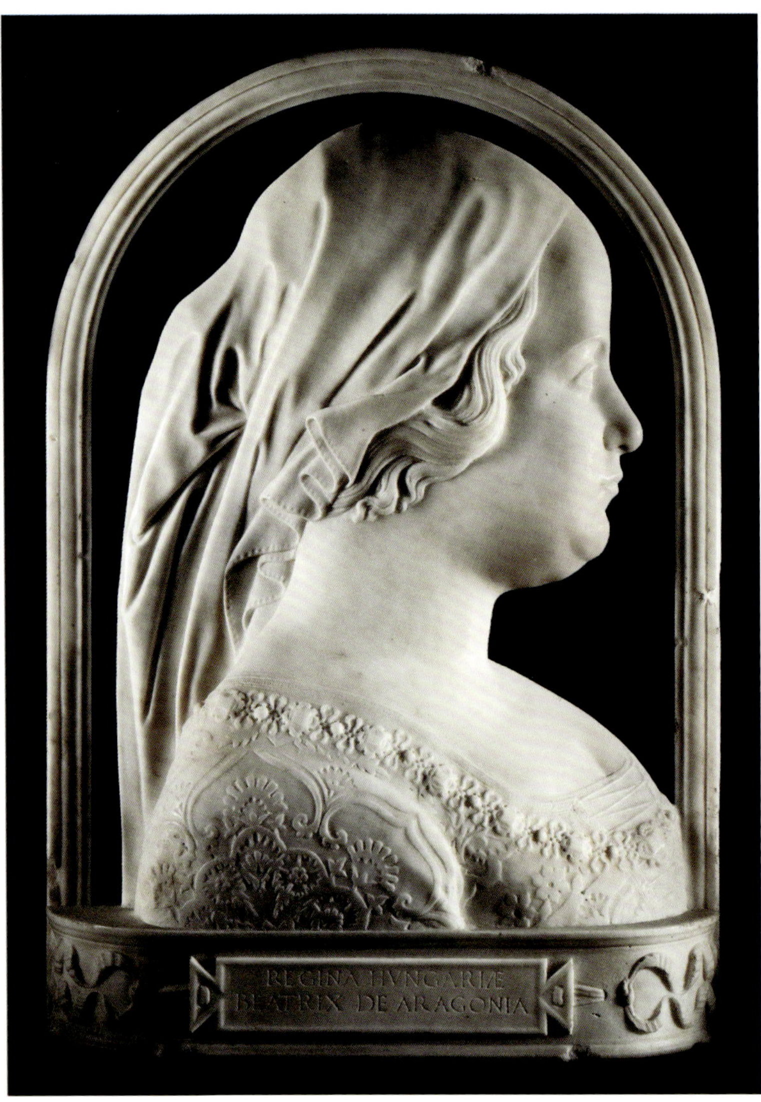

Attributed to Benedetto da Maiano (1442–1497)

Portrait of King Matthias Corvinus and Queen Beatrice

ca. 1476
Inscribed below on the front of the portrait of Matthias:
· REX ·
MATHIAS HVNGARIÆ

Inscribed below on the front of the portrait of Beatrice:
REGINA HVNGARIÆ
BEATRIX DE ARAGONIA

White marble, dark green serpentinite,
55 × 38.5 × 13 cm, 55 × 38.5 × 13 cm
Transferred from the former imperial collections in Vienna according to the 1932 Austro-Hungarian Agreement, 1934
Inv. no. 6711, 6712

The marble reliefs of King Matthias Corvinus (original name: Mátyás Hunyadi [1443–1490], King Matthias I of Hungary: 1458–1490) and his second wife, Beatrice of Aragon (1457–1508) are outstanding pieces of Italian quattrocento portrait sculpture. Matthias was the first European ruler to establish Italian Renaissance art north of the Alps. These antique-style relief portraits were carved from Carrara marble fitted with

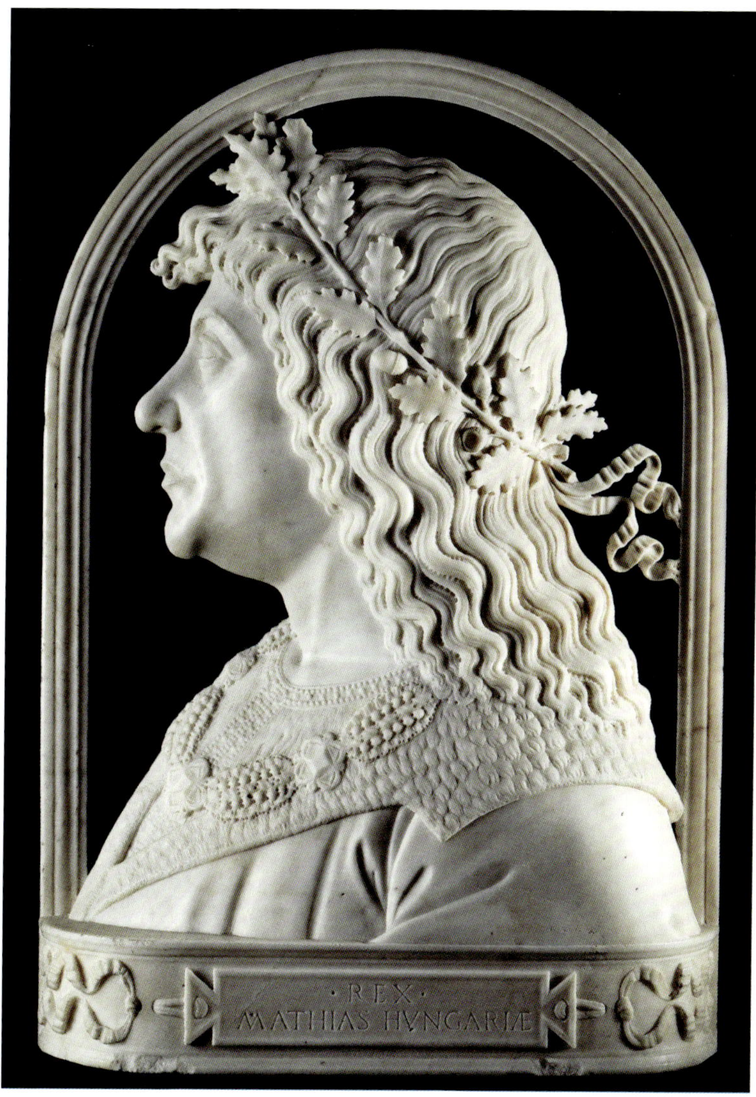

dark green serpentinite inlays. They were probably originally housed in the royal palace in Buda, although their first written mention is in a letter of 20 August 1571, written by King Maximilian, who was also, as Maximilian II, Holy Roman Emperor. At the time, the reliefs were held in Northern Hungary by Gergely Bornemissza, Provost of Szepes and Bishop of Csanád, and in the letter, Maximilian asked for them to be delivered to him. The portraits thus entered the imperial collection in Vienna on 14 March 1572, and were later acquired by the Kunsthistorisches Museum.

Hungarian history and art history writing only rediscovered the reliefs in the mid-nineteenth century. It used to be believed that the works were made by the sculptor Giovanni Dalmata (ca. 1440 – after 1509), who worked in Matthias's court from the early 1480s. More recent research, however, indicates that the twin portraits were carved in Florence around 1476 by Benedetto da Maiano, to commemorate the marriage between Matthias and Beatrice. The style of the reliefs and the use of different coloured materials recall other works by Maiano, who also, through the mediation of the Florentine banker and diplomat, Filippo Strozzi (1428–1491), regularly fulfilled commissions for Beatrice's father, King Ferdinand I of Naples (1423–1494, r. 1458–1494).

M I R I A M   S Z Ő C S

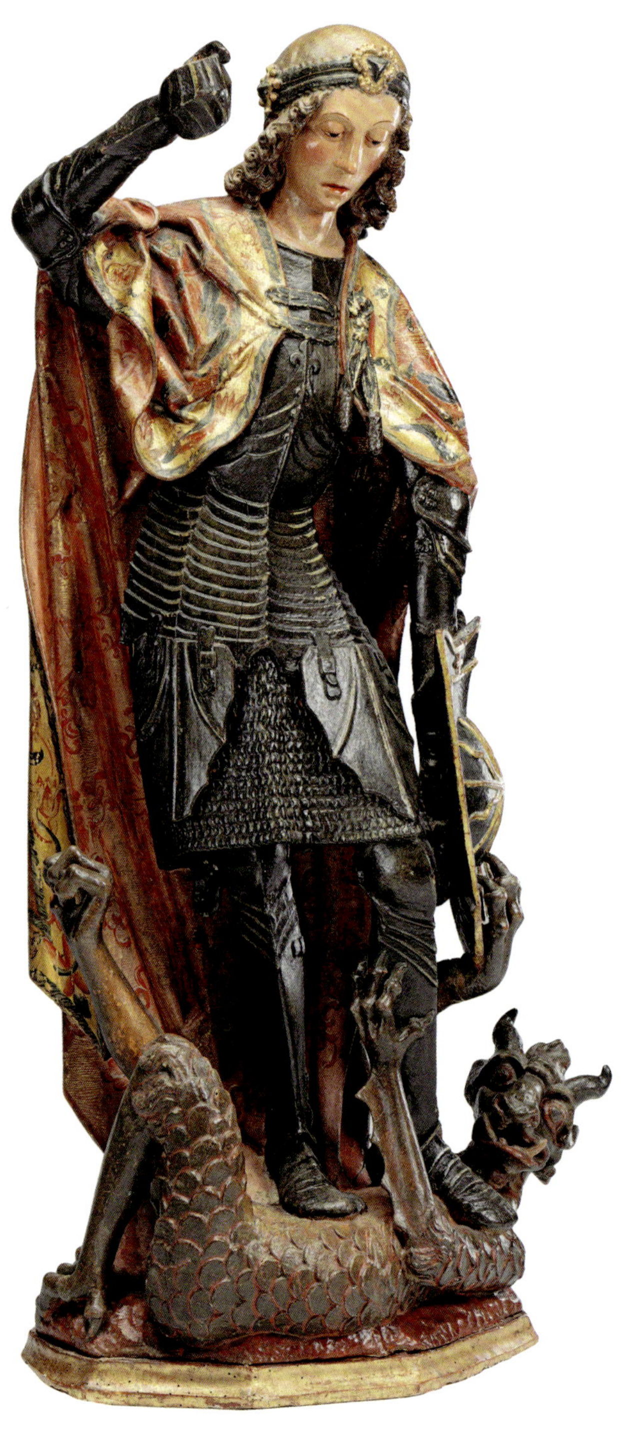

Saint Michael

ca. 1490
Painted, gilded, on carved wood, 110 × 50 × 30 cm
Purchased from the López de Aragón gallery
in Madrid, 2017
Inv. no. 2017.9

Gil de Siloé was one of the most important sculptors in Spain in the second half of the fifteenth century. Like many of his contemporaries working on Spanish soil, he originated from the Low Countries. He settled in Burgos in his youth, and one of his sons, Diego de Siloé, later acquired a reputation as a sculptor and architect.

Gil de Siloé's earliest surviving work is the altarpiece for the Chapel of Saint Anne in Burgos Cathedral, datable between 1486 and 1488. Between 1489 and 1493 he produced his most famous work, the double sepulchre of King John (Juan) II of Castile (d. 1454) and his wife, Isabella of Portugal (d. 1496), in Miraflores Charterhouse, not far from Burgos. Also here is the sepulchre of the royal couple's son, Infante Alfonso (d. 1468), which the sculptor completed in 1493, and the high altarpiece (retablo mayor), which he worked on between 1496 and 1499, in collaboration with Diego de la Cruz. The works of Gil de Siloé combine stylistic elements of Late Flemish Gothic with the densely crowded decorative tradition of Spanish art.

The authorship of this sculpture of Saint Michael was determined from stylistic comparison, as the saint's physiognomic features – emphatically rounded eyes and long, stern facial shape – are similar to those found on the figures of the high altarpiece in Miraflores Charterhouse. The figure, depicting Saint Michael as an archangel, originally had carved wings, and the place where they were affixed to the rear of the sculpture can still be seen. Saint Michael was extraordinarily popular in medieval Spanish art, as parallels were commonly drawn between the archangel's struggle against Satan and the fight against the Moorish occupation of Spain.

MIRIAM SZŐCS

Tilman Riemenschneider (ca. 1460–1531) and workshop

Virgin and Child

ca. 1505–1510
Painted limewood, 116 × 37 × 25 cm
Purchased in Frankfurt, 1923
Inv. no. 5898

Tilman Riemenschneider ran the largest sculpture workshop of his time, where with the help of over forty apprentices he fulfilled countless commissions. Not only were his works admired, but in time he was also elected a member of the town council of Würzburg. His unparalleled rise to fame ended in 1524–1525 with the German Peasants' War. Würzburg council sided with the peasants, so when the uprising was put down Riemenschneider too was incarcerated, and although he was soon set free in the years that followed he no longer received important commissions.

Riemenschneider belonged to the last generation of German late Gothic, and he raised woodcarving to a masterly level, introducing quite a few innovations. Monochrome unpainted wooden carved altars were disseminated largely through his works. In addition, his workshop was a model of organisation. Because he worked simultaneously on several commissions, the workshop produced one kind of sculpture for up to decades, almost unchanged in form. This Madonna is one of the popular types carved often, of which eight other versions are extant. They follow the pattern so closely that in addition to drawn designs it is conceivable that carved models were also used. Other evidence for this is that there are several small Riemenschneider wooden sculptures of barely half a metre high, which may have had just such a role in the shop.

MIRIAM SZŐCS

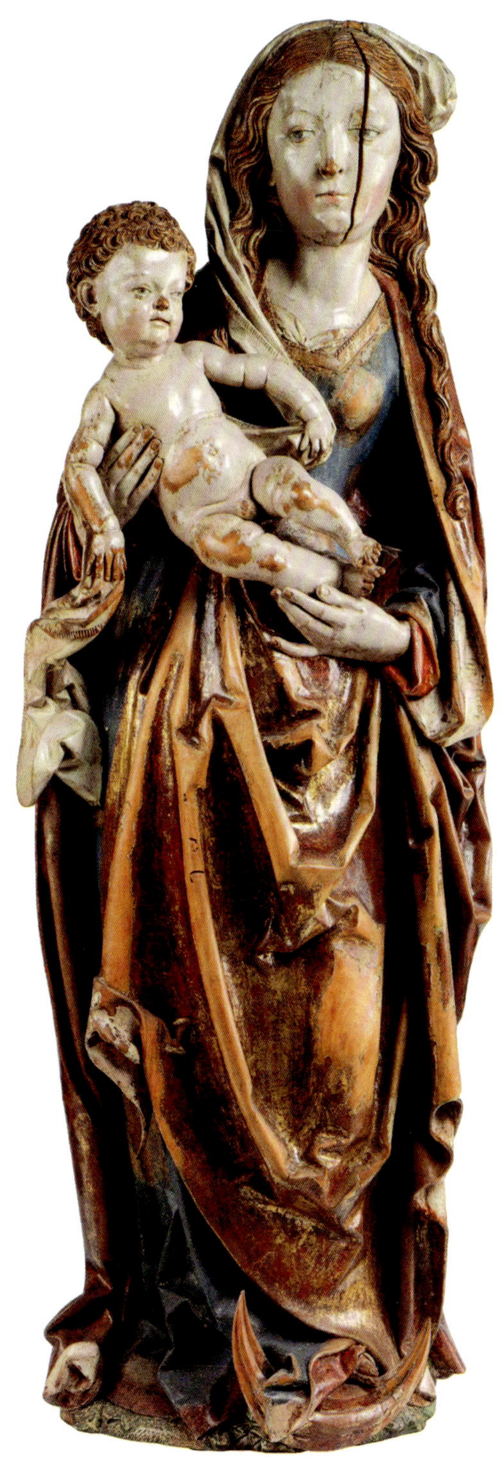

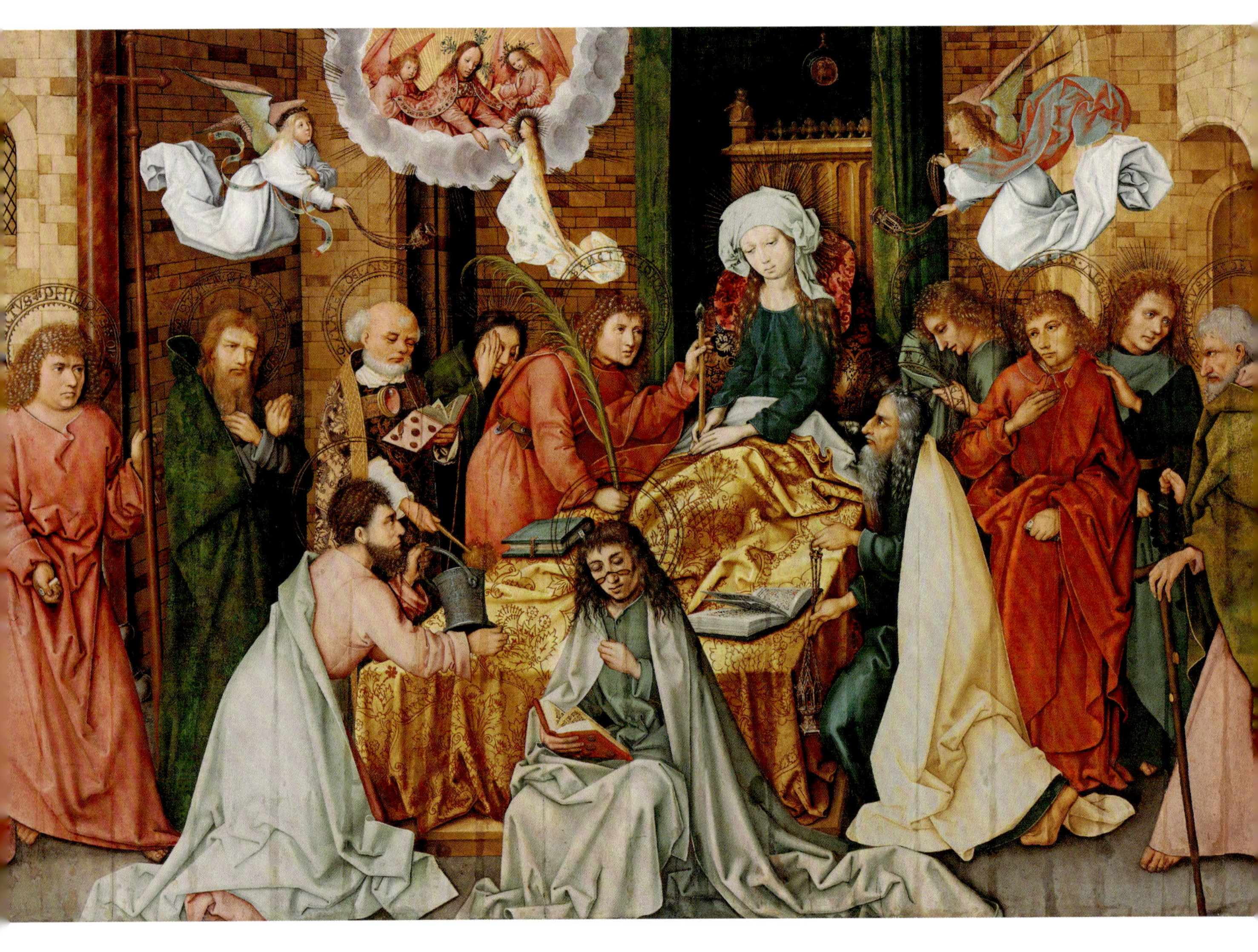

Hans Holbein the Elder (ca. 1465–1524)

Death of the Virgin

ca. 1491

Oil on oak, 150 × 228.5 cm

Gift of Ferenc Kleinberger, 1911

Inv. no. 4086

The Bible tells us little about the life of the Virgin Mary. People of the Middle Ages, however, wanted to know more about the woman who had become a focus of religion, and the supreme heavenly intercessor for the created world. Thus many apocryphal legends were born, and these episodes eventually appeared in church pictures. One of the most important stories was Mary's death. It is said that Jesus protected the body of his mother from earthly decay, and took her body and soul into heaven, where she was crowned Queen of Heaven. Medieval preachers often compared Mary's body, the vessel for the Redeemer, to the Ark of the Covenant, which "was of acacia, for that is incorruptible and the worms do not chew it away. Thus the body of the Virgin is worthy of being saved from corruption." Although today he is chiefly remembered as the father of the brilliant Hans the Younger, in his lifetime Holbein the Elder was also greatly esteemed. The *Death of the Virgin*, replete with small details taken from everyday life, is one of his most splendid works. The Virgin, with her unperishing young body prepares mildly for the end. The actions of the apostles gathered around the bed are consistent with the actual rite for the dead: Saint Peter sprinkles her with holy water, Andrew swings incense, and John puts a candle in her hand, the symbol of a peaceful death. Three read the scriptures, one of whom is, anachronistically, wearing spectacles. Meanwhile above the gate of heaven opens, and Jesus beckons his mother come hither.

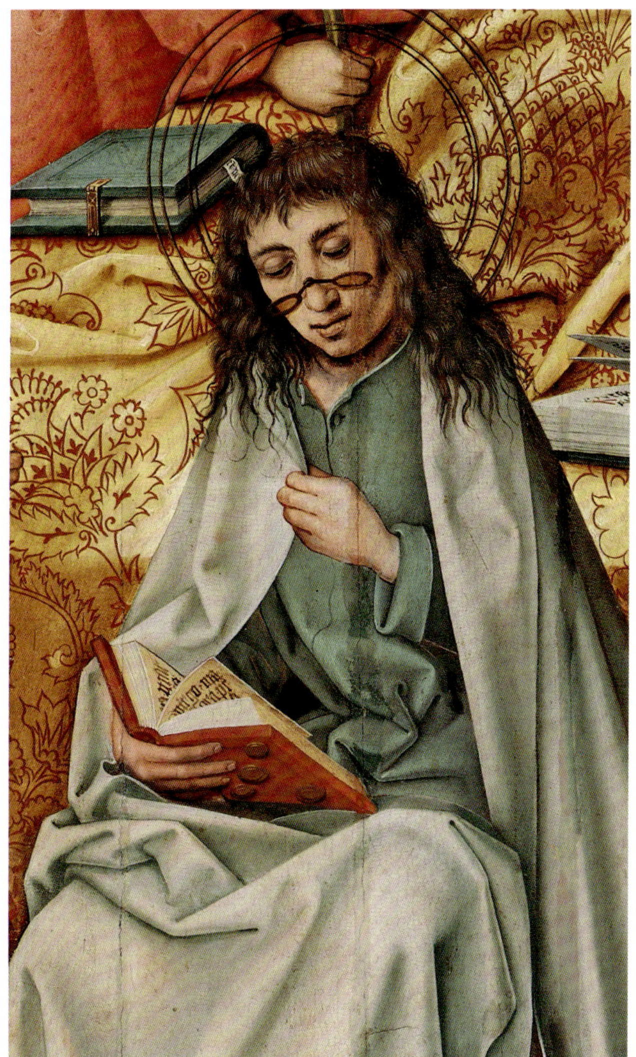

AXEL VÉCSEY

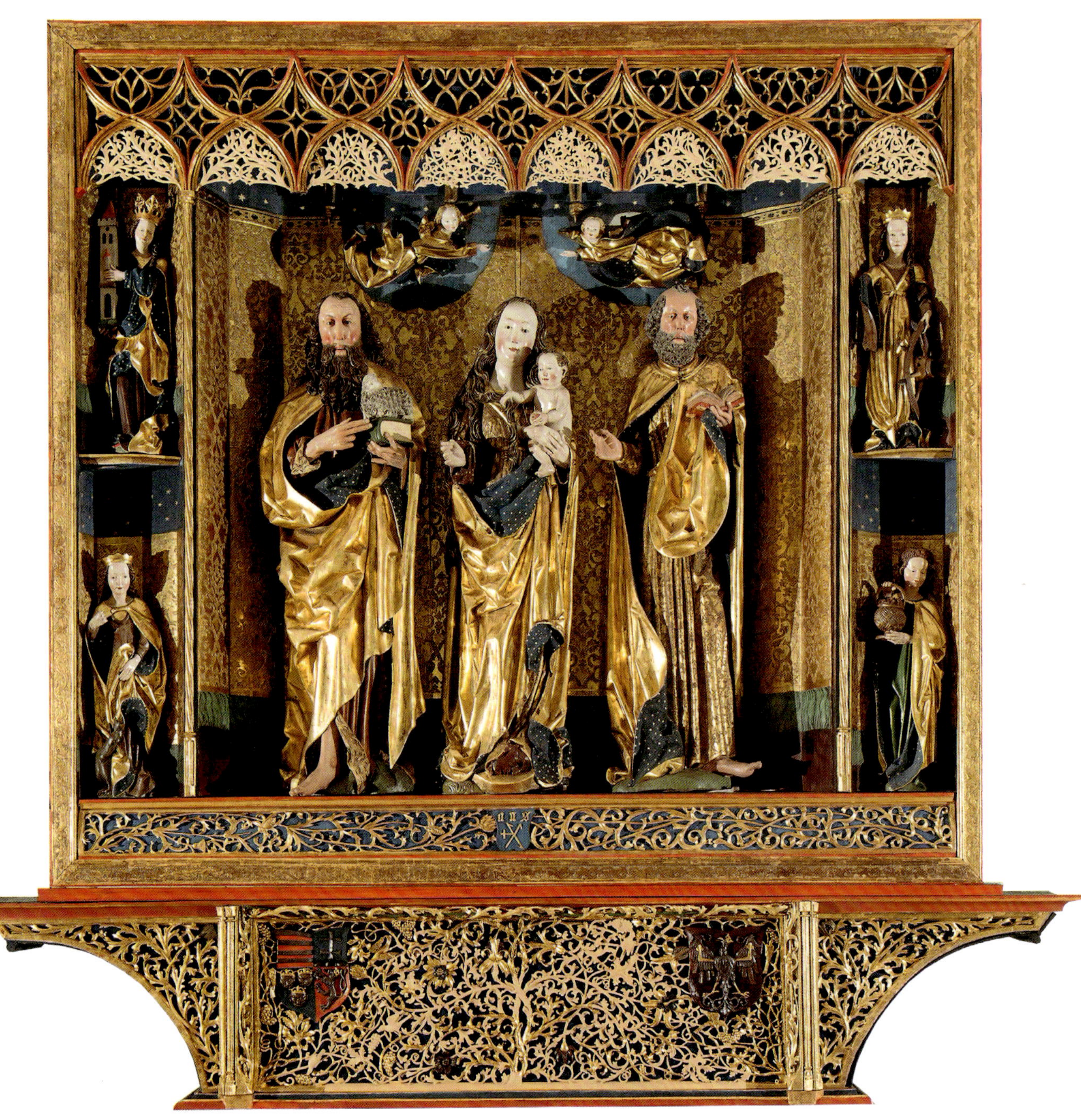

Altar of Saint John the Baptist

**Former main altar of the Church of Saint John the Baptist,
Kisszeben (now Sabinov, Slovakia)**

1496
Painted, gilded, on limewood and pine,
670 × 722 cm (when opened)
Transferred from the Museum of Applied Arts in 1909
Inv. no. 3916, 55.923, 64.1–2.M.

One of the largest and most ornate winged altarpieces from the medieval Kingdom of Hungary has the year 1496 written on the exterior of the wings. Inside the cabinet are larger-than-life-size statues of the Virgin Mary, Saint Peter and Saint John the Baptist, and the floating angels once held a crown above Mary's head. The richly decorated pinnacle originally consisted of several layers and bore some additional statues, but as this was the most fragile part of the altarpiece, it is no wonder that only fragments survive, especially given the work's troubled past. The brilliantly carved predella, featuring intricate foliage, grapes and birds, stands out as one of the most magnificent elements of the altarpiece. On feast days, when the altarpiece was opened, eight episodes from the life of Saint John the Baptist would be revealed to worshippers.

This high altarpiece, however, is remarkable for the scenes visible when the wings are closed, showing the so-called "workday side". Unparalleled among Hungarian altars, and indeed more broadly within the genre, the images follow the text of the Apostles' Creed, divided into sixteen episodes, with each scene illustrating one of the teachings. The symbolic depictions begin with a panel showing God the Almighty, Creator of Heaven and Earth, and progress through to an allegory of life everlasting. This unusual series was probably requested specifically by the commissioner of this exceptionally high-quality altarpiece.

GYÖRGYI POSZLER

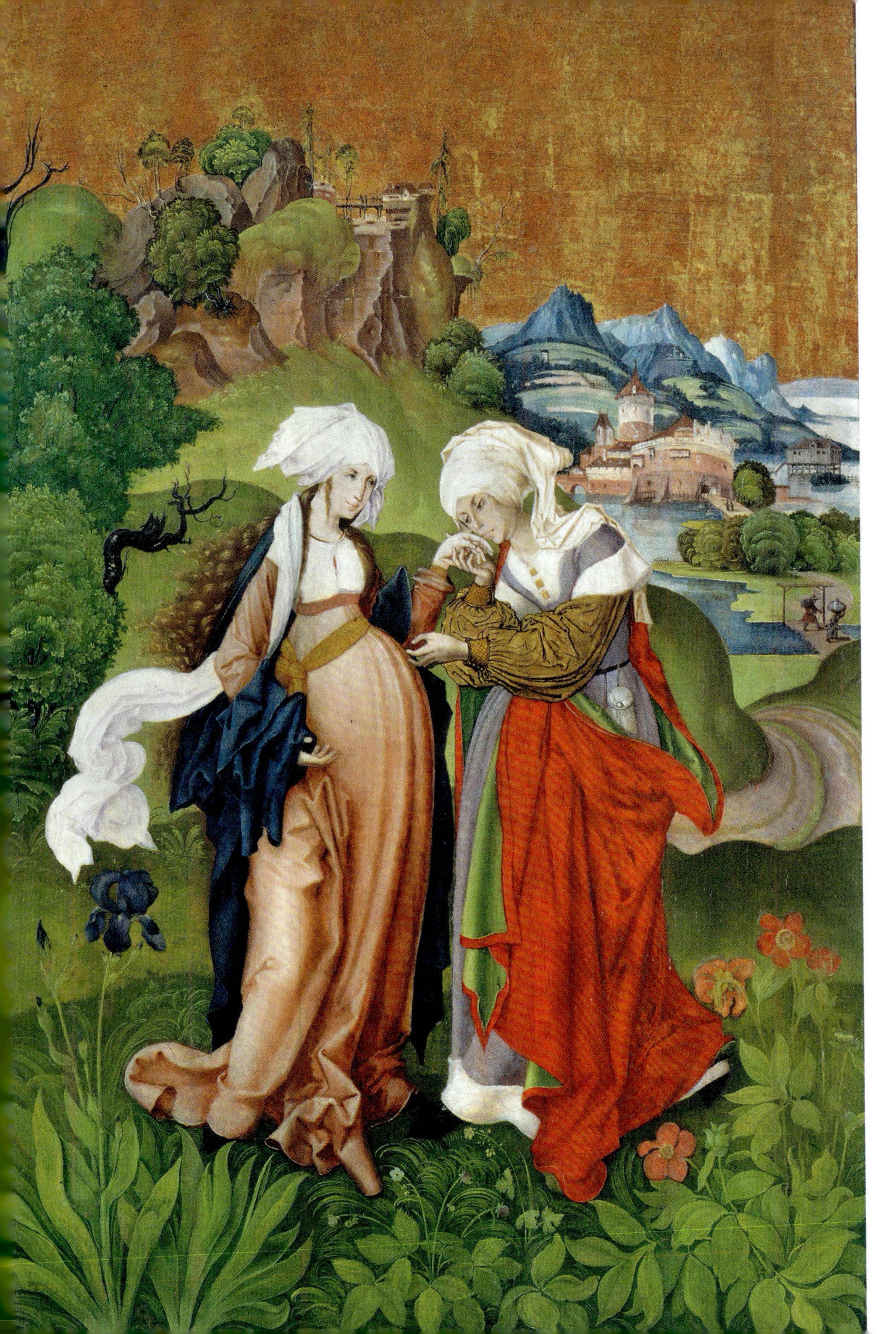

Master MS (Marten Swarcz?)

The Visitation

From the former main altar of the Church of Saint Catherine,
Selmecbánya (now Banská Štiavnica, Slovakia), 1506
Tempera on limewood, gilded · 140 × 94.5 cm
Purchased in 1902
Inv. no. 2151

This is one of the most magnificent and deservedly celebrated paintings from medieval Hungary, and all of the details – the holy women, the landscape, the plants and the objects – glorify the Lord, just as Mary does in the Gospel (Luke
1:39–56). This is the most intimate message of the painting,
expressed through the graceful postures, the subtle gestures,
the emotion-filled faces, the ecstatically fluttering drapery, as
well as the exquisitely painted flowers and foliage, the rocky
background, the gnarled, barren trees, the round-towered
castle surrounded by the flooded river, and the bluish mountain tops stretching into the distance. The thoughts and feelings evoked by the central theme of the work are constantly
echoed and reformulated in each painted motif.

The only parts of the altarpiece that still survive are three
larger-than-life-size statues (the Virgin Mary, Saint Catherine
of Alexandria and Saint Barbara), which were once housed
within the cabinet, and paintings from the "workday side", depicting Jesus in his infancy and episodes from the Passion.
The scene of the Resurrection contains the date and the master's monogram, consisting of the heavily faded letters MS,
with the master's mark between them, visible on the edge of
Christ's sarcophagus. The name has not yet been deciphered
with absolute certainty, but it was recently suggested that the
identity could be that of a certain Marten Swarcz, who arrived
in Kraków together with Veit Stoss, where he worked as a
painter on the famous Saint Mary's Altarpiece.

GYÖRGYI POSZLER

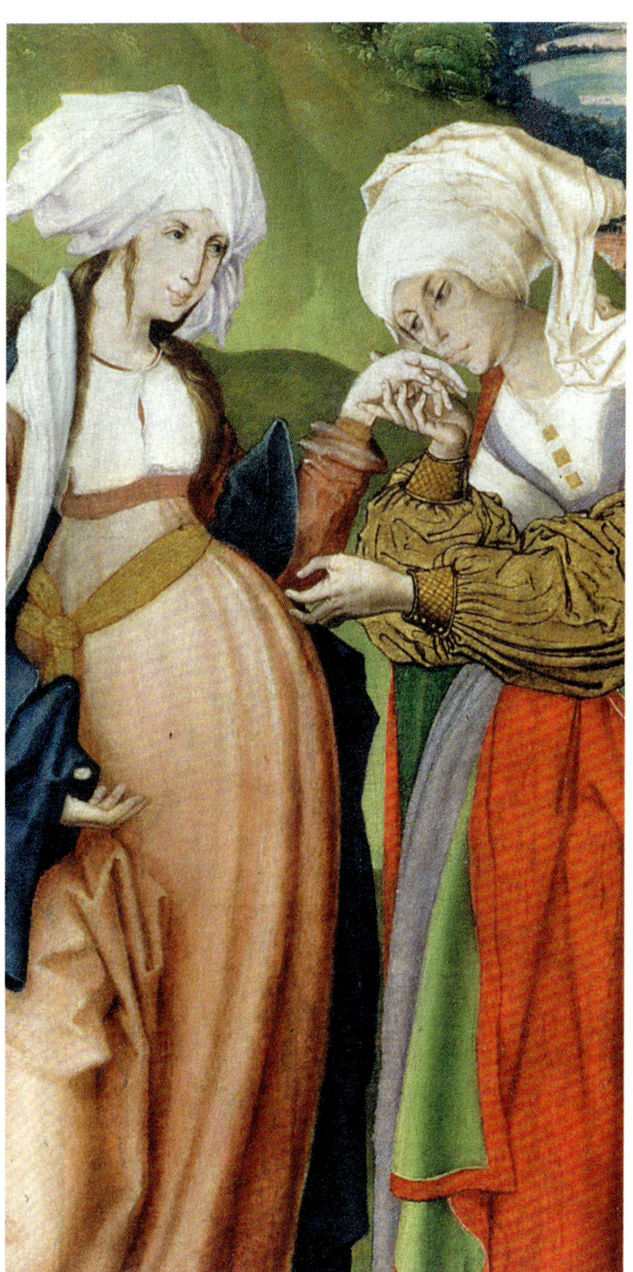

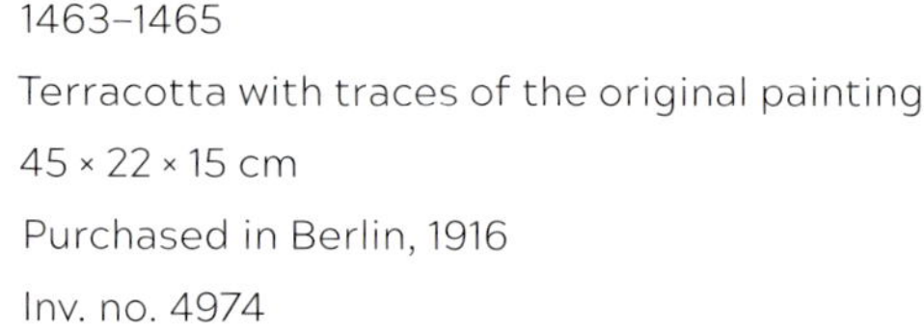

Luca della Robbia (1399/1400–1482)

Christ and Saint Thomas

1463–1465
Terracotta with traces of the original painting,
45 × 22 × 15 cm
Purchased in Berlin, 1916
Inv. no. 4974

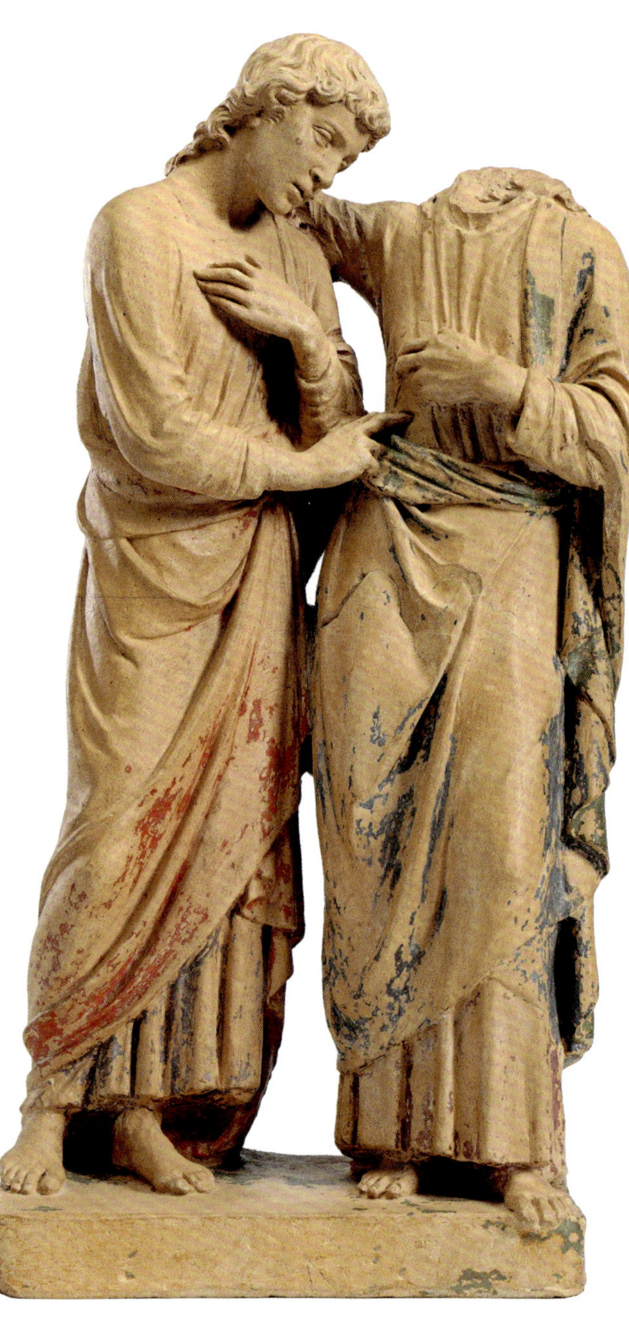

The craftsmen, artists and doctors of Florence attempted to defend their interests by forming guilds. They located the guilds' headquarters in the robust Gothic edifice originally intended as a market and wheat warehouse, the Orsanmichele, the facade of which was adorned with statues of each of the guilds' patron saints.

In 1463 the merchants' tribunal (Tribunale della Mercanzia) took over the statue niche of the Guelphs, a political party that supported the guilds, and commissioned Luca della Robbia, one of the most sought-after sculptors of the early Renaissance, to design a large statue group depicting Christ and Saint Thomas. As was custom at the time, the master made a small terracotta (fired clay) model of the planned monumental bronze. The apostle Thomas, doubting the resurrection, placed his hand in Christ's side (John 20:24–29), thus gaining proof that Christ had indeed died, but was risen again. The judges may have interpreted this story as a metaphor of their vocation: to "play the doubting Thomas" until tangible evidence is found. The scene is not dynamic; rather it is as if time stood still for the moment when Thomas accepts what for the human mind is incomprehensible.

The model, however, failed to please the commissioners, because in the end the bronze was cast not of this composition, but of one by another leading sculptor in the city, Andrea del Verrocchio. That group, far more dramatic, dynamic, and monumental than Luca's, can be seen to this day in Florence.

MANGA PATTANTYÚS

Domenico Ghirlandaio (1449–1494)

Saint Stephen the Martyr

ca. 1490–1494
Tempera and gold on poplar, 191 × 56 cm
Purchased in Paris, 1914
Inv. no. 4914

Domenico Ghirlandaio's shop, which employed many assistants (including the young Michelangelo), was the largest art company in Florence at the end of the fifteenth century, and practised not only painting, but jewellery, mosaics, and who knows what else. With Ghirlandaio's activity being so multifaceted, he was open to absorbing all the influences around him. No other of his Florentine contemporaries was as touched by Netherlandish painting, and nobody adopted its achievements with greater understanding than he. The painstaking details of the drawing, with a pin-sharp brushtip, the deep glow of the colours, betray the northern influence in this image too. The first martyr of Christianity, stoned to death a few years after Jesus's crucifixion, Saint Stephen appears with such transfixing power in three-dimensional realism, which for the contemporary viewer must have been shocking. Perhaps it was to dampen the effect, or in turn to reinforce it, that Ghirlandaio placed the figure in a feigned niche, and with this transposition, a painting imitating a statue imitating a human being, he blurred the line between fiction and reality even further. The panel was originally part of the high altarpiece of the church of Santa Maria Novella, which was painted on both sides and could be viewed from all round. There it stood in the centre of the choir, surrounded by one of the greatest achievements of the Florentine Renaissance, Ghirlandaio's celebrated fresco cycle of the lives of Mary and Saint John the Baptist.

AXEL VÉCSEY

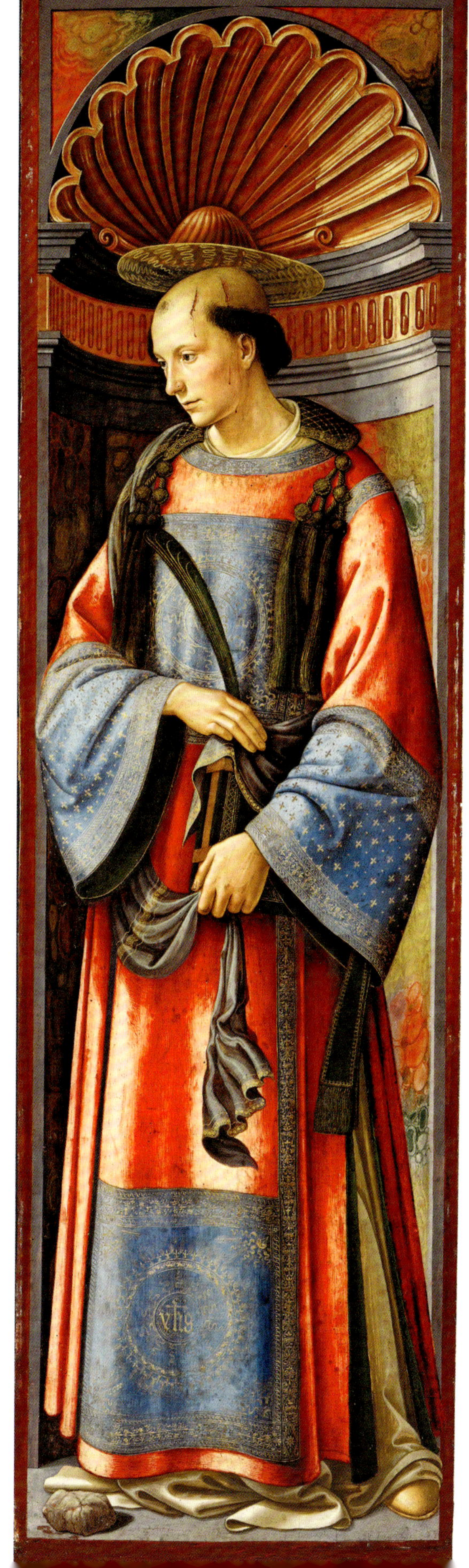

Leonardo da Vinci (1452–1519)

Study of Two Warriors' Heads

ca. 1504–1505
Black and red pastel on paper, 191 × 188 mm
Esterházy collection, purchased in 1871
Inv. no. 1775

Study of a Warrior's Heads

ca. 1504–1505
Black and red pastel on paper, 226 × 186 mm
Esterházy collection, purchased in 1871
Inv. no. 1774

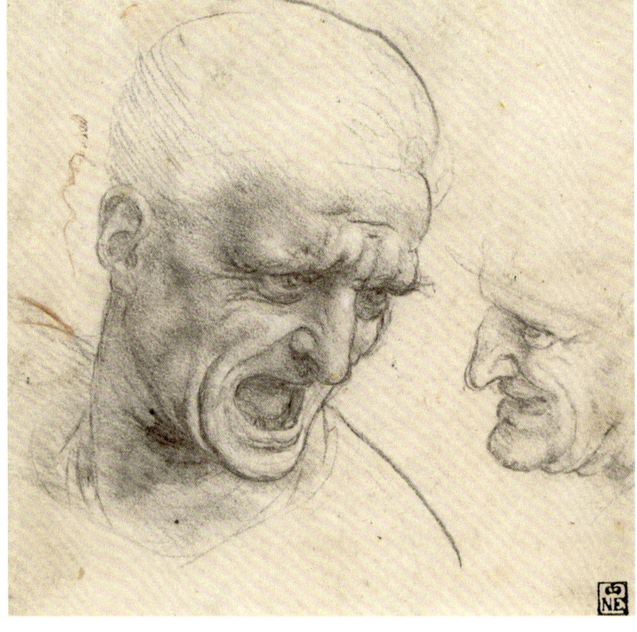

Leonardo was already over fifty when he was commissioned to decorate one of the long walls in the great hall in the Palazzo Vecchio, the Florentine town hall. The specified subject was the victory gained at Anghiari over the old rival Milan in 1440. Although such a prestigious commission must have been flattering to the painter, and his younger rival Michelangelo was working on a pair to the fresco, Leonardo once more began to work only after prolonged hesitation. Rather than the traditional fresco technique he experimented with a special slow-drying method, but met with failure. He had not yet finished the central scene when, in the poorly heated dank room the fresco began to decay. After this Leonardo abandoned the work completely, and a year later left Florence for good. While the fresco, which fell victim to subsequent alterations to the hall, is known through several contemporary reports and copies, barely half a dozen drawings for the work in Leonardo's own hand survives. Made in the last stage of the preparations, these head studies, with their vividness for being done from a live model, their dramatic expression, the highlights and deep tones creating the characteristic Leonardine chiaroscuro contrasts, count as some of the master's most excellent drawings. They also faithfully convey the staggering horror of the soldiers' cruel warring fury as they rush at each other with unbridled ferocity in the heat of the battle, a state Leonardo called *pazzia bestialissima,* the most bestial madness.

ZOLTÁN KÁRPÁTI

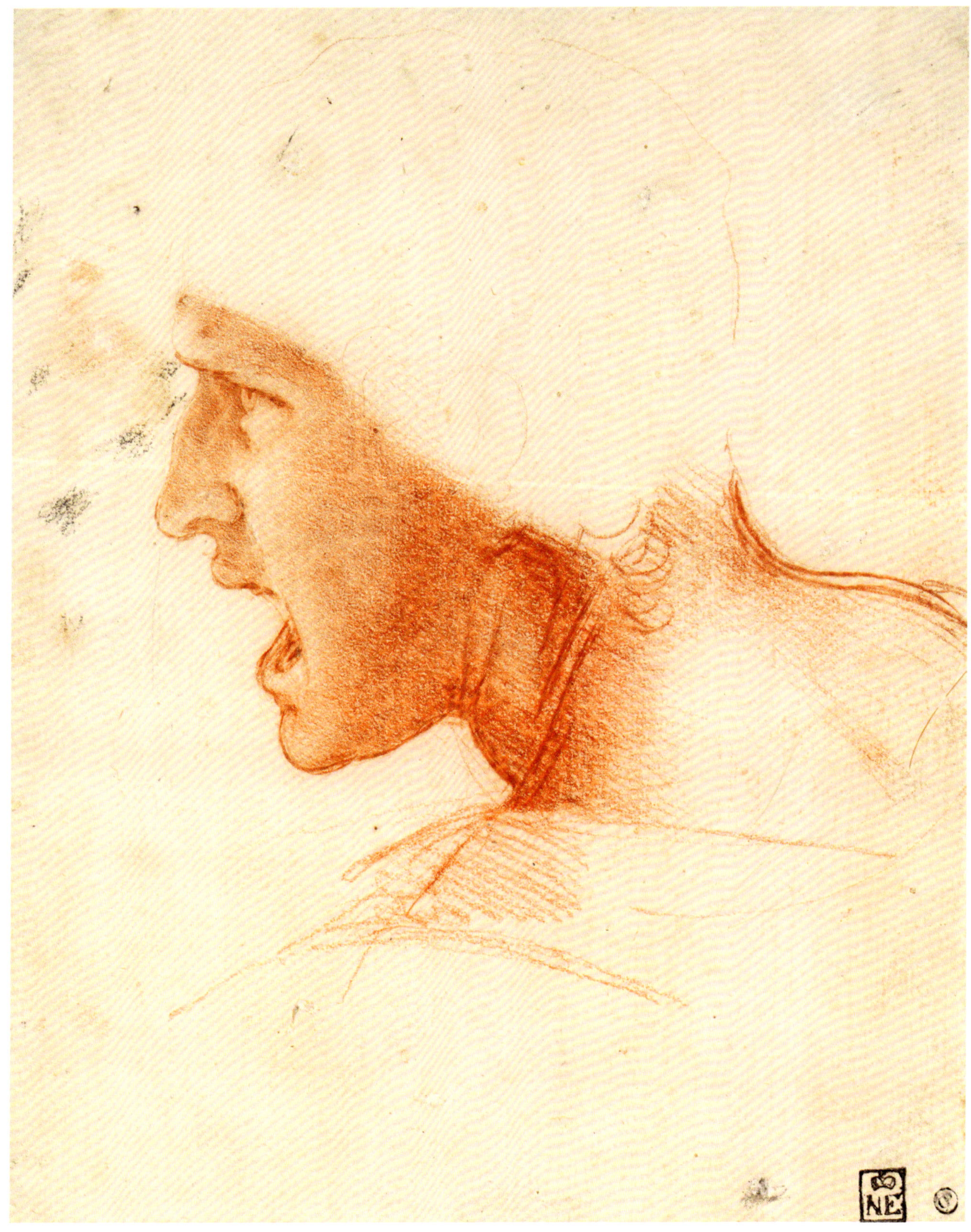

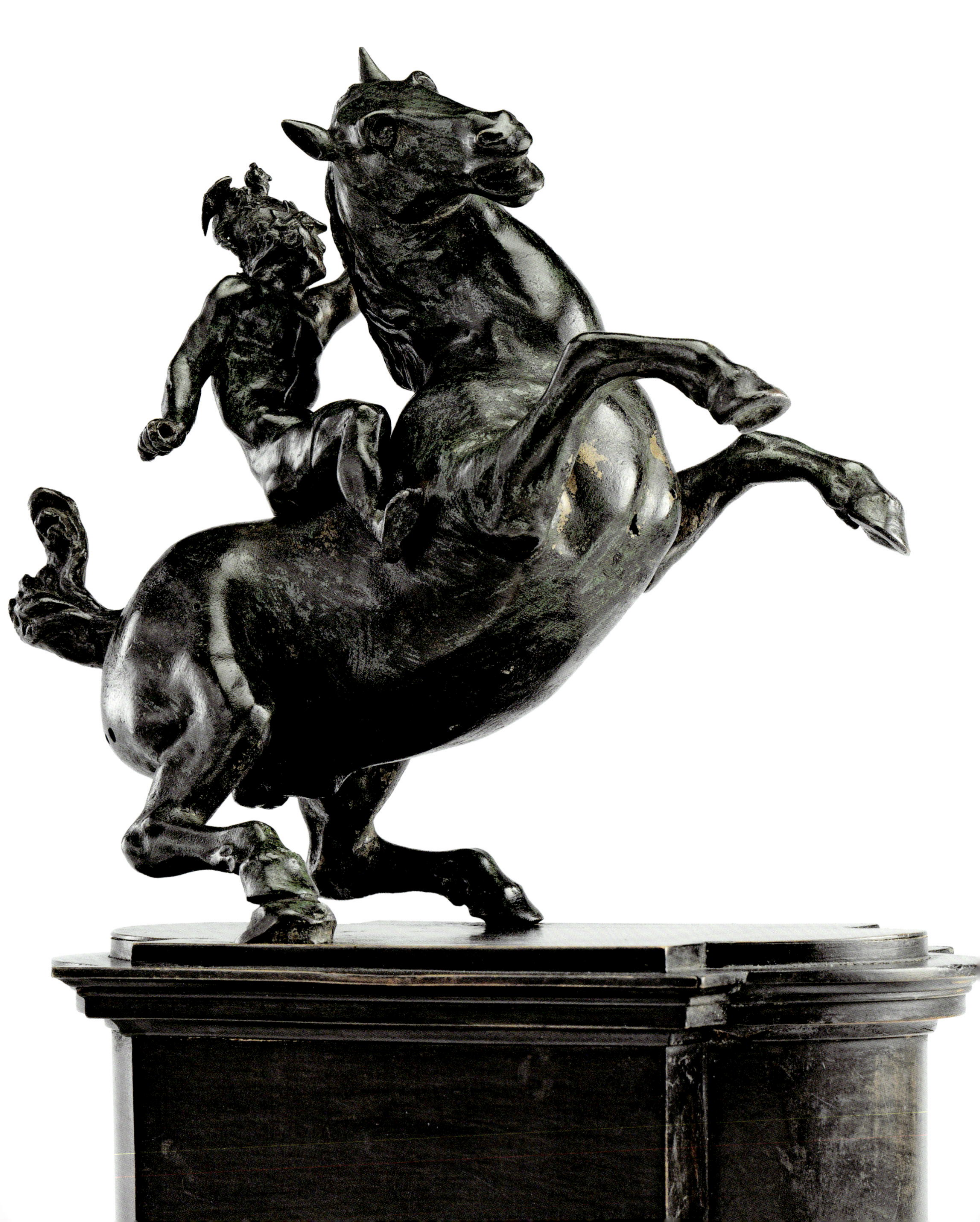

Attributed to Leonardo da Vinci (1452–1519)

Horse and Rider

Early 16th century
Bronze with green patina, 28 × 24 × 15 cm
Purchased in 1914, formerly part of the collection
of István Ferenczy
Inv. no. 5362

The small bronze *Horse and Rider* was purchased by the sculptor István Ferenczy in Rome between 1818 and 1824, who believed it to be a work from Ancient Greece. Shortly after the piece joined the collection of the Museum of Fine Arts, it was exhibited to the public as the only surviving sculpture by Leonardo da Vinci. Leonardo received several commissions for sculptures in his lifetime, and he designed two large equestrian statues for the city of Milan, neither of which was realised. His clay model for the equestrian statue of Francesco Sforza, which he worked on from the late 1480s until 1493, was destroyed by French mercenaries just before the work was cast in bronze. His memorial to Gian Giacomo Trivulzio (1508–1512) reached only the design stage, as did his intended statue for King Francis I of France. Leonardo devoted much thought to the process of bronze casting, as can be seen from his notes on the subject. Despite all this, there is no documentary evidence of any known equestrian statue by the master, which makes it difficult to identify the Budapest small bronze as an autograph work. Nevertheless, the precise composition of the statue is echoed in numerous drawings by Leonardo featuring dynamically rearing horses. The Budapest statue was conceived so that its weight would rest on the horse's rear legs, with no need for additional support. Leonardo initially designed both his Milanese horses in the same way, although executing this in bronze posed a significant technical challenge. This robust-bodied horse features certain imprecisely worked anatomical details, which suggests that the small bronze was the result of a series of experiments carried out in an attempt to resolve the complex structural problems.

MIRIAM SZŐCS

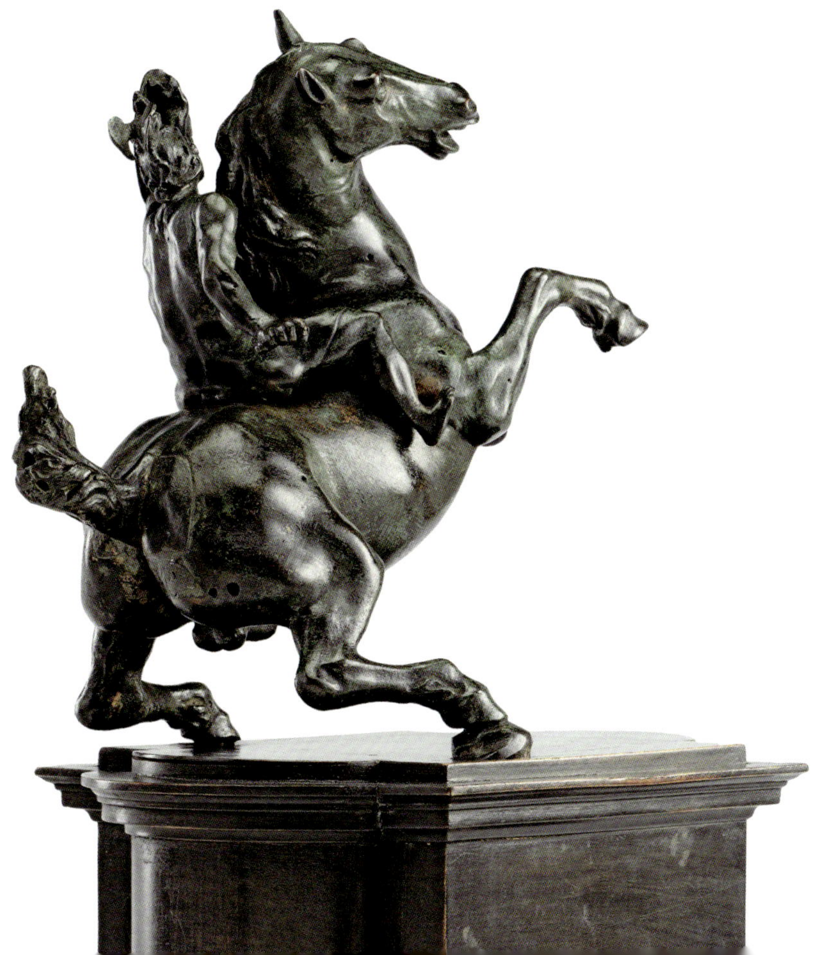

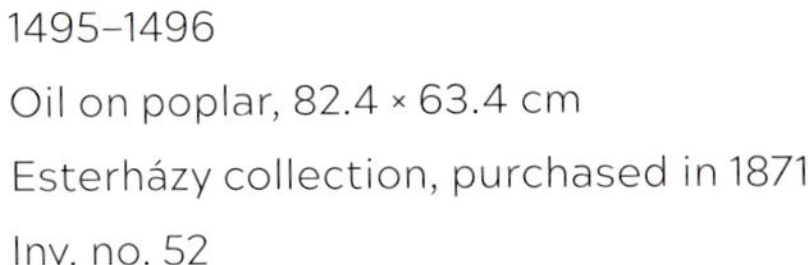

Giovanni Antonio Boltraffio (ca. 1467–1516)

Virgin and Child

1495–1496
Oil on poplar, 82.4 × 63.4 cm
Esterházy collection, purchased in 1871
Inv. no. 52

Leonardo da Vinci warned his fellow artists: "No one should ever imitate the style of another because he will be a grandson rather than a son of nature." But it seems that in his own workshop he did little to encourage his pupils to develop their own style. All over the world there are many Madonnas and portraits which only under the scrutiny of a practised, expert eye reveal that the brush that painted them was not held by in Leonardo's own hand. This is particularly true for this *Madonna* which is said to be "the finest Leonardesque picture not painted by Leonardo himself" – although some scholars believe the master may, after all, have guided the hand of his best pupil, Boltraffio, during the execution. The picture is perfectly Leonardesque in every respect: there is the famous sfumato, or the delicate shading softening the outlines of the forms, the Virgin's enigmatic smile and her characteristically large hands, and the pyramidical composition. Indeed, it was recently revealed that the wood on which it was painted was hewn from the same log as Leonardo's London *Madonna of the Rocks*. Yet the most Leonardesque part is the basic idea: the Christ Child reaches for something which has already disappeared, and it is forever a mystery to the viewer what the object might have been. It was once thought that the picture was unfinished, and that the master planned to paint a rose in the fine faience bowl, but technical examination has proved beyond doubt that this is the finished state.

AXEL VÉCSEY

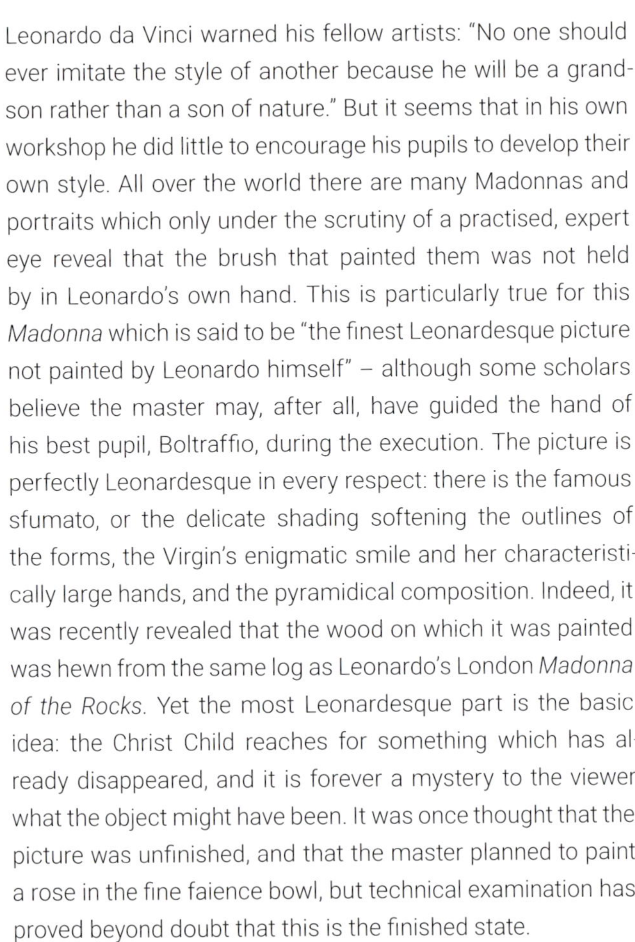
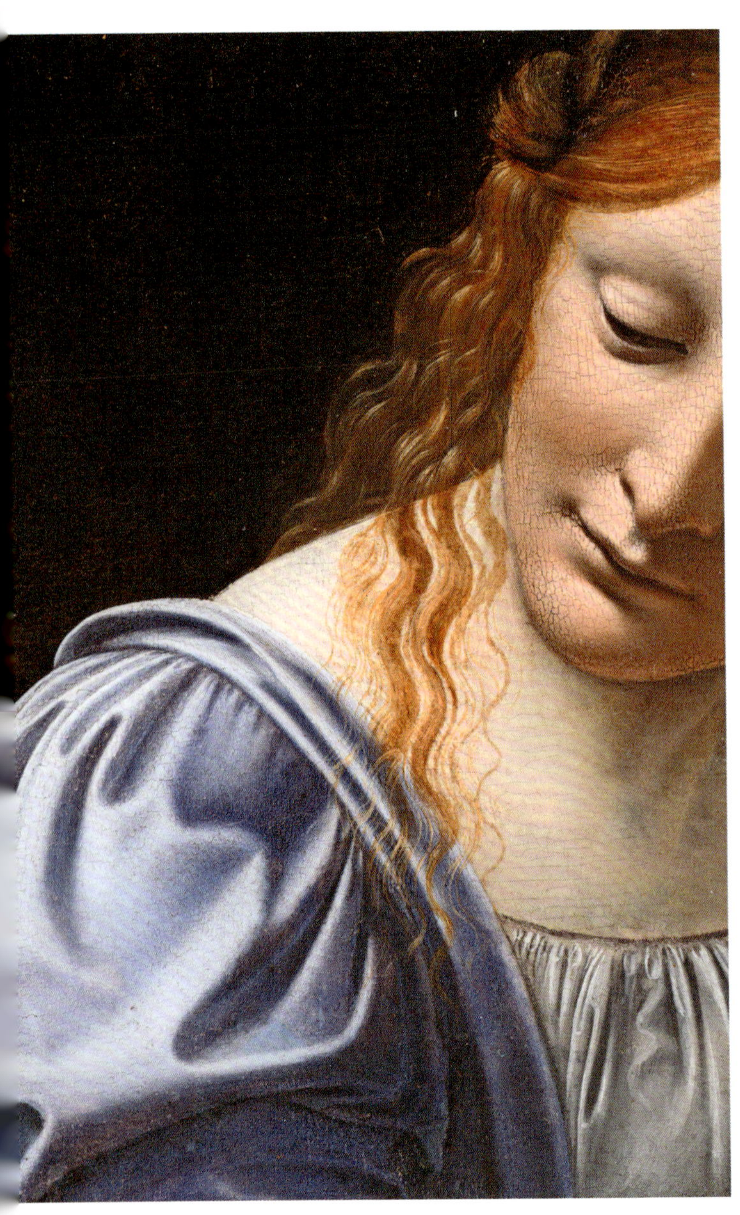

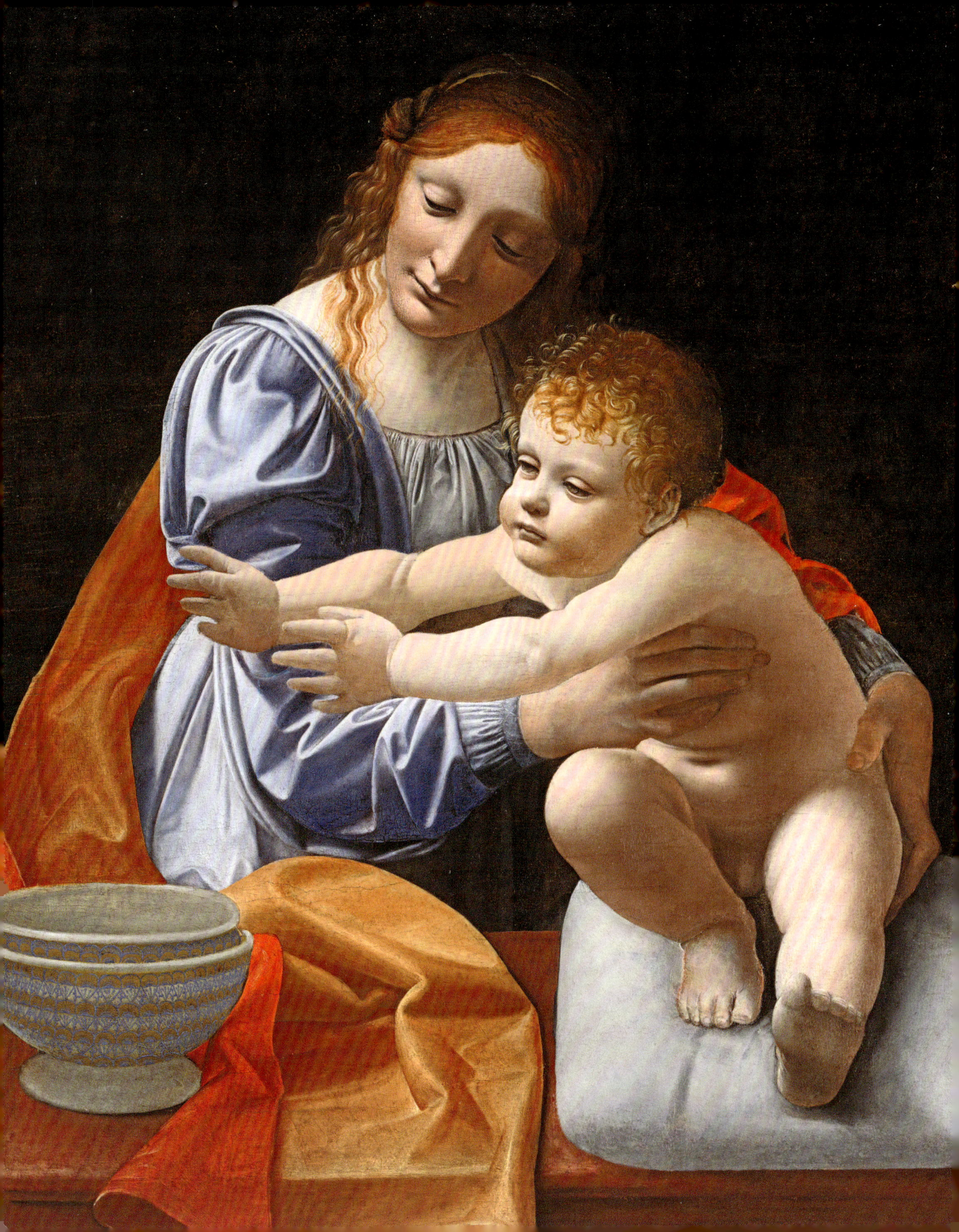

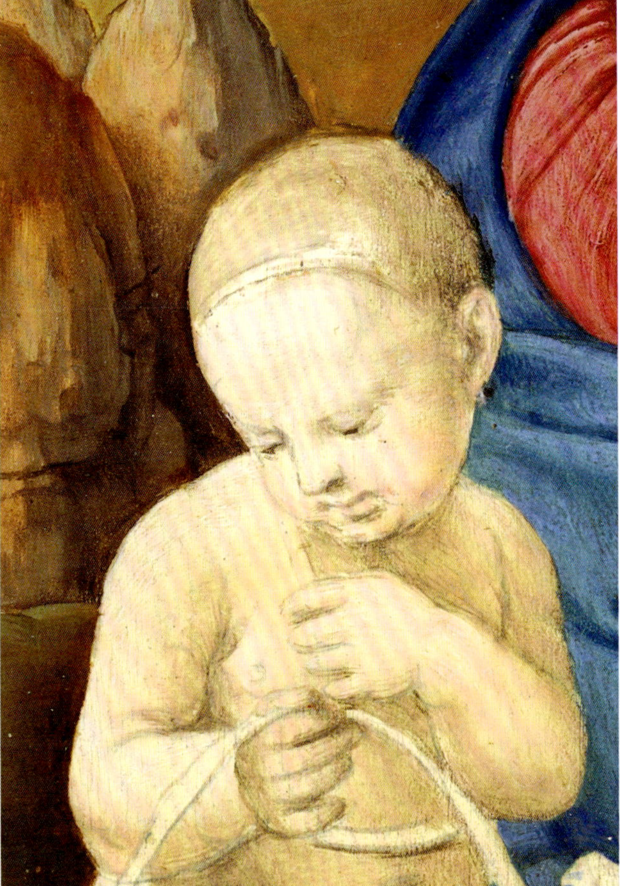

Esterházy-Madonna

ca. 1508
Tempera and oil on wood, 28.5 × 21.5 cm
Esterházy collection, purchased in 1871
Inv. no. 71

Right up to the end of the nineteenth century Raphael was honoured as the unsurpassable peak of painting: the master who recreated the spirit of classical antiquity and transcended its achievements. The timeless harmony, serene palette and peerless grace of his pictures served as a model for centuries. And if since then the public has come to feel closer to tortured geniuses wrestling with themselves, if the struggling torso pleases more than final perfection, the fact remains: every idea and aspiration of the Italian Renaissance reached its culmination and attained perfect synthesis in the art of Raphael.

In spite of being left unfinished (the Virgin's face and the figures of the children remain in the underpainting phase), the *Esterházy Madonna* represents the most perfect moment even of this absolute art: the end of the Florentine years, before Raphael moved to Rome where he would move on and begin to deconstruct the harmony. It is still the season of synthesis, and as if the express intention was to pay hommage to his predecessors, the posture of the Madonna was developed from Leonardo's paraphrase on an admired classical statue (the *Crouching Venus*). The pyramidal geometric structure, which masterfully directs the viewer's attention to the scroll held by Saint John the Baptist, also derives from Leonardo's ideas. If the picture reached completion, this scroll would bear John's prophecy on Jesus's role as redeemer: "Behold, the Lamb of God, who takes away the sin of the world!"

AXEL VÉCSEY

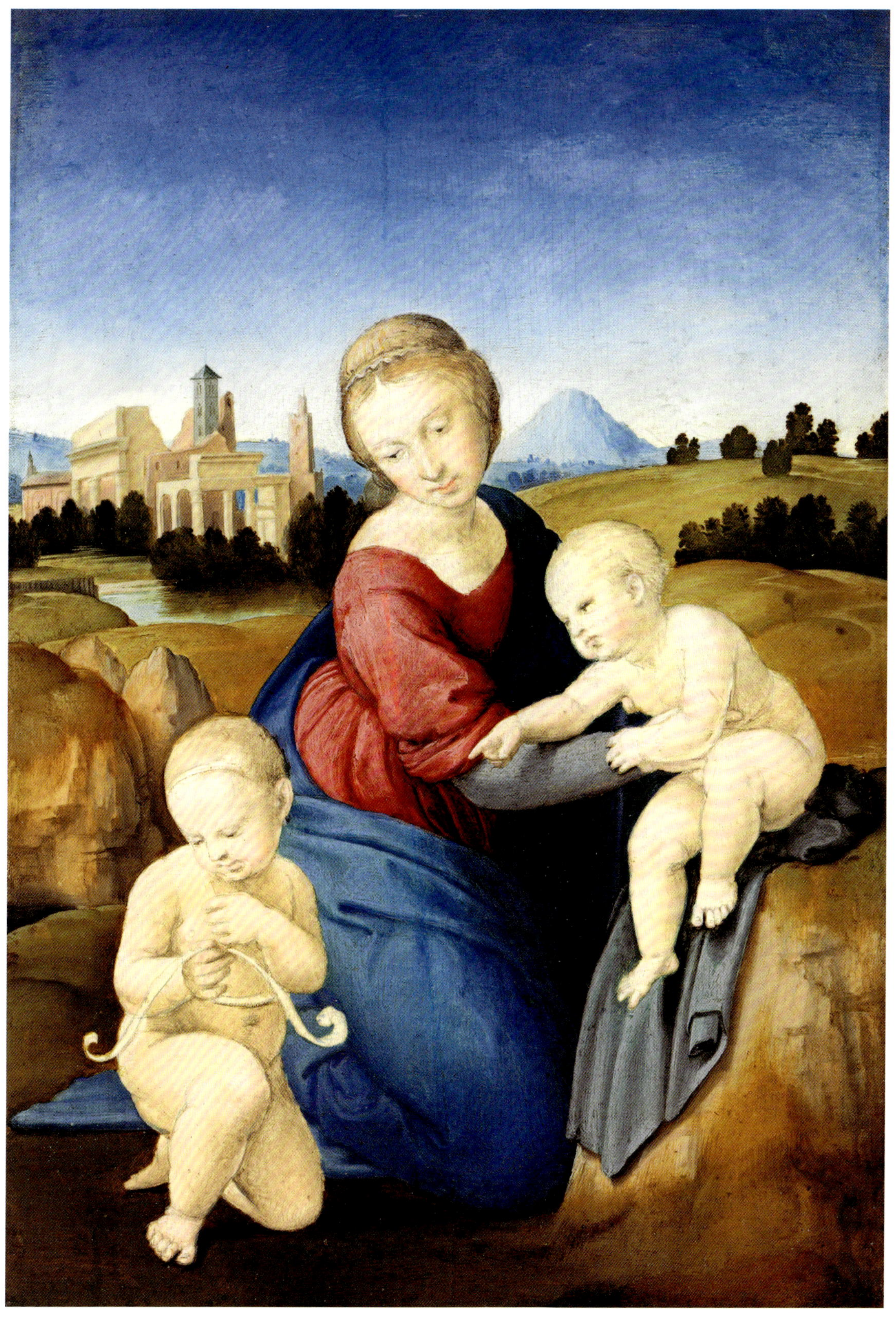

Gentile Bellini

(ca. 1429–1507)

Portrait of Caterina Cornaro, Queen of Cyprus

ca. 1500
Oil on poplar, 63.2 × 49.3 cm
Gift of János László Pyrker, 1836
Inv. no. 101

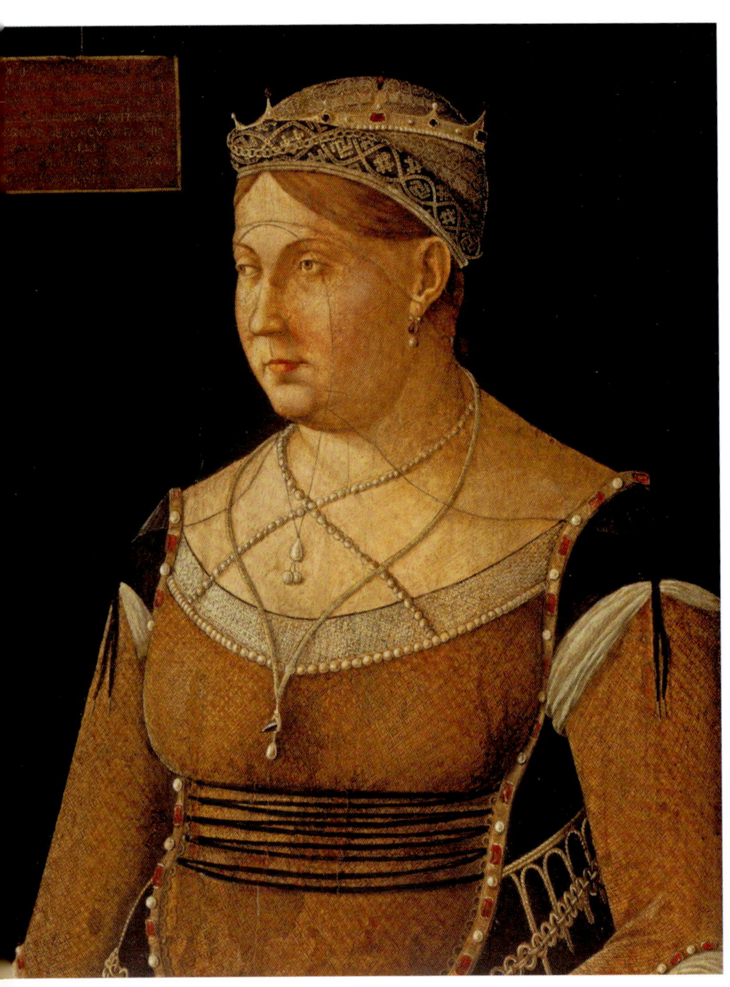

The heroine of Donizetti's opera, Caterina Cornaro was not born to the crown. The Venetian patrician girl was swept to the throne of Cyprus by her legendary young beauty and the caprices of politics. Rather than ruling, her role was to become a moral example – so decided Venice, which wanted the important trading post for itself. Thus she abdicated from the throne, but in exchange became the most feted celebrity in the city, a strange and exciting curiosity: a queen in the republic. When the leading Venetian master of the time, Gentile Bellini created this celebrated portrait, the bloom of her youthful beauty had waned. The painter made no bones about this, and approached his model with cartographical objectivity. The sumptuous gala dress is given as much attention as the face. The intricate rhythms of necklaces, veils, fabrics and jewels seem to combine to form a kind of eastern ornamental pattern: like those that Bellini studied so enthusiastically during his years at the Constantinapole court. The braiding seems to symbolise the restraint of duty: it seems to fetter the woman, biting into her flaccid flesh, while she stands firm, without so much as a tremor. This makes the image an epitome of the ruler's virtues: the dual triumph over external challenges and selfish inner desires. And this makes it the very masterpiece claimed by the confident words put into the mouth of the queen in the inscription: "You see how great I am; but even greater is the hand of Gentile Bellini which portrays me on such a small panel."

AXEL VÉCSEY

Giorgione (Giorgio da Castelfranco)

(ca. 1478–1510)

Portrait of a Young Man ("Broccardo" Portrait)

ca. 1508–1510

Oil on canvas, 72.5 × 54 cm

Gift of János László Pyrker, 1836

Inv. no. 94

"Even today it is difficult to define what the advent of Giorgione means for the history of taste. Like Proust, he taught that the world could be looked at in a more pleasurable, more subjective way. His recipe for doing so was to infuse painting with the lyricism and romance that were already current in the prose and poetry of his time." It would be hard to find a better summary of Giorgione's significance than the words of the great art historian John Pope-Hennessy. Though he died young, Giorgione utterly overturned the world of Venetian painting, and enshrouded not only narrative scenes in a magical, poetical atmosphere, but also transferred this approach to portraiture. So was born the introspective, emotive type of male portrait, of which the most inspired example is the *Portrait of a Young Man*. Yet the image is also the most perplexing image in our collections. Its author and sitter are the subject of endless dispute, as are the meaning of the hieroglyphic emblems on the parapet, and even the very nature of the emotion which infuses the picture. Is the sitter in a reverie, tormented by the bittersweet pain of love, or does he exude some quiet melancholy from the depths – perhaps grief? Perhaps the painter captured a hallowed moment of religious devotion or poetic inspiration? Some even claimed it may be an inauguration into some secret society. Of course there is no objective answer: everyone interprets the mood according to his own inclinations. One thing is certain: nobody can resist the picture's spell.

A X E L   V É C S E Y

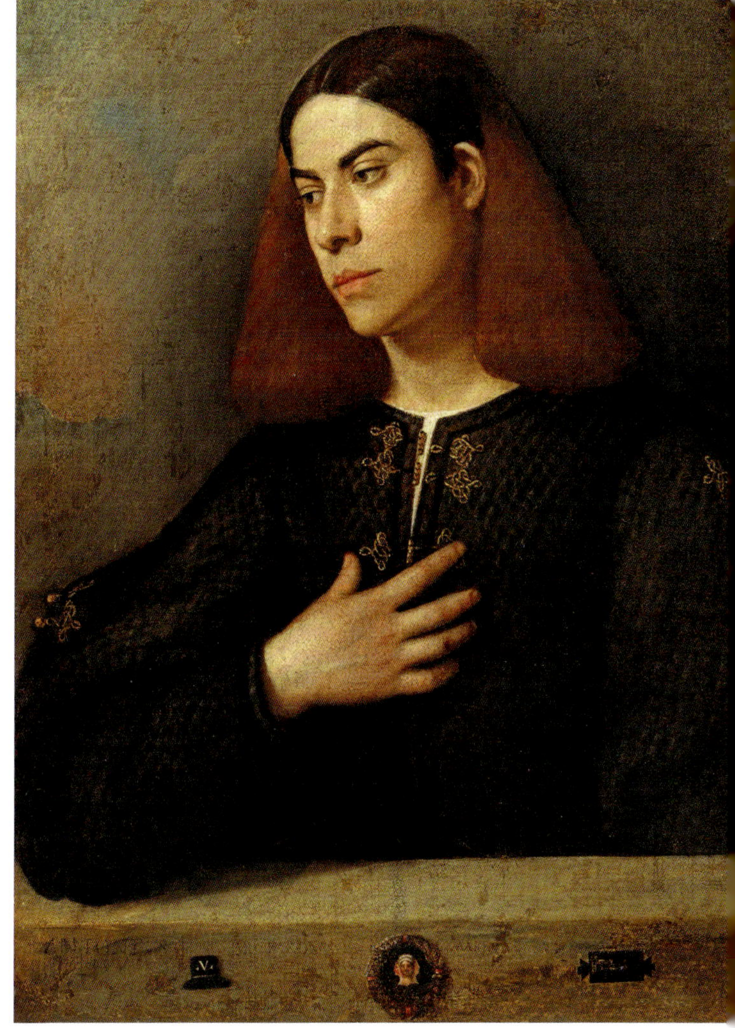

Albrecht Dürer (1471–1528)

Portrait of a Young Man

ca. 1500–1510
Oil on pine, 43 × 29 cm
Transferred from the Buda residence
of the President of the Treasury, 1848
Inv. no. 142

Rider with a Lance

1502
Pen and dark brown ink on paper, 272 × 215 mm
Esterházy collection, purchased in 1871
Inv. no. 75

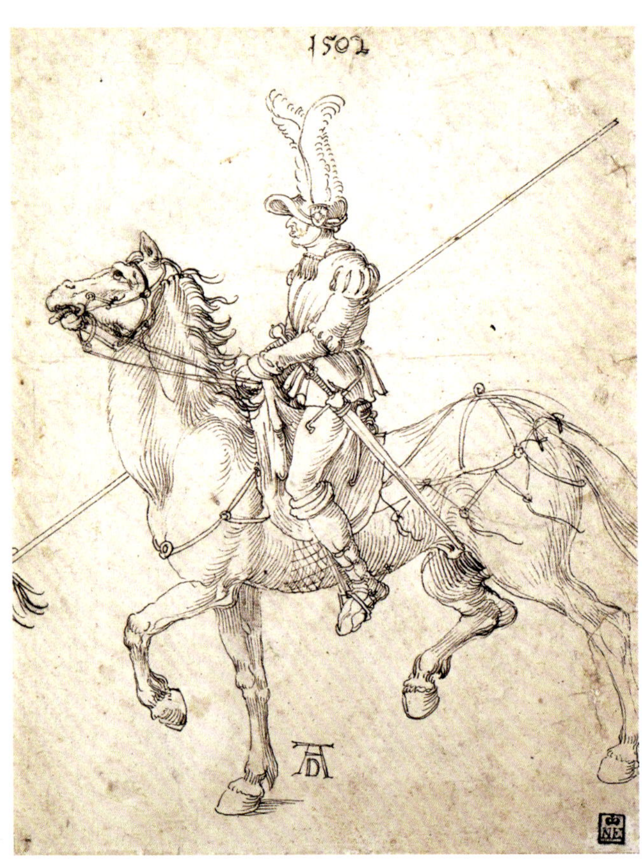

Albrecht Dürer was indisputably the greatest sixteenth-century painter north of the Alps. Not only did he have a God-given talent, he was also an exceptionally deliberate and self-aware master. He travelled round Italy several times, thoroughly working through everything important, and making use of what he considered good. But he found his home tradition more beneficial, and since the theoretical basis was lacking, he decided to create it. "The more rigorously your work adheres to life, the better it will appear. So you should never wonder whether you could do better than that with which God has endowed the natural world he created", runs Dürer's alternative to the idealising Italian aesthetics.

In the small painted portrait he did not wish to "correct" the work of nature, the strange, asymmetrical smile of this young German. How right he was! For it is precisely this lopsided smile that is the key to the aura, which makes the man enigmatically interesting, but also magically alive. A host of scholars have claimed for decades that the mysterious smile could only have been inspired by Leonardo, yet it is an integral outcome of Dürer's own principles.

The *Rider with a Lance* does however reveal that behind the apparently artless naturalism there was actually thorough research of the proportions of the human body. This splendid study drawing, bursting with life, was very likely made from live models, but two tiny holes betray that a pair of compasses was used in drawing the outline of the horse.

AXEL VÉCSEY

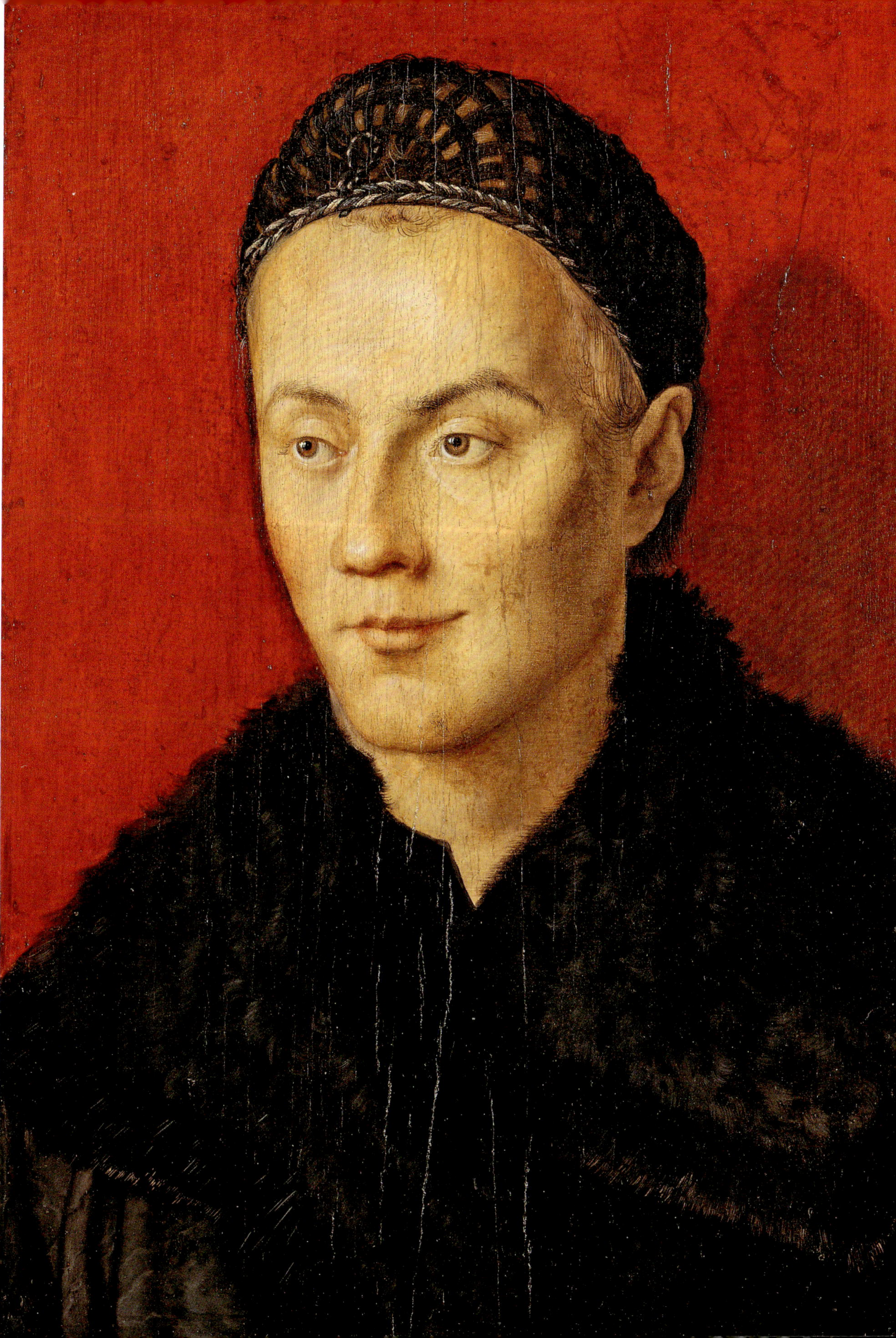

Barend van Orley (ca. 1488–1541)

Portrait of Emperor Charles V

ca. 1519–1516
Oil on oak, 71.5 × 51.5 cm
Purchased in Cologne, 1894
Inv. no. 1335

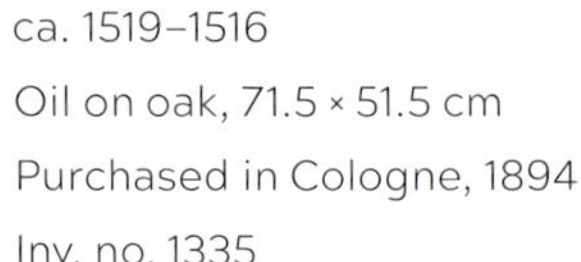

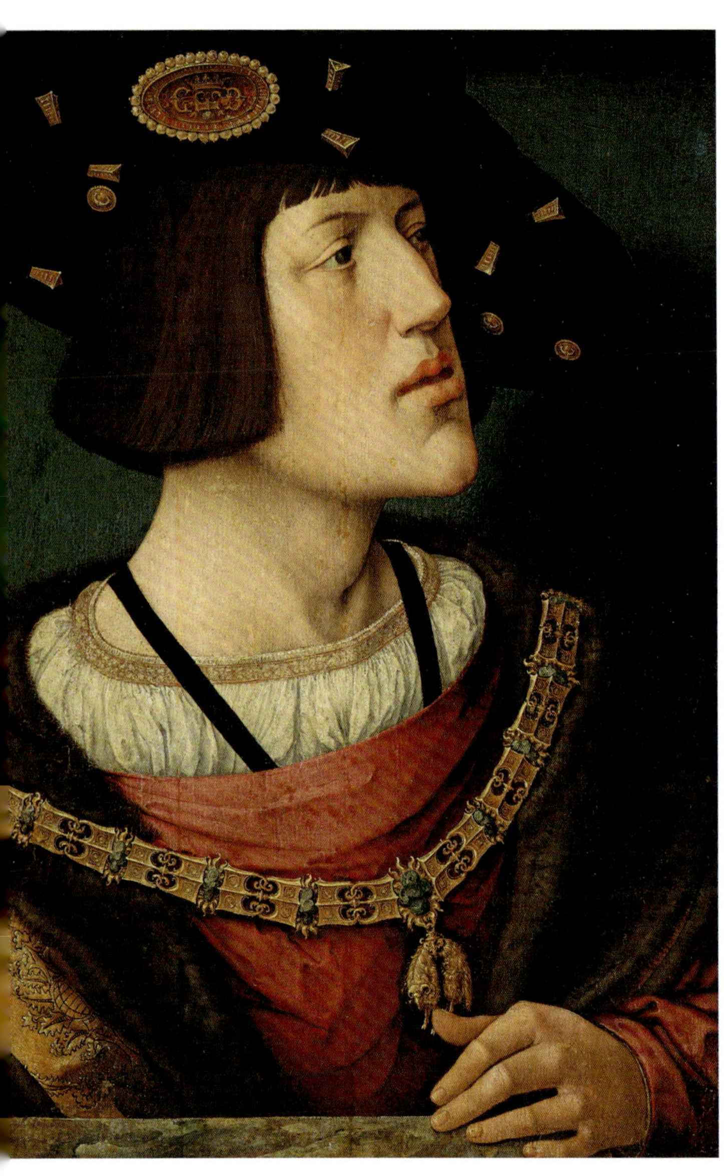

Emperor Charles V, perhaps the most powerful ruler of all time, had an empire on which, it was said, the sun never set. He ruled over Spain, Germany, the Low Countries, Southern Italy, and had extensive colonies in America and Asia. His portrait was painted by the greatest artists of Europe, from Dürer to Titian, so that through copies of the portraits, albeit metaphorically, he could be present in every corner of his empire. Yet Charles was not a particularly attractive man, as attested to by contemporary accounts: "His lower jaw is unwieldy and protrudes, as if it were not a natural part of him, but some additional imitation; and so if he closes his mouth, a space the size of a row of teeth is left between the upper and lower teeth."

One of Charles's first portraitists was Barend van Orley in Brussels. This image was made about the time the adolescent young man had been elected (at the cost of enormous bribes) Holy Roman Emperor. However, there is no reference here to this title or to the Spanish throne he had inherited earlier; only the royal emblem of Burgundy, the flint and steel, appears on the large hat brooch, between the large doubled initial of his name, and around his neck hangs the badge of the famous order of the golden fleece. Van Orley created an ideal fusion of northern and Mediterranean styles to lend an imposing realistic air to his portraits: the forms of the body are captured with masterly Italianate plasticity, while the jewels and clothes have a Netherlandish richness of detail.

A X E L   V É C S E Y

Wolf Huber (ca. 1485–1553)

Landscape with Willows and Mill

1514
Pen and brown ink on paper, 153 × 207 mm
Esterházy collection, purchased in 1871
Inv. no. 191

In the early sixteenth century a small group of Austrian and German artists developed a special interest in nature. The "Danube school" was not a movement in the traditional sense: the term covers artists who depicted the Danube river valley and Alpine landscapes in the same spirit and style. Although they were all painters, it was primarily in their drawings that they created a new genre in German Renaissance art. Their drawings, which show mainly dense woodland and high mountains, are the earliest examples of independent representation of nature. The most famous exponents of the "Danube school" are Albrecht Altdorfer from Regensburg, and Wolf Huber, a native of Austria who worked in the court of the bishop of Passau.

The date on the Budapest sheet reveals that Huber made this lyrical, virtuoso pen-and-ink drawing around 1514, while travelling in the Alpine region. Showing trimmed willows lining the winding road and the watermill next to the brook, it may once have belonged to Huber's sketchbook. The bare branches sketched with calligraphic lines, and the treetrunks shaded with small, dense penstrokes, lend a particularly decorative quality to the composition. Huber's contemporaries were fond of copying his "land portraits", and the works influenced engravers too, including Augustin Hirschvogel. A contemporary drawn copy reveals that the Budapest composition was originally wider: a considerable part of the right side is now missing.

ESZTER KARDOS

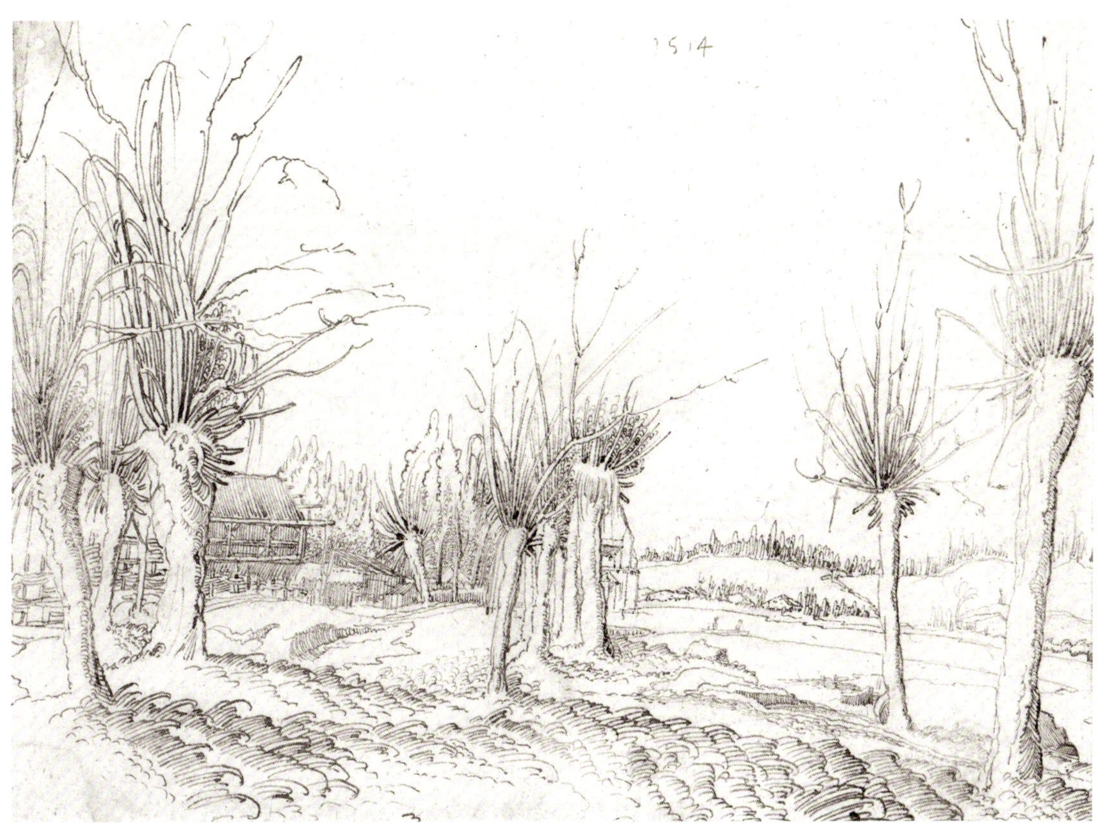

Attributed to Andrea Riccio (Briosco)

(1470–1532)

The Rape of Europa

ca. 1505–1510

Bronze with green patina, 18.2 × 16.5 × 7.5 cm

From the collection of István Ferenczy, 1914

Inv. no. 5363

Zeus, the untiring seducer, took on the image of a tame bull in order to draw near to the Phoenician princess playing on the shore with her companions. After the bull, bedecked with flowers, had managed to trick the beautiful Europa onto his back, he swam across the sea to the island of Crete. In the oft-depicted Ovidian version of the story there is no mention of the pugnacious resistance apparent in the Budapest small bronze. In Ovid's *Metamorphoses* the princess was quite taken by the overtures made to her by Zeus turned bull. It is likely, then, that the author of the Budapest sculpture took inspiration not from this popular work, but from a less known ode by Horace, in which the Roman poet writes of Europa's desperate protestations.

This is the only cast known of this small bronze. Although the identity of its author remains doubtful, the unusual choice of source betrays he was familiar with humanist works. The style of this outstanding piece is closest to the works of Andrea Briosco, given the sobriquet Riccio (curl) after his dense, curly hair. Riccio, known for his excellent bronzes, nursed close relations with the humanist circles of the prestigious University of Padua, and influenced by this made a whole series of classically inspired small bronzes. Renaissance small bronzes are now considered sculptures, but at the time many were intended as functional objects. Such is the *Europa*, the interior of which is designed to hold incense.

MIRIAM SZŐCS

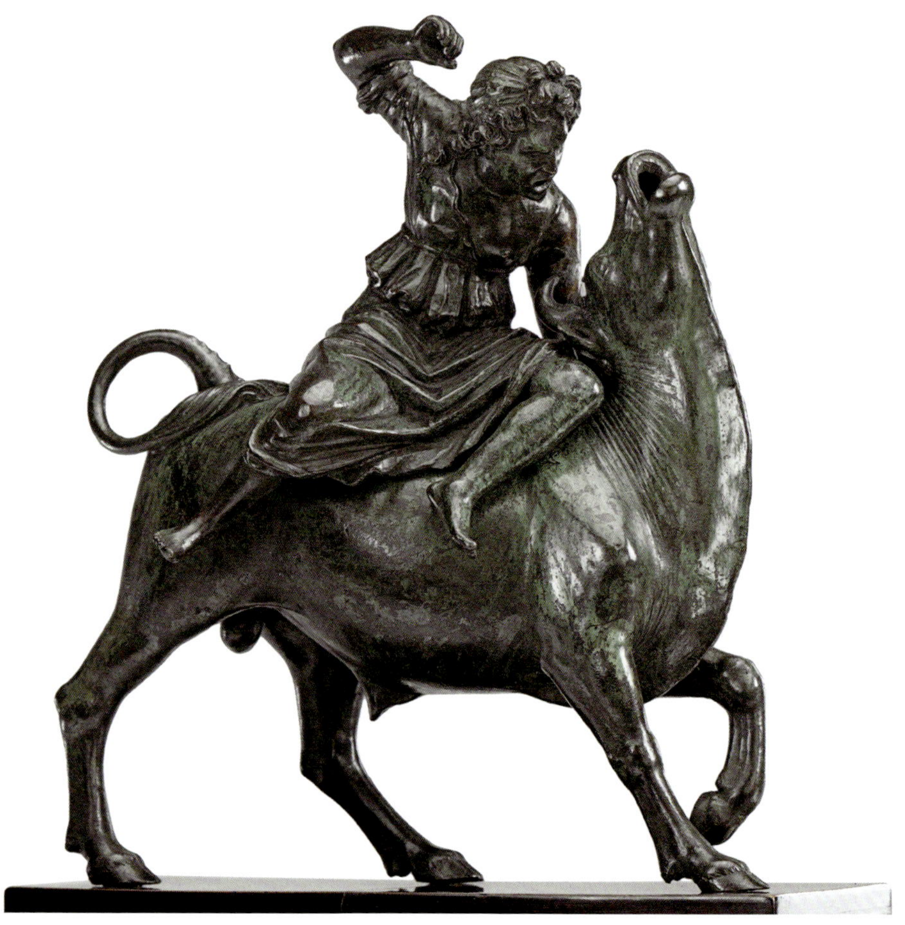

Jacopo Sansovino (Jacopo d'Antonio Tatti)

(1486–1570)

Virgin and Child

ca. 1510–1511
Wax and gilt canvas, 65.5 × 23.5 × 19 cm
Purchased in Florence, 1895
Inv. no. 1177

When the sculptures adorning public spaces in Renaissance Florence were commissioned, artists was often selected in an open competition. The participants had to make a model from clay or wax, which was judged by a jury consisting of artists were, town aldermen, or delegates from aristocratic families. This small-scale sculpture by Jacopo Sansovino was made for such a competition.

Around 1510–1511 it was planned to erect a marble statue of the Madonna on the facade of the market Mercato Nuovo, and Sansovino entered the competition with this wax model. Because wax is highly malleable, it was particularly suitable for making models: if the artist wished to alter the form, he simply had to warm it, and he could add or remove the material as he pleased. One unusual technical feature of the statue is that the bodies of the two figures are not supported by an armature. They were so cleverly composed by Sansovino, who was both a sculptor and an architect, that they support one another with their own weight. The artist dipped the drapery serving as the Virgin's attire in glue and coated it with a layer of wax of varying thickness, then covered the surface of the entire statue in gold.

Although this maquette won Sansovino the competition, the commission went to a rival with political connections, Baccio Bandinelli. Sansovino's winning entry must then have passed to one of his painter friends, Andrea del Sarto, who used it as a model for two works.

MANGA PATTANTYÚS

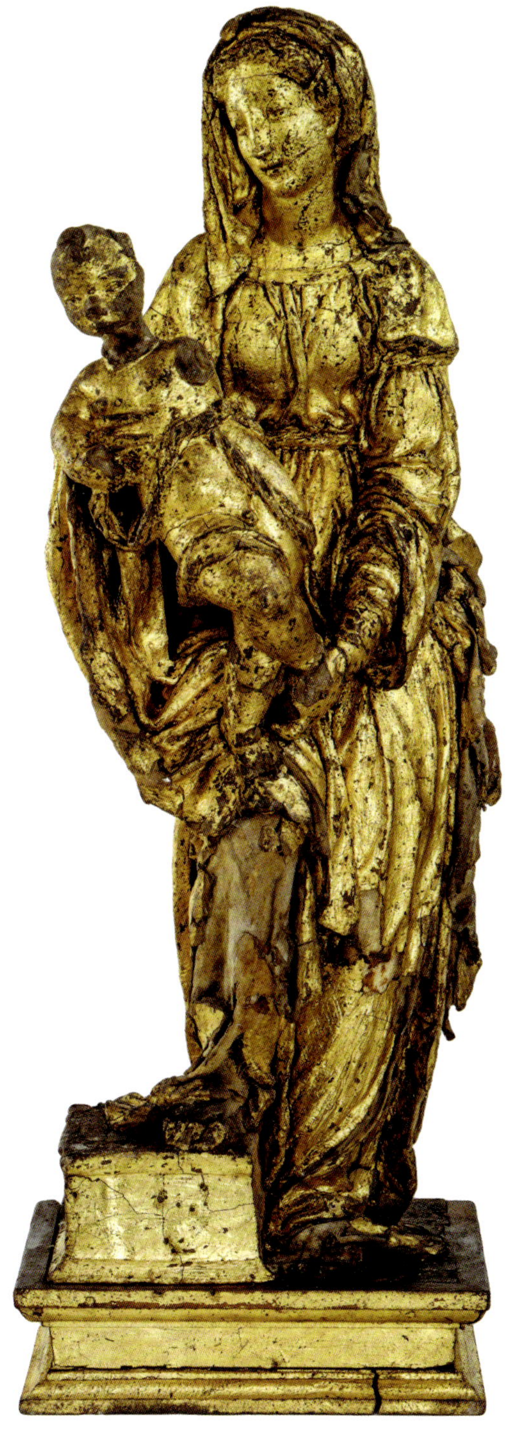

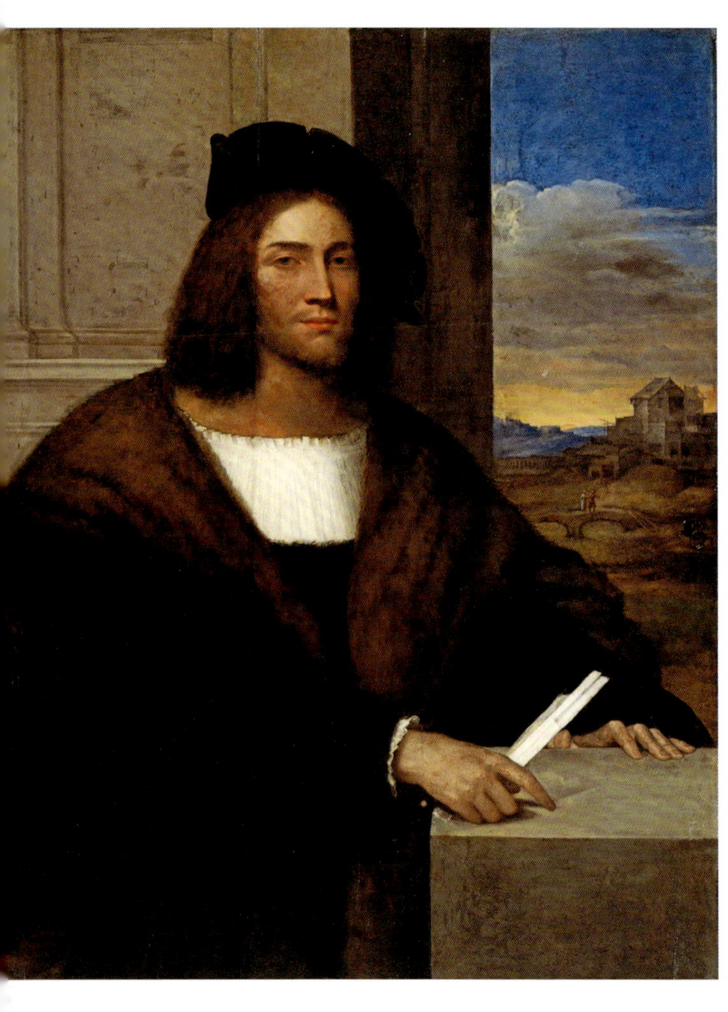

Sebastiano del Piombo (Sebastiano Luciani)

(1485/1486–1547)

Portrait of a Man

ca. 1512–1514
Oil on poplar, 115 × 94 cm
Purchased in Milan, 1895
Inv. no. 1384

Thanks to Giorgione's new style, Venetian painting rose to become the greatest rival in Italy to Tuscany. News of it spread to Rome too, and thus one of his best pupils, Sebastiano, received an invitation to the papal court. Here he came under the spell of Michelangelo's classical, epic heroism, which he tried to combine with the poetic style inherited from Giorgione. And when Michelangelo left for Florence, and Raphael died a couple of years later, Sebastiano became Rome's leading painter.

This extraordinary portrait, perhaps of a scholar, was painted shortly after he arrived in Rome. The Venetian legacy still predominates: in spite of the man's tangible, monumental presence he seems to fade in from the mist of some nostalgic poem. The soft atmospheric effects and the twilight hues cast an enigmatic aura about him, although in the rigorous composition Sebastiano had already departed from his master.

Piombo's masterpiece is one of the greatest achievements of Renaissance portraiture. But Károly Pulszky, founding director of the museum, was vilified for the purchase, and finally driven to suicide. Pulszky acquired the picture as a Raphael, and his witless political opponents thought that the quality of a work of art is determined by the reputation of its author. The *Portrait of a Man* is today one of the emblems of the museum, and perhaps this fact may serve as a late appeasement for the excellent connoisseur, and as a memento to the public that lives under the spell of "great names".

AXEL VÉCSEY

Lorenzo Costa

(ca. 1460–1535)

Venus

ca. 1515–1518
Oil on poplar, 174 × 76 cm
Purchased in Brescia, 1895
Inv. no. 1257

In the Renaissance, as works of art became more widely appreciated, their role in diplomacy also grew. This painting was a diplomatic gift, sent to King Francis I of France by the Marquis of Mantua. In a letter dated 20 March 1518, the mercenary commander, Luigi Alessandro Gonzaga, who was in Ambroise as a guest of the French king, wrote to his cousin, Marquis Francesco Gonzaga, "… the most Christian of kings spoke to me, and when he mentioned a highly esteemed painter in his service [probably Leonardo da Vinci], he told me that he would like nothing more than to possess a painting of a human figure by every leading artist, and he then asked me whether your Grace happened to have such an excellent painter. I replied that you do, the master Costa, whom everybody praises. His Highness then confided to me that it would please him to have a nude figure by him, or a painting of Venus." On 30 November that same year, the Marquis of Mantua dispatched the longed-for painting, accompanied with the message, "… I hereby send your Highness a painting that I commissioned from my artist as soon as I learned that your Highness wished to obtain a picture of this kind. I am fully aware that the picture will come before the eyes of a great and distinguished expert in physical beauty, especially the beauty of the female body, and therefore it is with even greater pleasure that I send it to you." In Italy at the time, the figure of Venus embodied Neo-Platonist ideals, but as is apparent from these excerpts of written correspondence, among princely art patrons, the philosophical content was not always the primary consideration.

VILMOS TÁTRAI

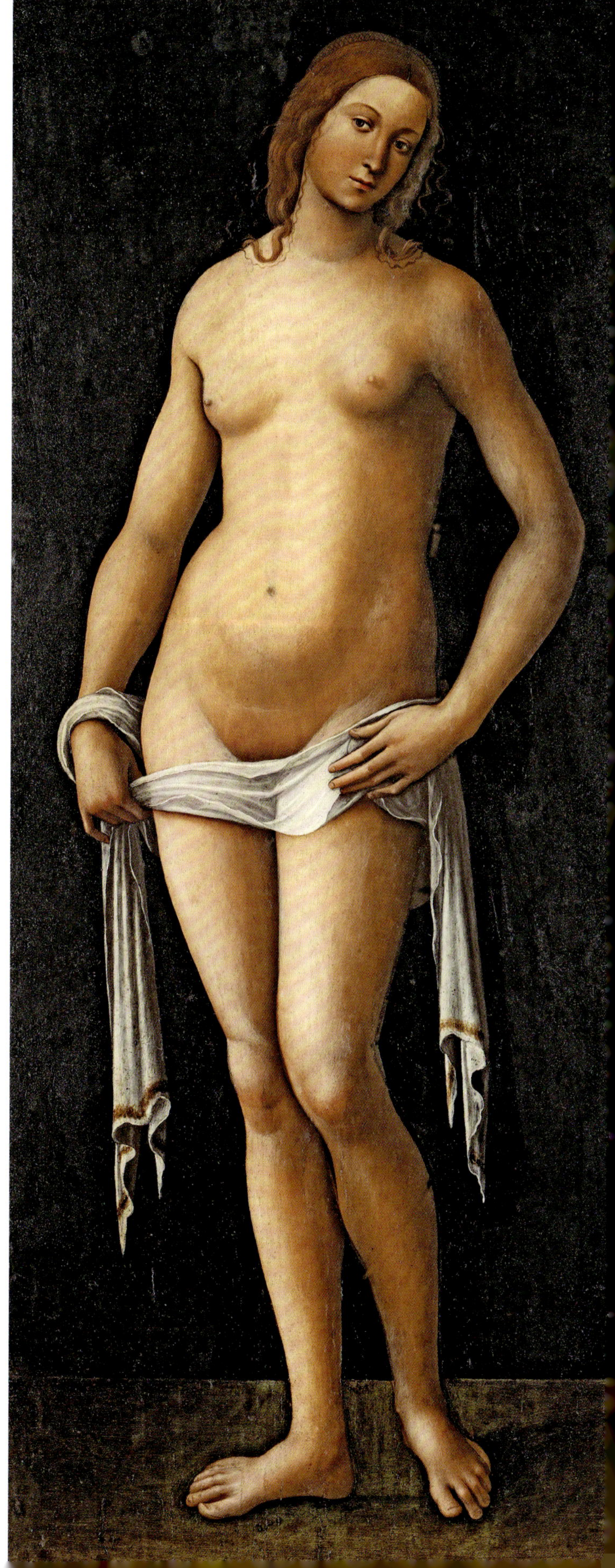

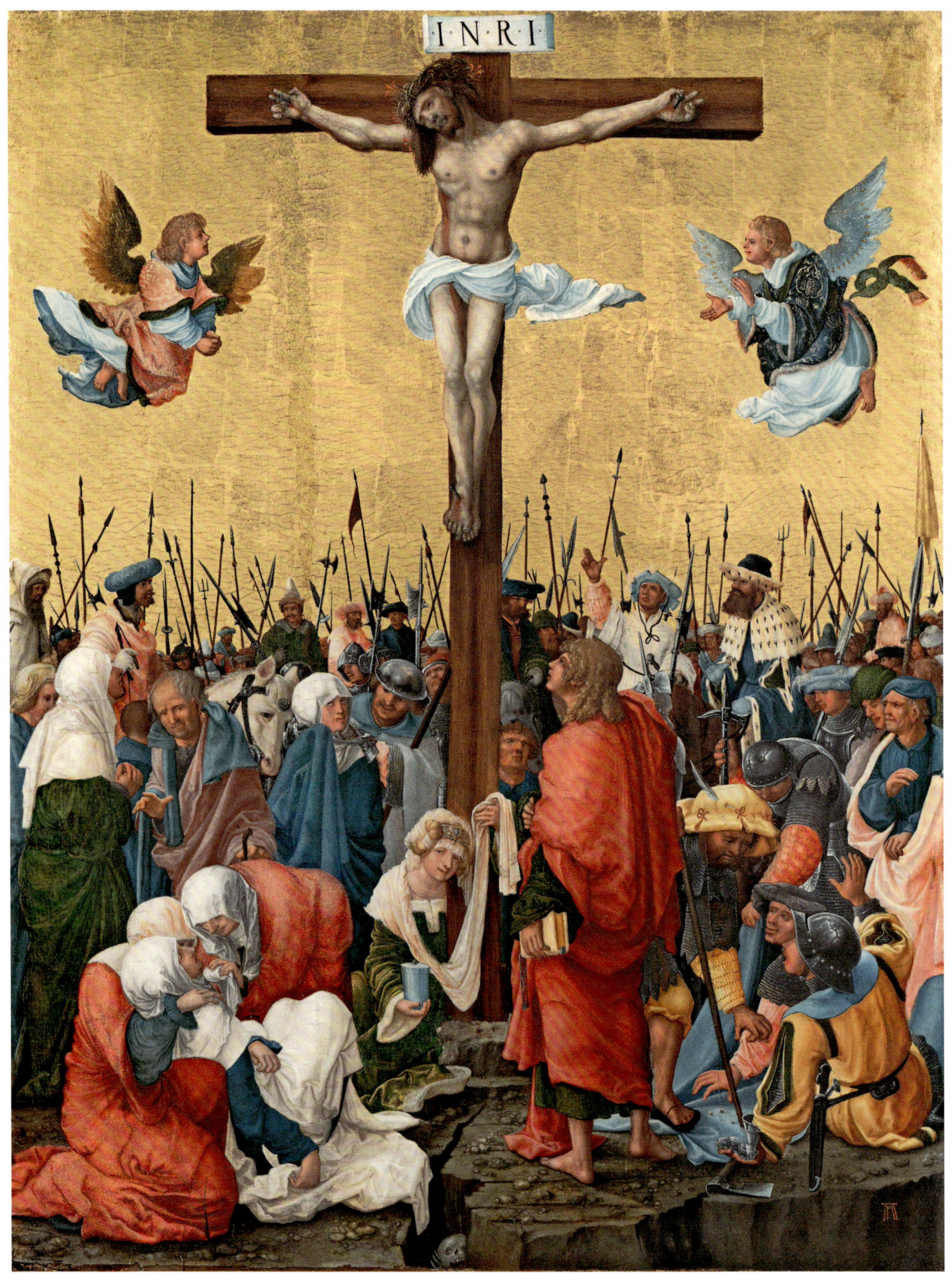

Albrecht Altdorfer (ca. 1480–1538)

The Crucifixion

ca. 1516–1518
Oil on limewood, 75 × 57.5 cm
Purchased from Countess Imre Erdődy,
née Irma Migazzi, 1922
Inv. no. 5892

Vibrant yellows, reds and blues imbue this painting, but most emphatic of all are the patches of brilliant white, the cloths and shawls, worn by the Mother Mary, swooning on the ground, the nuns attending to her, the weeping woman standing on the left, and Mary Magdalene, leaning with her left arm around the base of the cross, a jar of anointing oil in her right. Thanks to the overhead perspective and the foreshortening, the group of figures closest to the picture plane, with Mary at their centre, is etched into our memories, while the dice-playing soldiers across from her are confined to the role of minor characters. Standing with his back to us, John is another key protagonist on the bleak stage of Golgotha. Christ on the Cross, and the two mourning angels, dressed as ministrants, are delineated by the winding contours of their drapery against the gold background. Altdorfer, the first painter of landscapes in the German territories, eschewed the inclusion of a landscape vista in this work, following the precedent from decades before, and probably complying with the request from the commissioner, the provost of the Monastery of Sankt Florian, near Linz. The ever decreasing figures in the midground and background throng together in a tumultuous mass, while the flagpoles, halberds and spears held swaying in the air suggest that the crowd stretches far into the distance. The features of the visible faces are individualised, often to the verge of caricature, and the postures and gestures have a look of authenticity about them, yet the overall impression is defined by something completely different: the abstractly expressive pattern composed of dazzling colours and labyrinthine calligraphy. This is what gives the moment of action a sense of biblical finality, while the Late Gothic stylisation makes us feel that we are witnessing the inhabitants of an enchanted realm.

VILMOS TÁTRAI

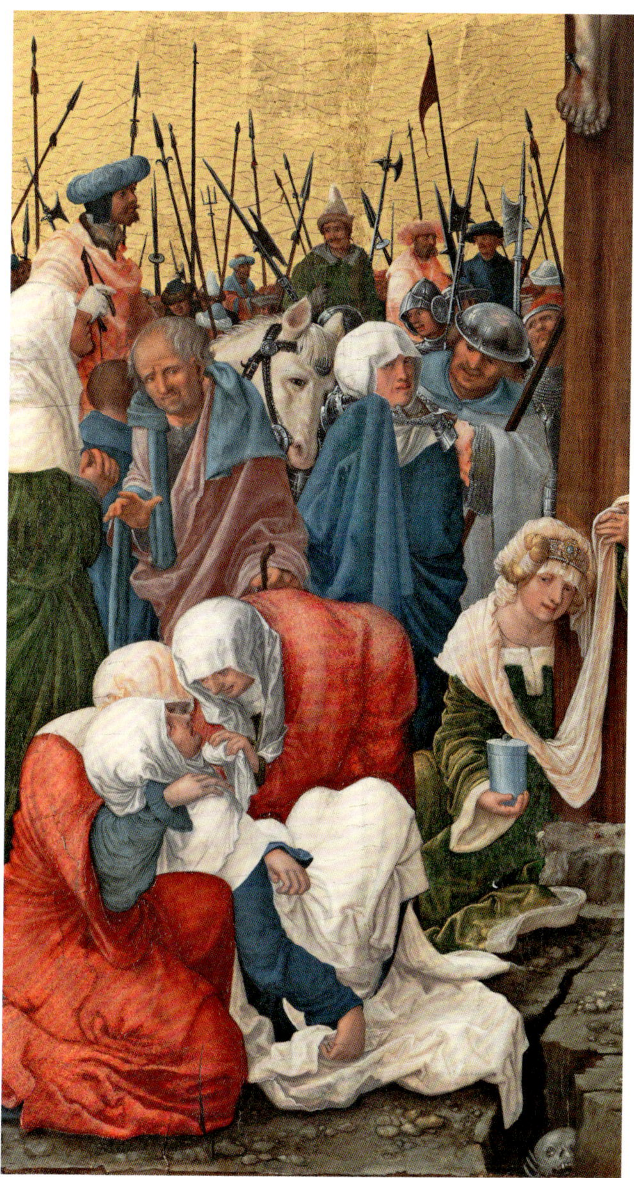

Correggio (Antonio Allegri)

(ca. 1489–1534)

The Virgin Nursing the Christ Child

ca. 1522–1524
Oil on panel, 68.5 × 56.8 cm
Esterházy collection, purchased in 1871
Inv. no. 55

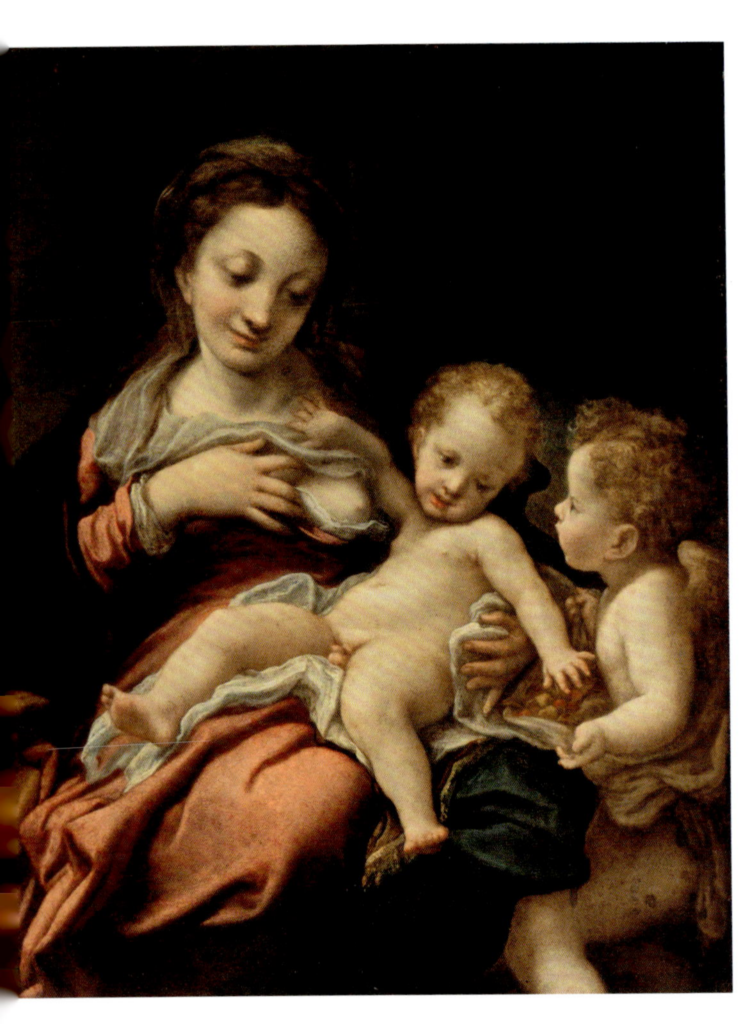

"No craftsman ever painted with greater delicacy, such was the softness of his flesh painting, and such the grace with which he finished his works", wrote Giorgio Vasari, in his chronicle *Lives of the Artists,* of Correggio. Later writers were just as enthusiastic. Stendhal was moved to tears by one of his works, and even flint-hearted Goethe was touched by the beautiful Correggio he saw in 1787 at an art dealer's in Naples. He wrote: "It shows the mother of God with the Child at the very moment when the babe hesitates between the mother's milk and some pears proffered by a cherub. The theme is thus the weaning of Christ. The idea is most tender, and the delightfully executed composition is dynamic, natural, and splendid."

The picture, which had passed through famous collections and was widely admired, could not of course be bought by Johann Wolfgang von Goethe, only by an immensely rich and refined collector like Prince Miklós Esterházy. For the lines above refer to the Budapest *Madonna* – indeed, it could not be put better today. Scholars have recently argued that the picture attempts, through an intricate system of symbols, to express the dogma of the Immaculate Conception. It may does, but even at that time only the most erudite and initiated believers would have understood. The simple viewer both then and now truly sees in the image but this deeply humane, vivid moment of motherhood, the weaning of the child. A theme that befits nobody so perfectly as Correggio's intimate, emotional style.

AXEL VÉCSEY

Unknown Master (before 1526)

Báthory-Madonna

before 1526
Marlstone, 68 × 51 cm
Transferred from the Hungarian National Museum,
1936–1939
Inv. no. 55.982

Florence, the birthplace of Italian Renaissance art, was decorated with countless depictions of the Virgin Mary and the Infant Jesus, not only in paintings, but also in relief works, made of marble, terracotta, gypsum or papier-mâché. Pieces carved in stone were unique, as the process for making them was more time-consuming and required greater skill.

Outside Italy, Renaissance works showing the Virgin and Child often followed compositions invented by famous Italian artists, as was the case with the Báthory Madonna, named after András Báthory, who commissioned the work, whose name is included in the carved inscription. This work is similar to pieces produced by the workshop of the outstanding Florentine painter and sculptor, Andrea del Verrocchio. The Báthory Madonna was carved from marlstone quarried near the royal seat of Buda, which proves beyond a doubt that the work originates from Hungary. Moreover, the broad, round faces of the Virgin and Child contrast sharply with the facial type found in Italian-made counterparts, as do the spiralling curls of Jesus's hair and the technique employed for carving the stone, in which the shallow relief used for the figures is combined with the bold and intricate undercarving of the details in the ornate crown held above the Virgin's head by angels.

In spite of the wars that ravaged Hungary during the period of Ottoman rule, the relief has survived surprisingly intact, probably thanks in part to its small size, its portability, and its handling as a framed "picture". The exact location where the Báthory Madonna was originally housed cannot be identified, but the inscription, offering greetings of peace to those who enter, clearly implies that it was placed above a gate or door, possibly at one of the estates of the Báthory family, in Ecsed (now Nagyecsed) or Nyírbátor.

MANGA PATTANTYÚS

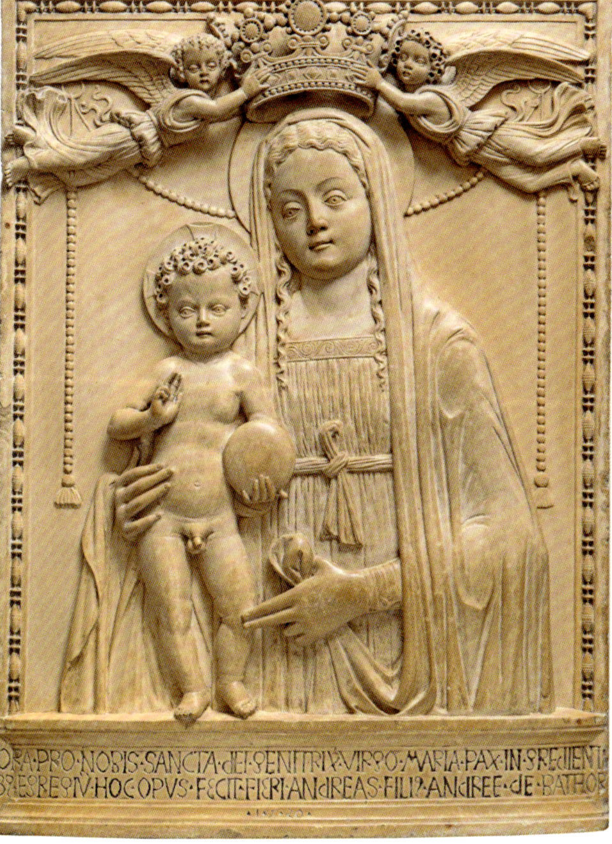

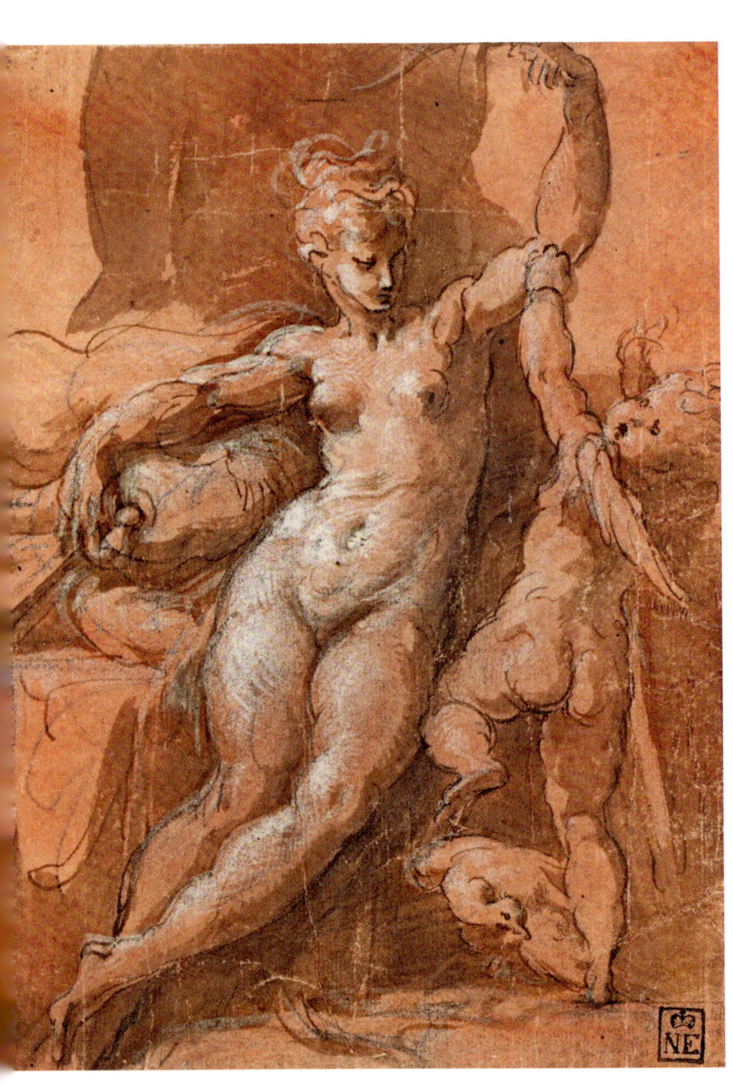

Parmigianino (Francesco Mazzola)

(1503–1540)

Venus Disarming Cupid

ca. 1524–1530
Pen, wash and brown ink on paper, 188 × 143 mm
Esterházy collection, purchased in 1871
Inv. no. 1890

Although during his two-decade career Parmigianino painted very little, few of his contemporaries had such a great influence as he did. His popularity was largely due to the fact that his tastefully elegant style reflected with self-evident unaffectedness the ideal of beauty shared by the young generation of mannerists who followed Raphael. Parmigianino liked to draw, and produced many drawings: more than one thousand of his sketches survive, and one of the finest of these is Venus Disarming Cupid. In the Metamorphoses Ovid tells of how Cupid once wounded his own mother, Venus, with an arrow, and she fell in love with the athletic but mortal hunter, Adonis. Thus the goddess of love came to know all the anguish of consuming passion. On this finely detailed sheet Venus is shown plucking away the unguarded bow from the child. The goddess is a masterful example of the figura serpentinata beloved of mannerist and baroque artists, a figure in unnatural, calculated elegant serpentine twists.

We do not know Parmigianino's purpose in making the drawing, but the coloured ground of the paper, the richly toned wash and the marked whitewash are akin to the preparatory drawings for his woodcuts. Though no contemporary woodcut version is known of, the drawing may be one of those Parmigianino made for the woodcutter Antonio da Trento in Bologna.

ZOLTÁN KÁRPÁTI

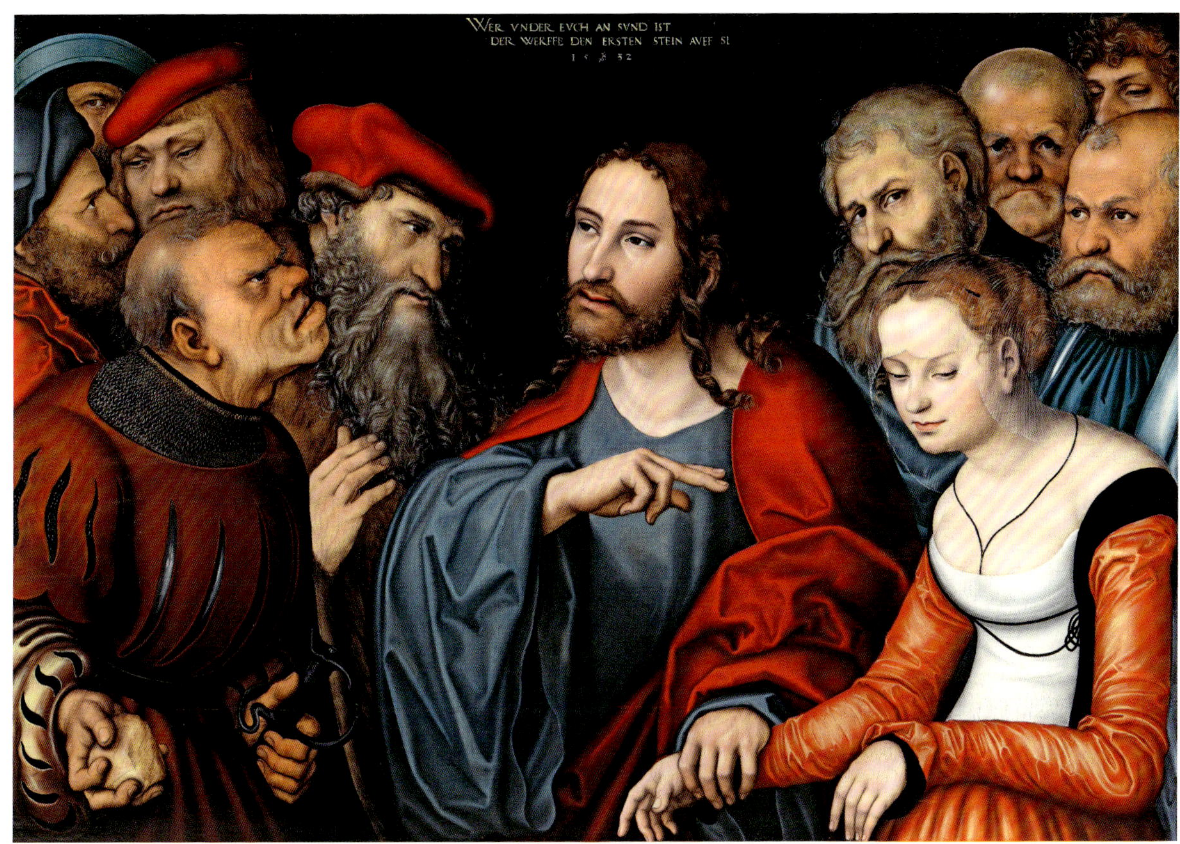

Lucas Cranach the Elder (1472–1553)

Christ and the Adulteress

1532
Oil on limewood, 82.5 × 121 cm
Esterházy collection, purchased in 1871
Inv. no. 146

"Let any one of you who is without sin be the first to throw a stone at her." These words, which have grown into an adage, appear inscribed at the top of the painting. The year written below – 1532 – not only dates the work, but also implies that Christ's teaching is still valid in the present, just as the costumes also belong to Cranach's own times. The half-length, close-up portrayal is based, indirectly via Dürer, on Northern Italian forebears, and the emphasis is transferred from the gestures to the facial expressions. The would-be henchman, who wears, over his coat of mail, a jacket that is decorated with vertical slashes, grips a stone in his right hand and clutches the haft of his sword in his left. With his gormless, bestial appearance, he is an embodiment of brute force. One of the Pharisees has an avid look on his face as he tries to catch Jesus speaking against the law, while another casts a corrupt and conspiratorial glance at his companion, who is shown in profile. Between them is a solitary eye, a perfectly conceived and executed motif of horror, the chilling look of an anonymous member of a lynch mob. The men assembled beside the adulteress, drinking in the words of Jesus, could be four of the apostles. The man closest to Jesus looks out at us directly in gentle admonishment, while behind him, shown fully frontally, the almost caricature-like face of the bald and toothless old man reassures us that ugliness, in Cranach's visual vocabulary, is not necessarily a synonym for Evil. Cranach often poked fun at his female figures, as can be seen in his earlier depictions of Lucretia and Salome, and here too, as the adulteress casts her eyes downwards in shame, it seems that Cranach could not resist his customary mockery.

VILMOS TÁTRAI

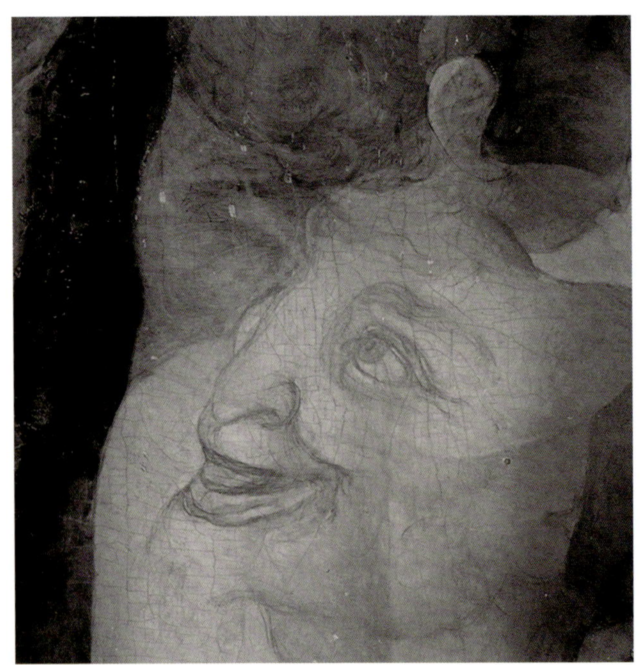

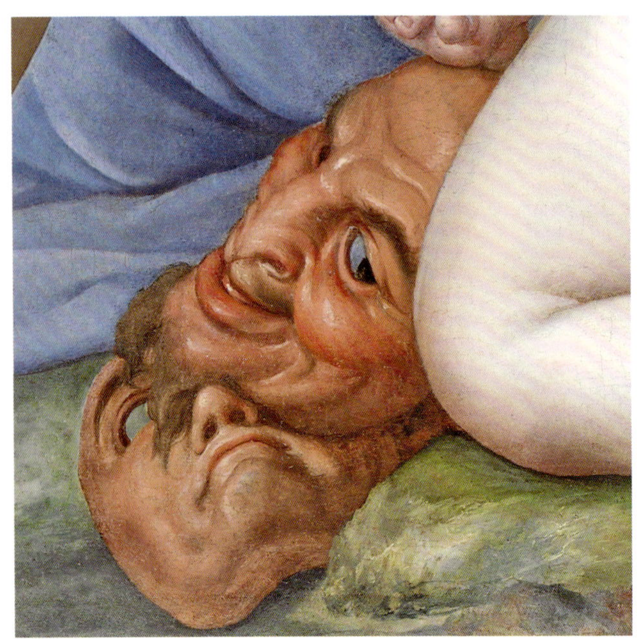

Bronzino (Agnolo di Cosimo di Maiano)
(1503–1572)

Venus, Cupid and Jealousy

ca. 1550
Oil on poplar, 192 × 142 cm
Gift of Count István Keglevich, 1863
Inv. no. 163

"The human eye cannot see like this", stated Wölfflin, the authoritative art historian, of Bronzino's art. And perhaps a healthy human mind cannot think so crookedly as Bronzino's did, for this bizarre picture is able to jolt even today's jaded viewer. A blatant dissonance lies between the brazenly indiscreet erotic content and the annoyingly restrained form. There is body, but no soul, no instinct, no passion, no torrid arousal. There is no flesh, for bodies are hard as marble and cold as ice, as every outline is mercilessly sharp – this is what Wölfflin meant. Nor is there blood in them, they are blindingly white, like gesso (indeed, that is what they are made of: the gesso ground vibrates from beneath the thin, transparent colours). The tyranny of intended artifice weighs the picture down with sadistic overtones. The subject is no less contrived, in that the precise meaning of the picture, and that of its famous twin, the *Allegory* in the National Gallery in London, will perhaps never be unravelled. Whereas in the London image jealousy and fraud seem to triumph over love, here, in turn, desire seems happy, mutual, and the hideous monstrosity of Jealousy scurries away in the background. But in the laboured world of mannerism, nothing is so simple. When looked under infrared light, it turns out that in the place of the children Eros and Anteros, representing requited love, there was originally a satyr baring its teeth with a demonic grin, similar to the mask beneath their feet.

A X E L   V É C S E Y

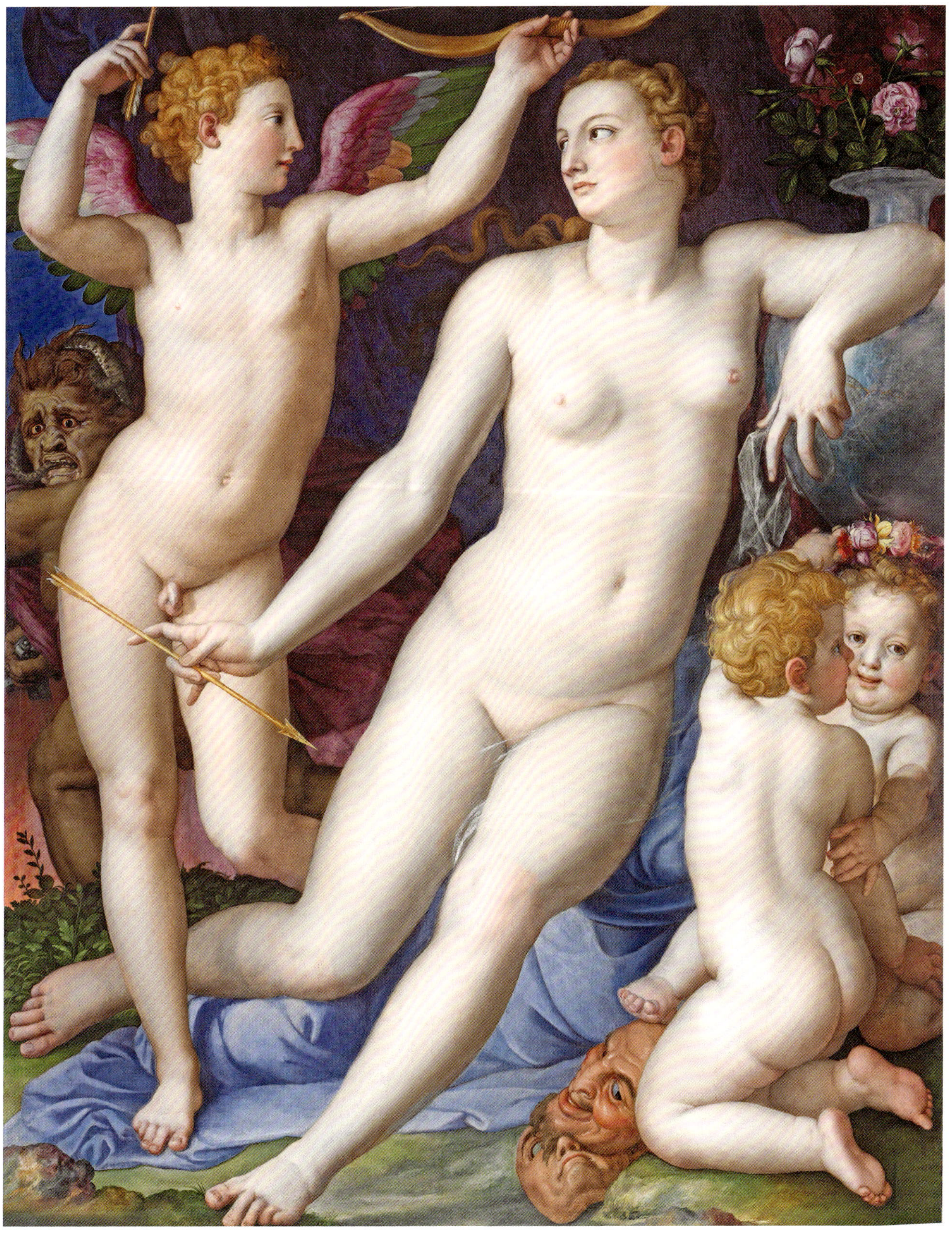

Hans Baldung Grien (1484/1485–1524)

Adam and Eve

1525
Oil on limewood, each 209 × 83.5 cm
Purchased in Vienna, 1900
Inv. nos. 1888, 1889

Sixteenth-century Europe loved scintillatingly provocative pictures of women twisting men round their little fingers with cunning stratagem, thereby driving them to destruction. Particularly fond of the theme of the demonic power stemming from female sexuality was Hans Baldung, perhaps Dürer's best pupil, who was dubbed "Grien" after his favourite shade of metallic green which here covers the snake's body. The obvious prototype for the role is Eve, the ancestral mother. Through her eating of the fruit, sinful but sweet to taste, the human body became the source of knowledge and pleasure, but also subjected to death. Baldung's pair of pictures (originally part of a series complemented by Judith with the severed head of Holofernes, and Venus and Cupid) focuses clearly on the story's erotic content. The sin is already done, the progenitors cover their loins with leaves, but their movements are wanton rather than shy. Evil has triumphed. Adam is tormented by lust: his body convulses, and he presses his right hand to the place of his missing rib. The locks of his hair form horns, his lips are parted, and his face is covered by a beard and moustache – all traits of contemporary depictions of satyrs. While Adam is portrayed as a victim, Eve is the active seductress, who finds unabashed pleasure in the power of her desirable beauty. The smile playing on her lips reflects self-satisfaction; her gaze and her every movement are directed to the man's body, as if to take possession of it.

AXEL VÉCSEY

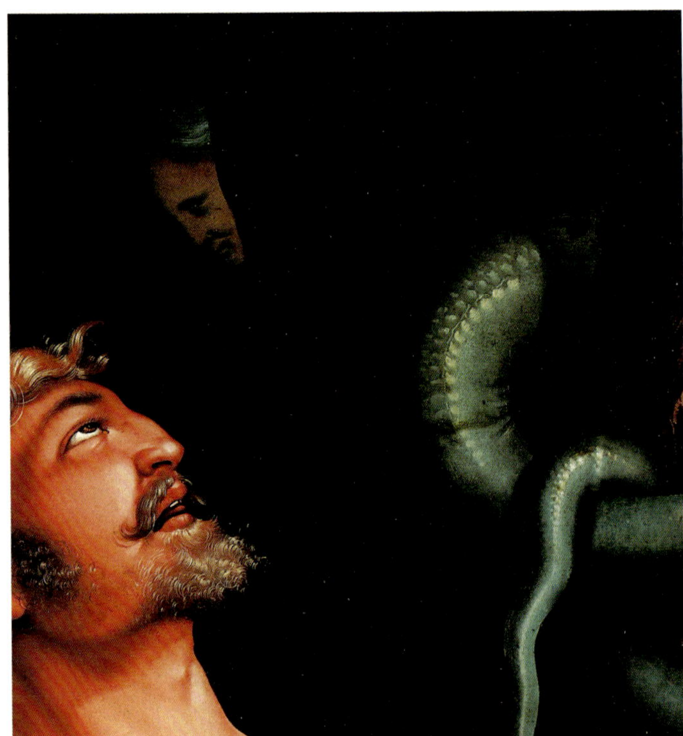

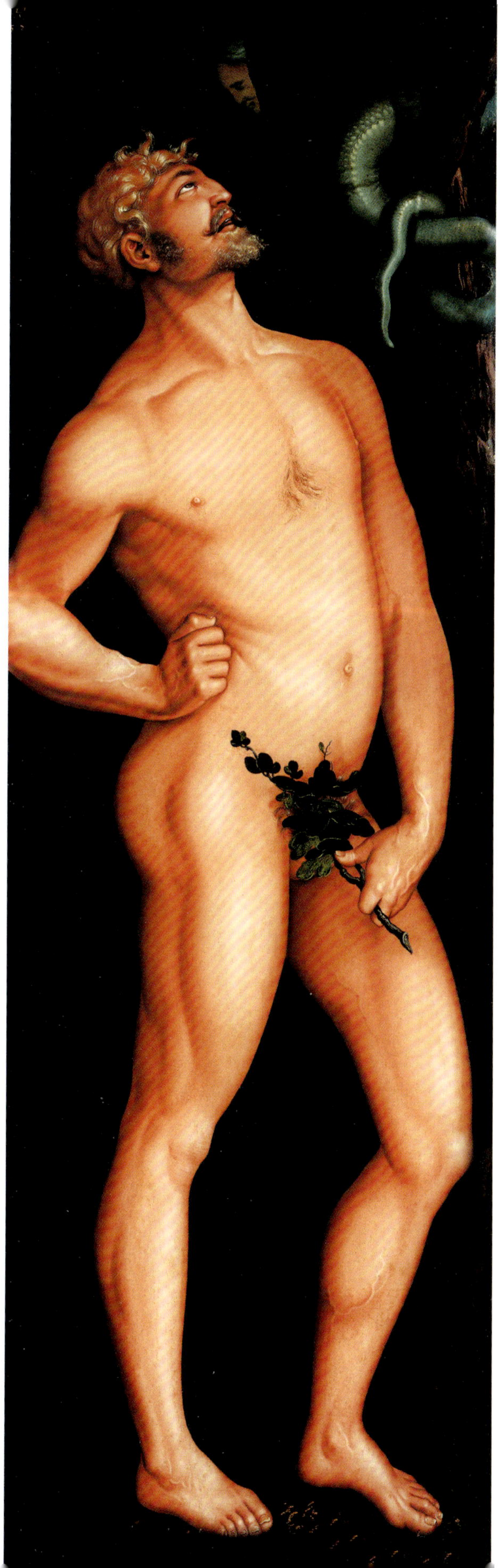

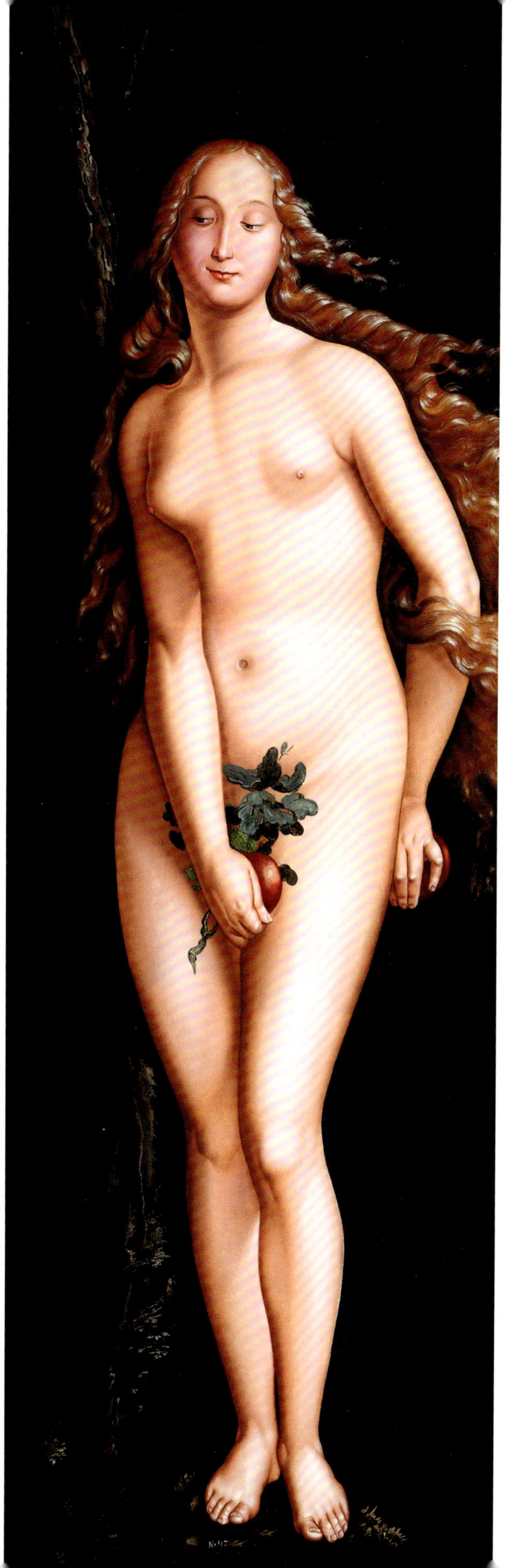

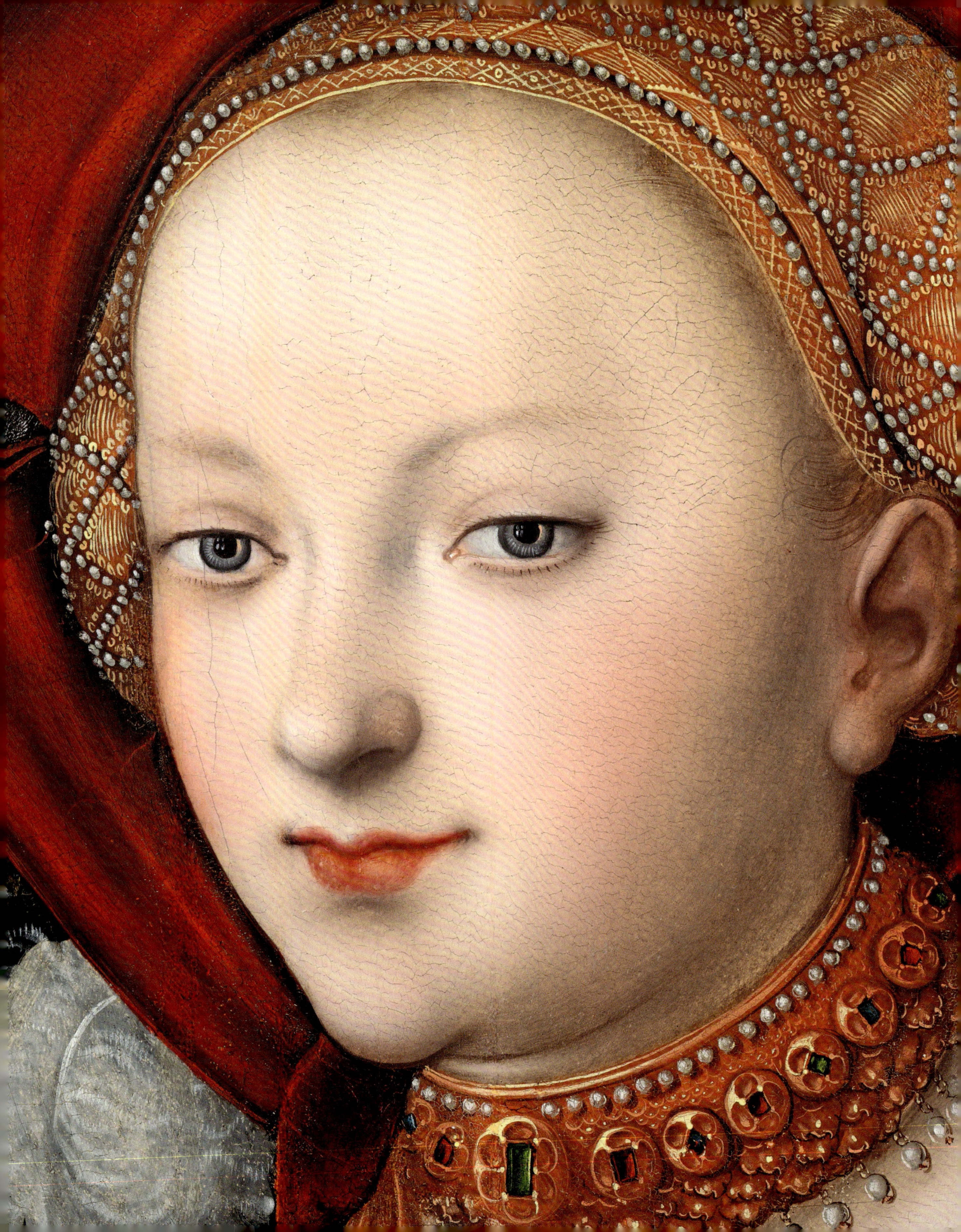

Salome with the Head of Saint John the Baptist

1530s

Oil on poplar, 87 × 58 cm

Esterházy collection, purchased in 1871

Inv. no. 132

The painter prince of the pReformation, Lucas Cranach was a close friend of Martin Luther, and also the godfather to his children. He made the illustrations of Luther's Bible translations, just as he did his portraits and allegories of his theses. Still, he had no qualms about providing his Catholic clients with pictures suiting their own faith, nor did he baulk at ribald subjects. Of course, we can if we wish interpret his piquant works as moral parables, which point out man's destiny if he surrenders to his lecherous desires. Indisputably, though, the host of Salomes, Judiths and other demonic women of fate that swarmed from Cranach's studio owed their popularity rather to their thrilling sensuality. They are icy, sadistic and triumphant, in the extreme attire of classy ladies of the time, and what is more they are endowed with the facial features of the illustrious beauties of the Wittenberg court.

Salome's name is not mentioned in the Bible; she gained popularity only in the sixteenth century, to be revived by the decadent aesthetics of the late nineteenth century. Strictly speaking she was little more than a tool for her mother, Herodias, to get revenge on Saint John the Baptist, who had spoken out against her sinful relationship with the king. The payback came during a banquet, when Salome performed a maddening dance, and prompted by her mother, asked the spellbound king for her reward: John's death. She then handed her mother the disembodied head on a platter.

AXEL VÉCSEY

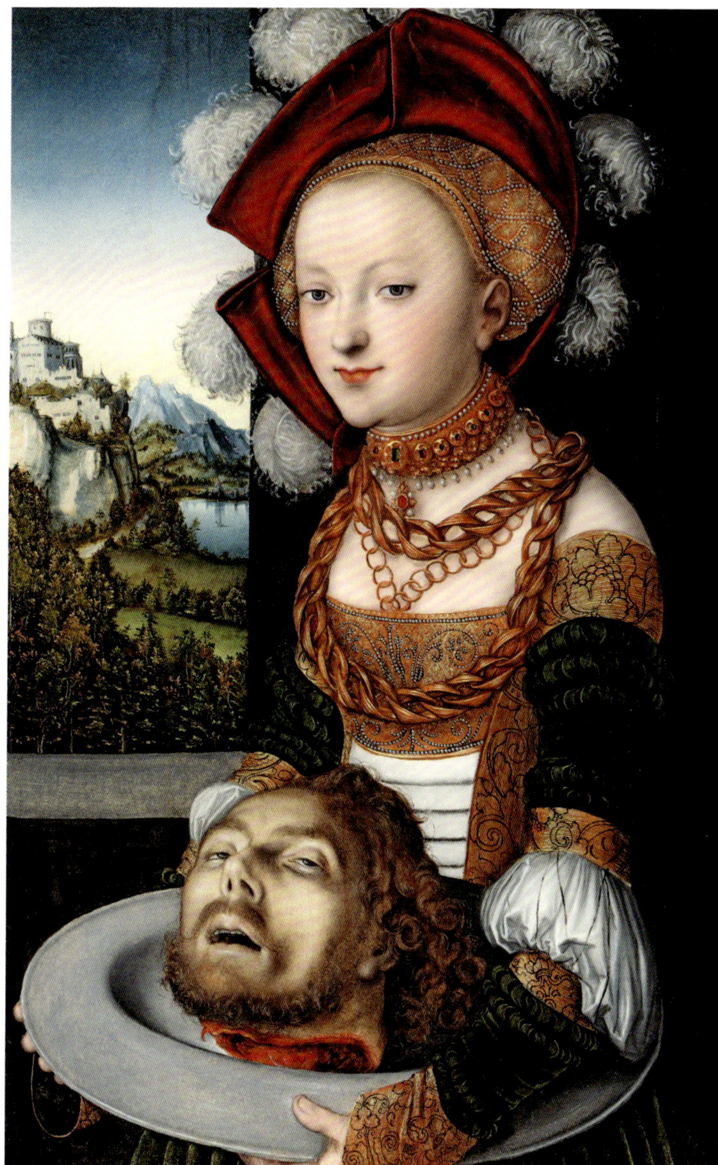

Titian (Tiziano Vecellio)
(1488/1490–1576)

Virgin and Child with Saint Paul

1540s
Oil on canvas, 108 × 96.5 cm
Deposit of the Hungarian National Bank
Inv. no. L. 3.745

This painting gives us a clear idea of what is meant by Titian's famed colourism, which served as a template for several generations of later artists. What it does not mean is a kind of multi-coloured cavalcade. The great innovator of the Venetian Renaissance tended to limit his palette to relatively few colours, which he usually mixed into deep, warm and sensuous shades. The other essential element of his colourism was the manner with which he handled his brushes. Like nobody before him, with loose brushstrokes, touches of thicker or more thinly applied pigments, multiple layers of glazing, and a softening of sharp contours, Titian produced compositions of unprecedented vividness. Colourism, in Titian's hands, achieved the powerful illusion of verisimilitude. In this work too, worshipful Saint Paul (dressed as a Roman officer, that is, as the recently converted Saul), the humble Virgin Mary, recalling the idealised beauty of the Venus of Urbino, and the divine Infant Jesus, gazing into infinity, are portrayed so that we can almost feel the physical presence of all three figures.

Knowledge of this painting as an autograph work by the prince of Venetian Painters was forgotten for approximately a century. Only after it reappeared at auction in Budapest in May 2005 was it established that the work had, from the mid-seventeenth until at least the mid-eighteenth century, been part of the Este collection in Modena, where it was attributed to Titian himself. A substantial part of the Este collection was acquired by the Dresden Gallery, but numerous paintings remained in Modena and were later dispersed, including this piece, which was described in one source from the year 1800 as being in Vienna.

VILMOS TÁTRAI

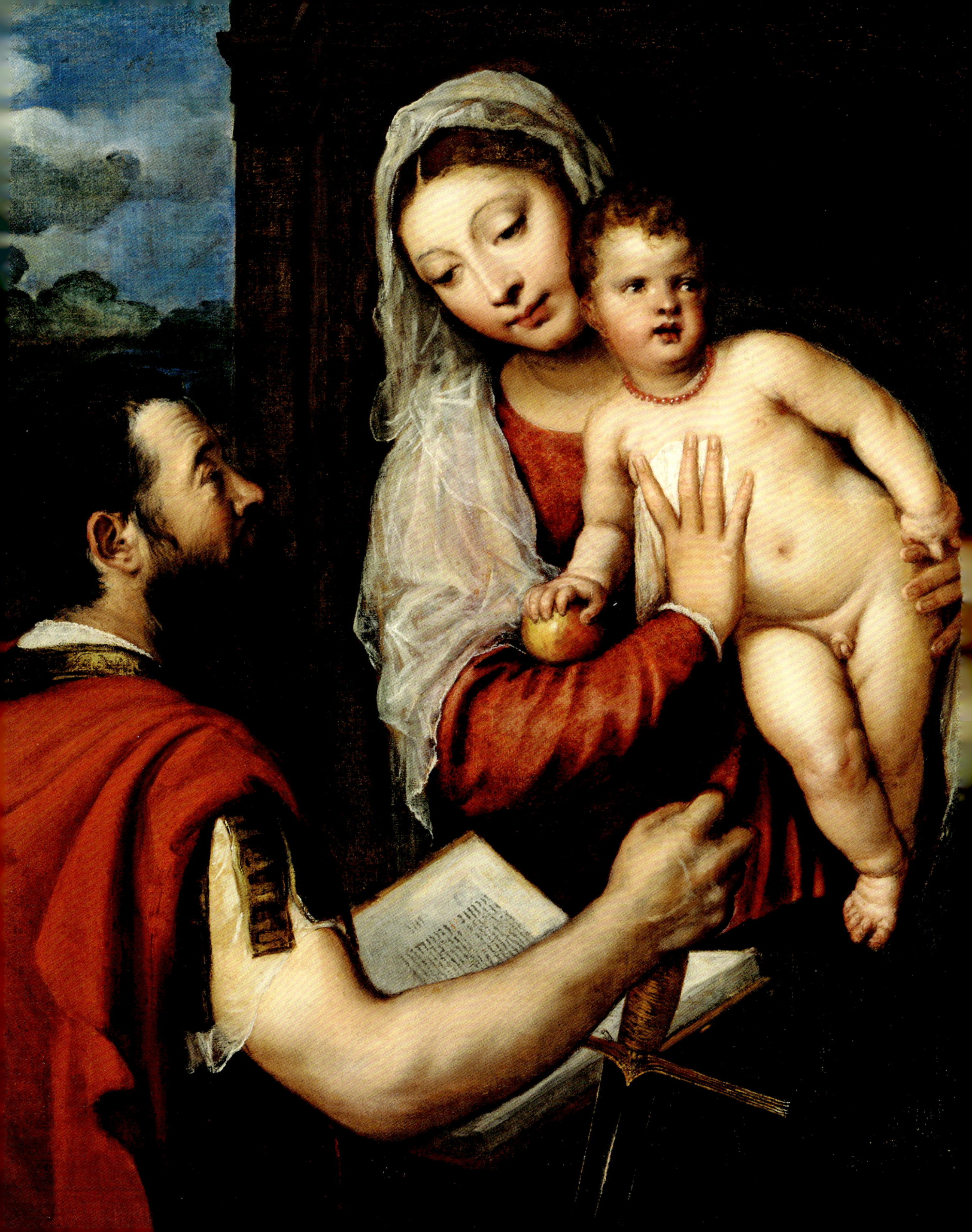

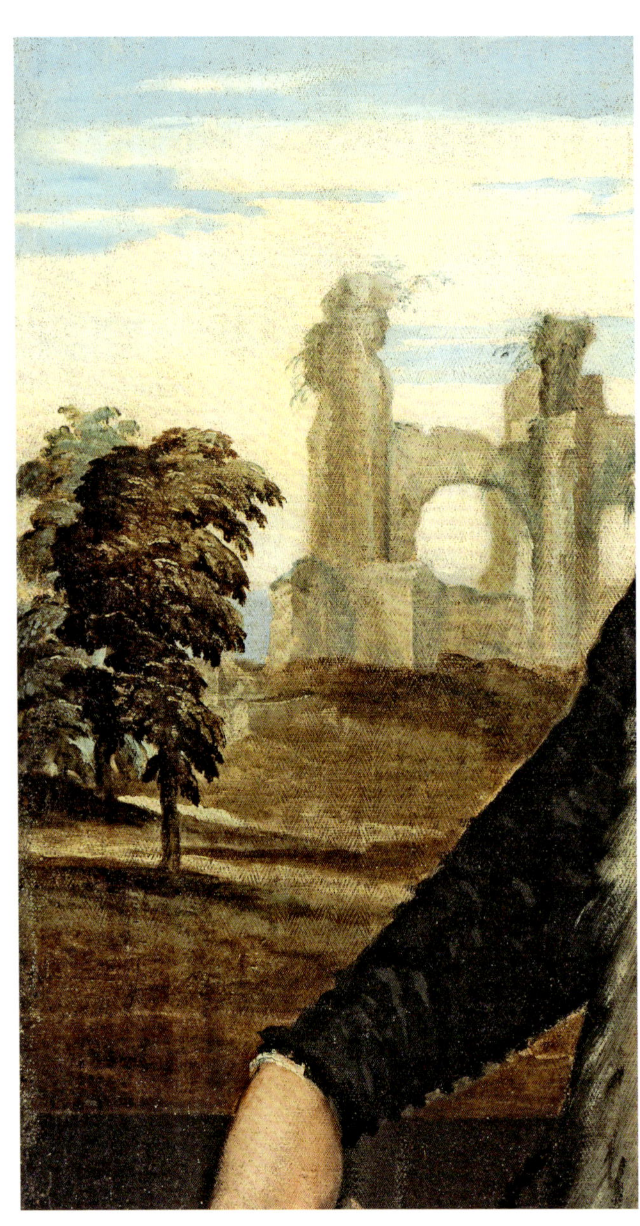

Paolo Veronese (Paolo Caliari)
(1528–1588)

Portrait of a Man

ca. 1555
Oil on canvas, 120 × 102 cm
Bequest of Count János Pálffy, 1912
Inv. no. 4228

"There is one man who makes easy what we have always been told is impossible; and that is Paolo Veronese. In my view he is the only man who has penetrated the whole secret of nature", praised Delacroix his great predecessor. And indeed, in superior virtuosity, and in graceful elegance only Tiepolo could compete with Veronese in the history of painting. He wallowed in formal tricks, yet remained classical in his spirit: his colours are pure as crystal, and create clear harmony; the locations are spacious and bathed in light; and underlying all the flamboyant cavalcade is a perfectly balanced geometric structure. And if others received more praise in the form of verse or statues, perhaps there was no painter whose direct influence was greater in the following centuries. This portrait of a young man posing in a sumptuous lynx fur not only conveys the dense essence of Veronese's genius, but also that of the aristocratic cultural milieu which was the hotbed for his art. The structure appears infinitely simple, and the execution also seems effortless, yet so many little ruses create the unquestionable air of authority about the man. His direct open gaze, his relaxed posture (as recommended by contemporary manuals of ambitious courtiers) is the embodiment of nonchalance. The character is shown through gesture, and just as the painter proclaims his model, he announces himself too: this confident, vigorous, yet easy manner of painting suggests a person born to absolute dominion over matter.

A X E L V É C S E Y

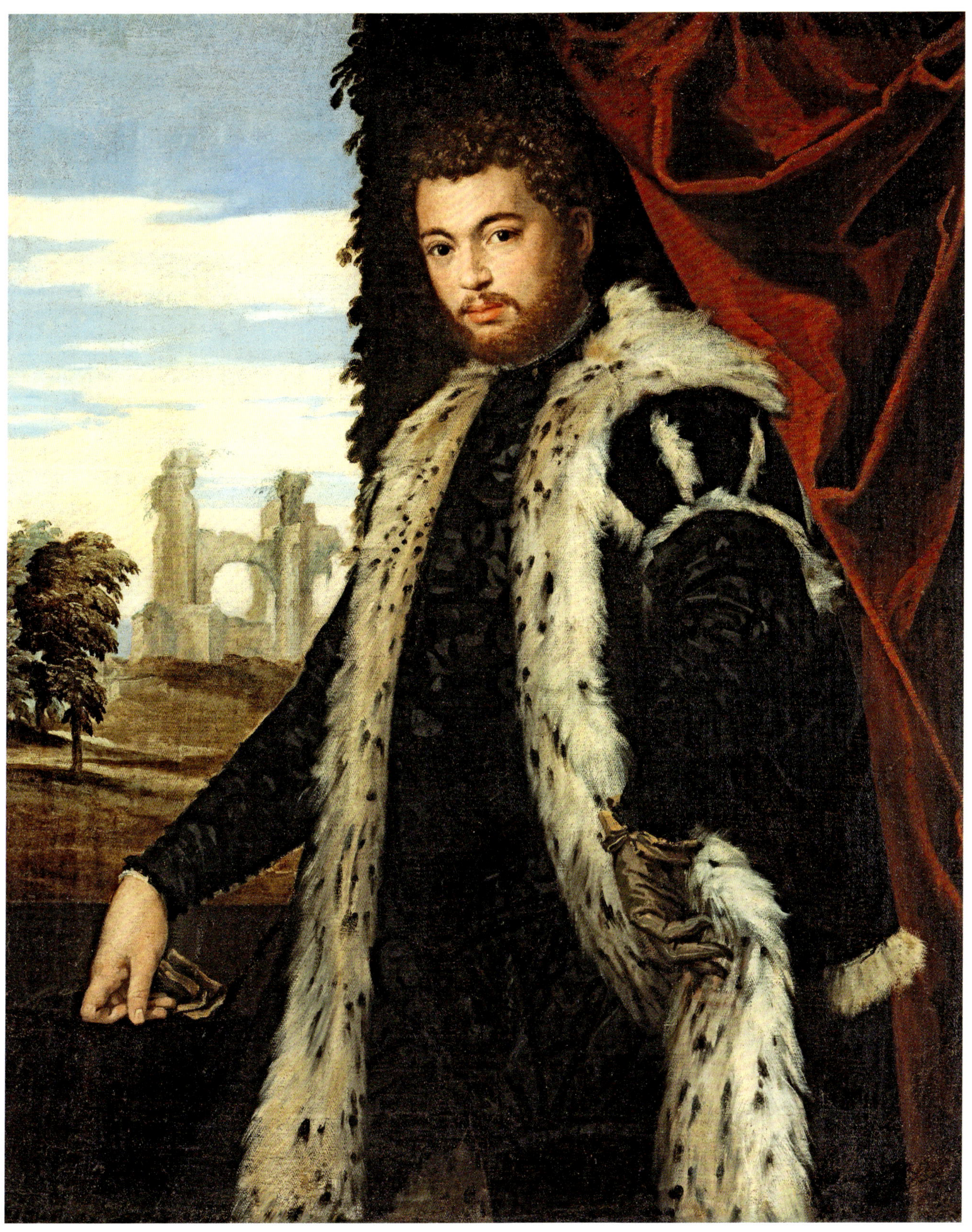

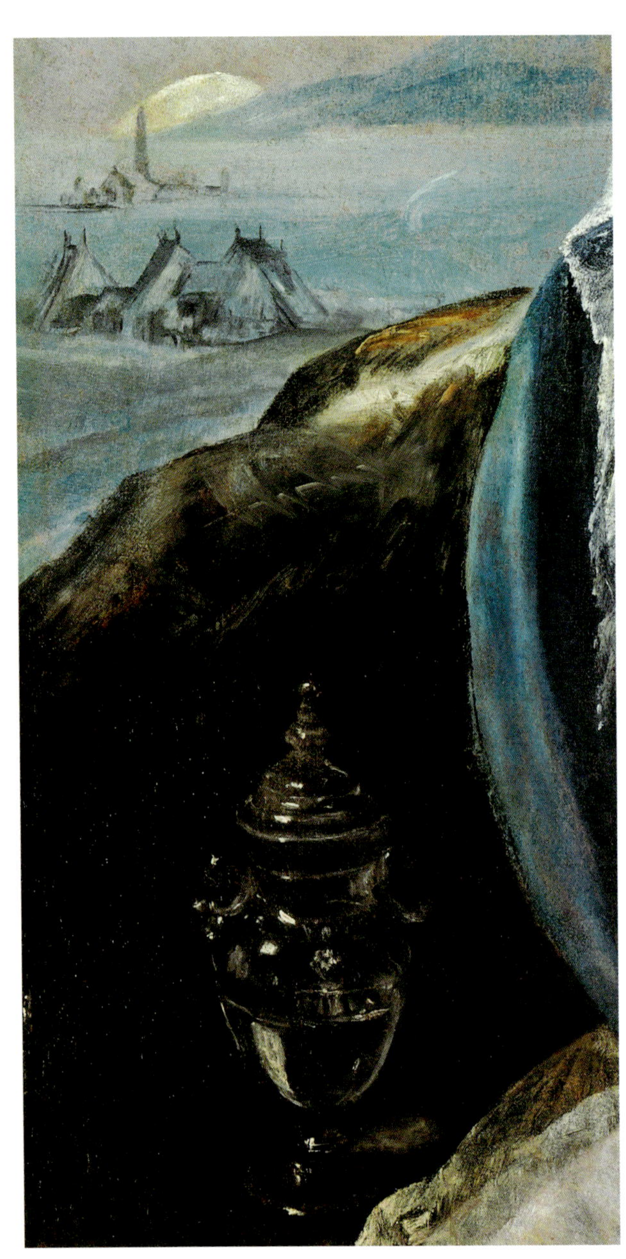

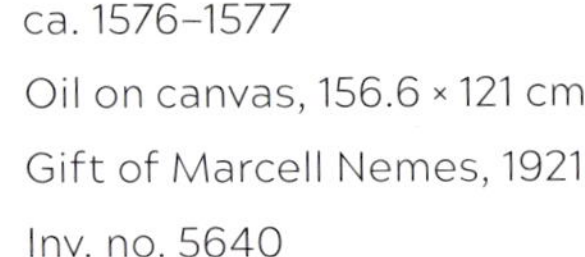

Penitent Magdalene

ca. 1576–1577
Oil on canvas, 156.6 × 121 cm
Gift of Marcell Nemes, 1921
Inv. no. 5640

It was said of El Greco that he painted with a piece broken off a wooden cross, without making any corrections, so that "every patch of paint corresponds to God's will". The story is not factual, yet it speaks volumes: it is as if the febrile visions evolved from the roughly defined, impetuous forms at the touch of some mystic power. Yet it is not, after all, God's hand at work, but their painter's passionate faith and talent, which forged a new organic unity from Christendom's two great painterly traditions. Domenikos Theotokopoulos from Crete was already a recognised master of the old-style icon painting before he was captivated by the modern western style of Titian and Tintoretto. Wherever fate took him, to Venice, Rome, and finally to Spain, in his soul he remained "El Greco", "the Greek".

A former harlot, Magdalene turned to Jesus's most devoted believer. Following Titian, Greco condensed her story into the single moment of ecstasy: the moment when she, meditating in the wilderness on death and immortality, converts. But while for Titian her passionate revelation is accompanied by erotic overtones, here the blinding beam of light seems to purify her, almost uplifting her from the bonds of corporeality. The skull, which refers to earthly mortality, has rolled out of her hand, and behind her ivy, symbol of eternal life, stretches heavenwards. The dawn landscape, bathed in cold moonlit pale tones, is a delicate echo of the emanating experience of spiritual catharsis.

AXEL VÉCSEY

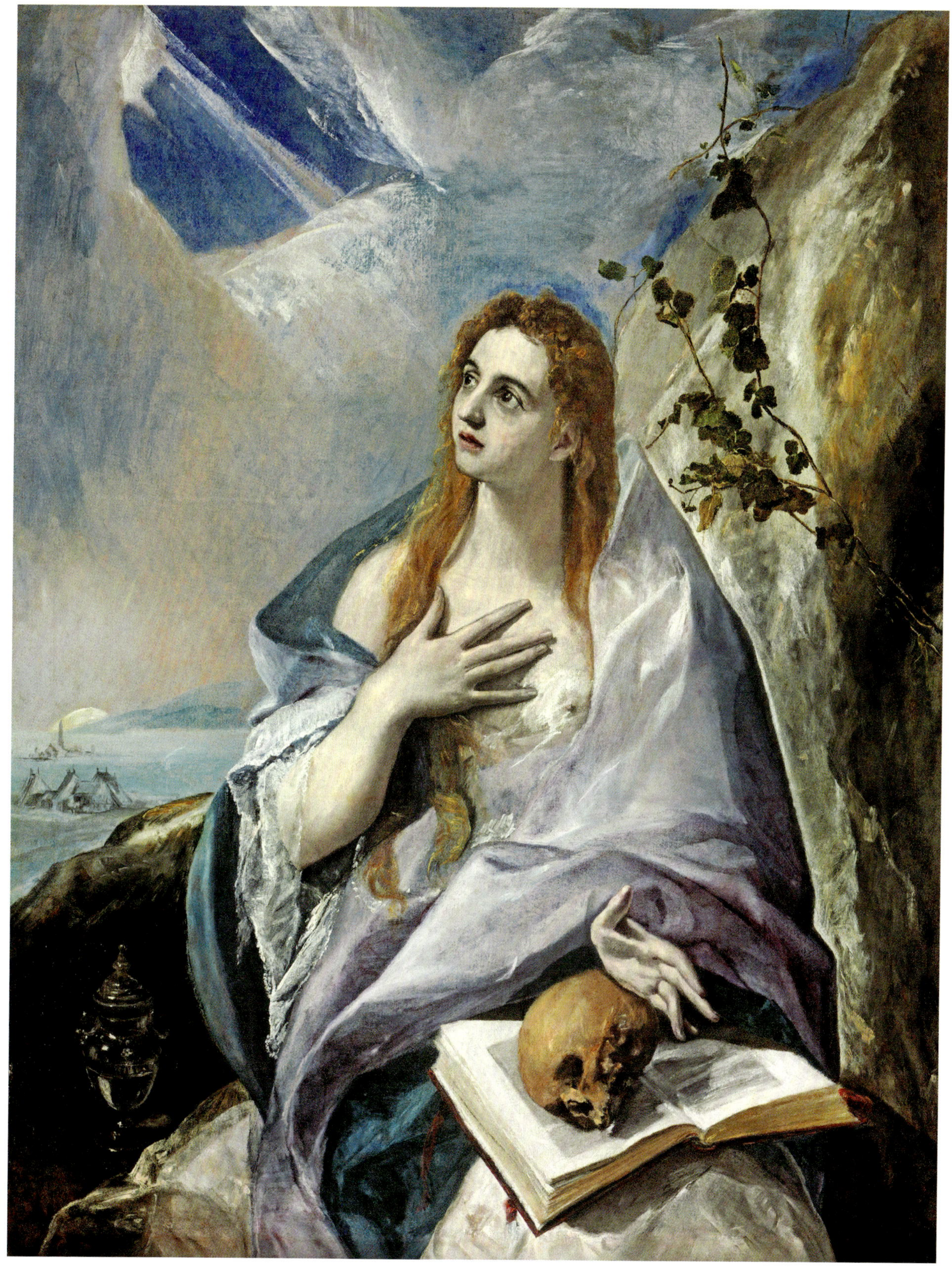

Pieter Bruegel the Elder (ca. 1525/1530 – 1569)

The Sermon
of Saint John the Baptist

1566
Oil on oak, 95 × 160.5 cm
Deposit of Veronika Batthyány-Strattmann
and Ádám Batthyány
Inv. no. L.3.788

"The peasant": this is the name that has become associated with Pieter Bruegel the Elder, the greatest genius of sixteenth-century Netherlandish art. Not that he tilled the land (he was an erudite townsman), nor simply because he took pleasure in portraying peasant life with sympathetic irony. Yet his pictures do indeed seem to smack of the earth, for he had a worm's-eye view of the world. He was interested not in the heroes from the grand stories of mankind, but in what simple folk grasp of events, and how they affect them in everyday life. For sure, sometimes the conclusion is that they remain unaffected, as in the famous Brussels picture, *The Fall of Icarus,* where the ridiculous rebellion of man remains an imperceptible speck in the divine order. Not so in the *Sermon of Saint John the Baptist,* a key work in his oeuvre. Here the whole world draws up, in captivating diversity: nobles, priests, soldiers, burghers, peasants, Flemings, Spaniards, Jews, Gypsies, Turks, the healthy, and the infirm. Yet this story tells not of differences, but of togetherness, of the new covenant that Christ would make with all mankind, and of the words of the prophet, by which it is foretold. This experience in common surges throughout the colourful throng, and resonates in their souls. Every sense is pervaded by the recognition that this is a special moment; that the Redeemer, as the prophet says, stands there in the crowd, and if he has not yet announced himself, the time when he will do so is near.

AXEL VÉCSEY

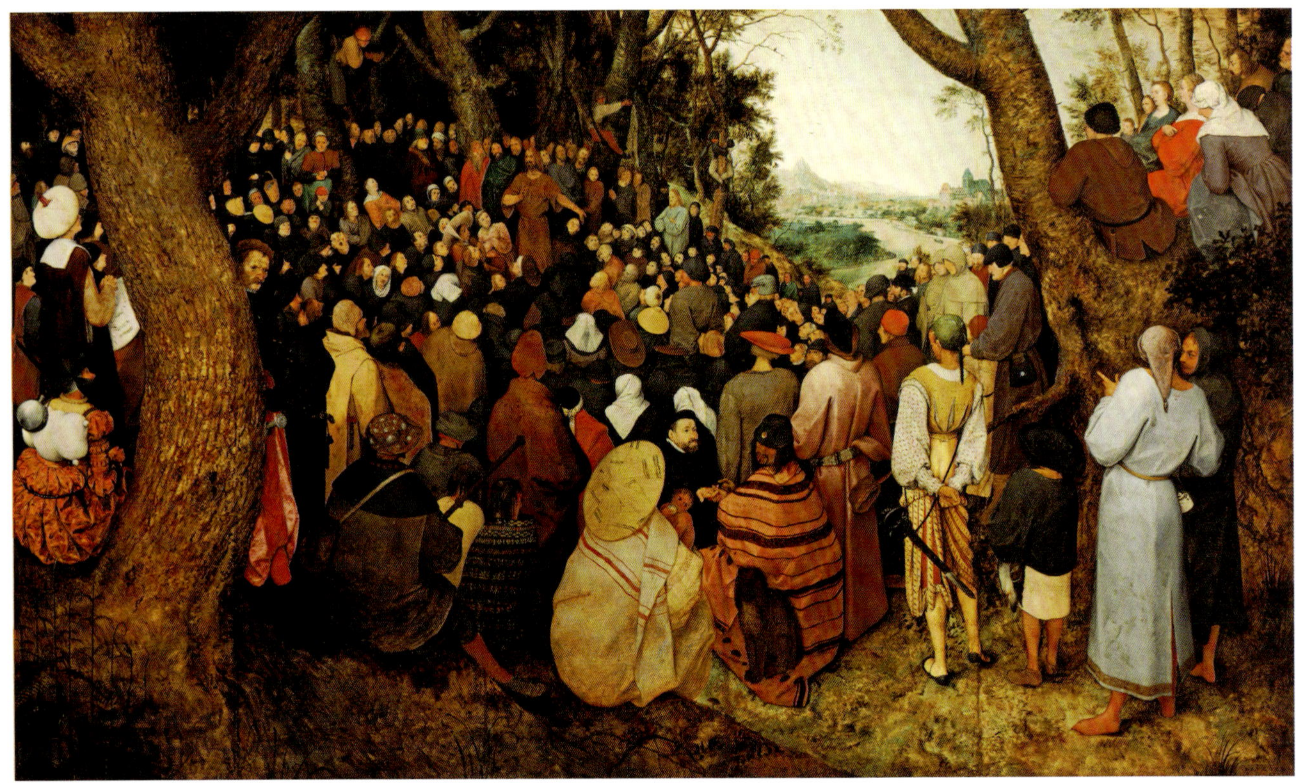

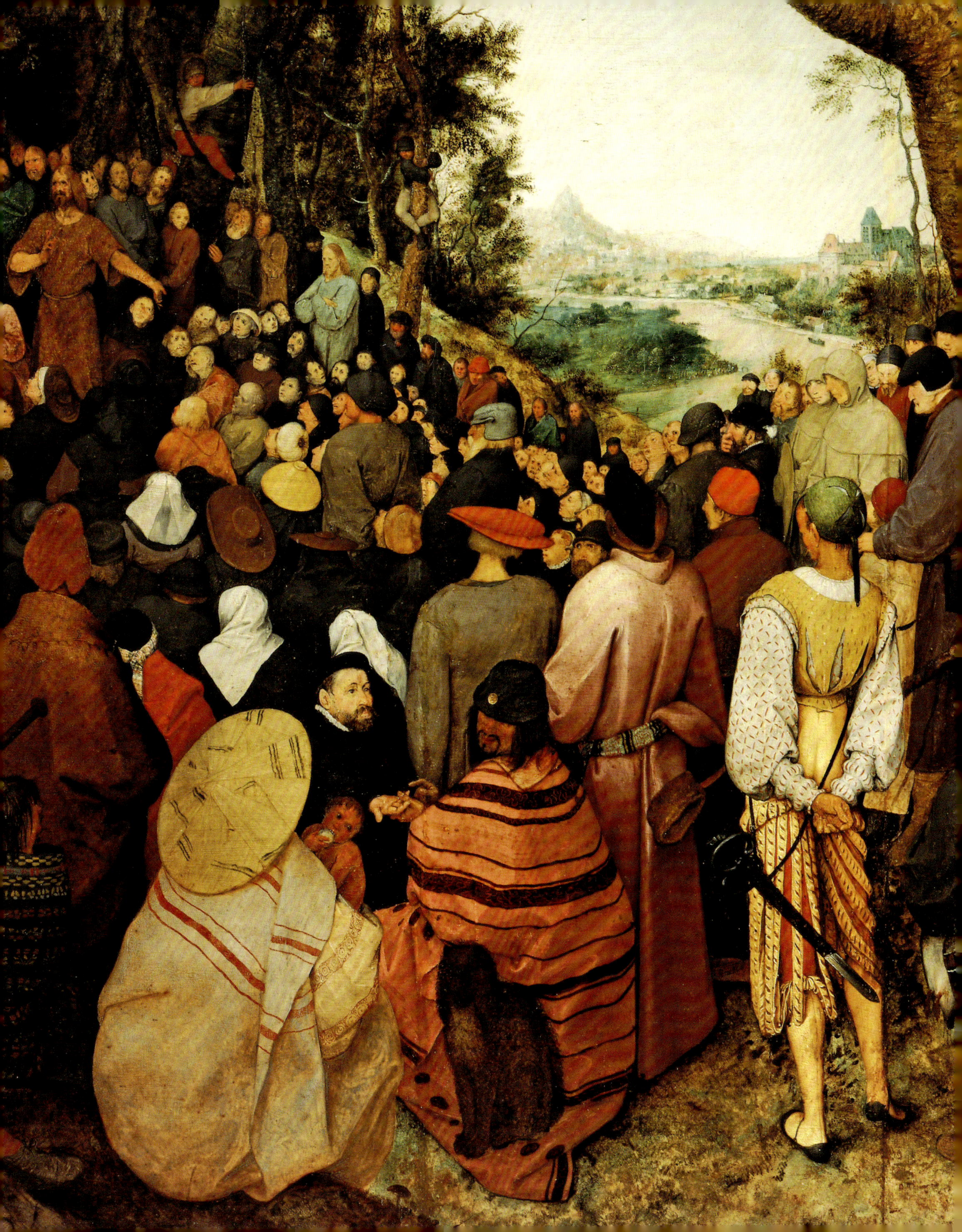

Frozen River with Skaters

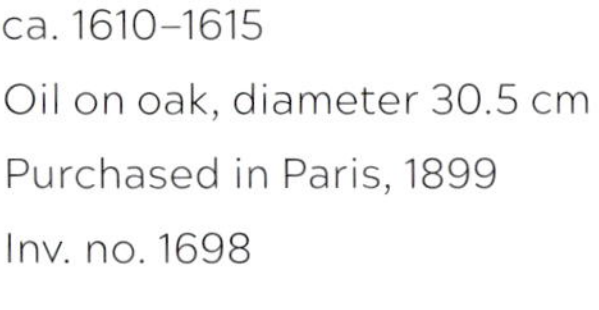

ca. 1610–1615
Oil on oak, diameter 30.5 cm
Purchased in Paris, 1899
Inv. no. 1698

A decisive moment in the history of European painting was when during the sixteenth century artists first dared to paint pictures with no "history". No saints, no Greek gods: just a forest clearing, a shepherd driving his flock, or a table laid with food. Such a picture was a self-contained world, free of all literary references. And as new genres were born, so they soon had their specialists. Avercamp was the first Dutch master to specialise in winter landscapes, populated with many small figures, merrily sliding and skating. The popularity of this deaf and dumb painter peaked in the 1610s when exceptionally harsh winters visited the small town of Kampen, where he spent most of his life.

The inquisitive eye can delight in many charming little episodes within the refined structure of the picture. A peasant pushes his wife and child on a sledge; figures in noble attire play *ijskolf*, the ancestor of ice-hockey; further back two gentlemen make towards a horse-driven sleigh. Many folk are skating, but not everyone is practised in the sport: one lad has fallen flat on his tummy on the ice, and lost his hat. Those who like ribald jokes can chuckle over the woman squatted down by the prow of the ship to relieve herself, while a dog bustles about her bare behind. The noble, the fisherman and the peasant take pleasure together, and perhaps this is the picture's underlying message: the unity of the newly independent Dutch nation.

AXEL VÉCSEY

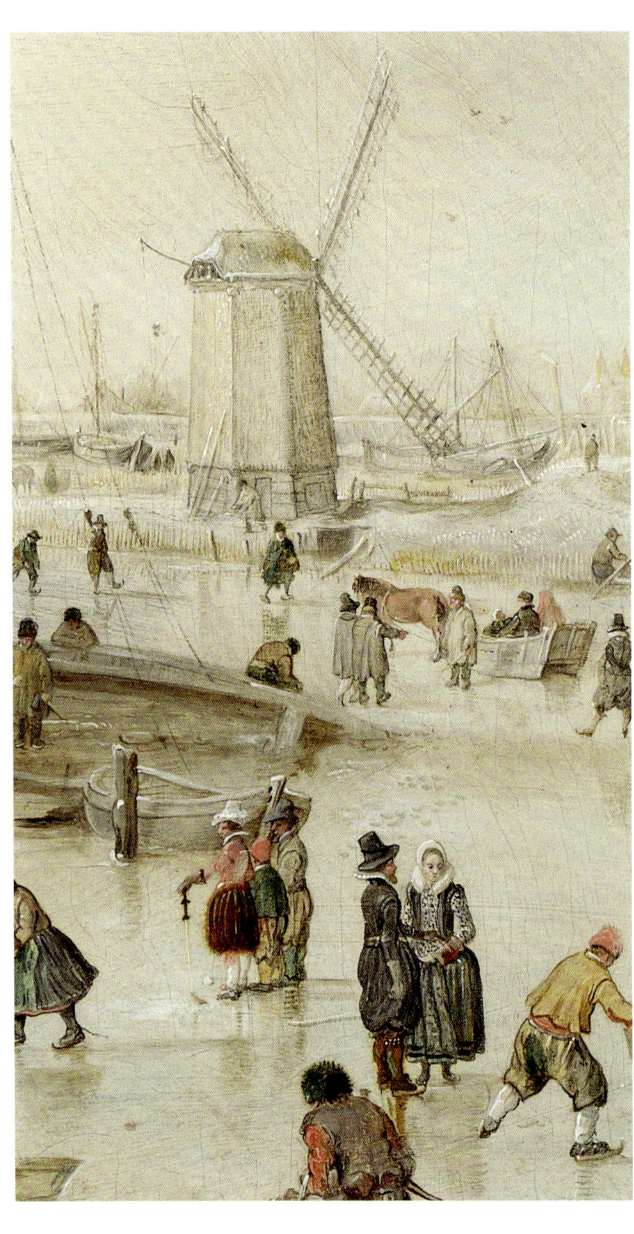

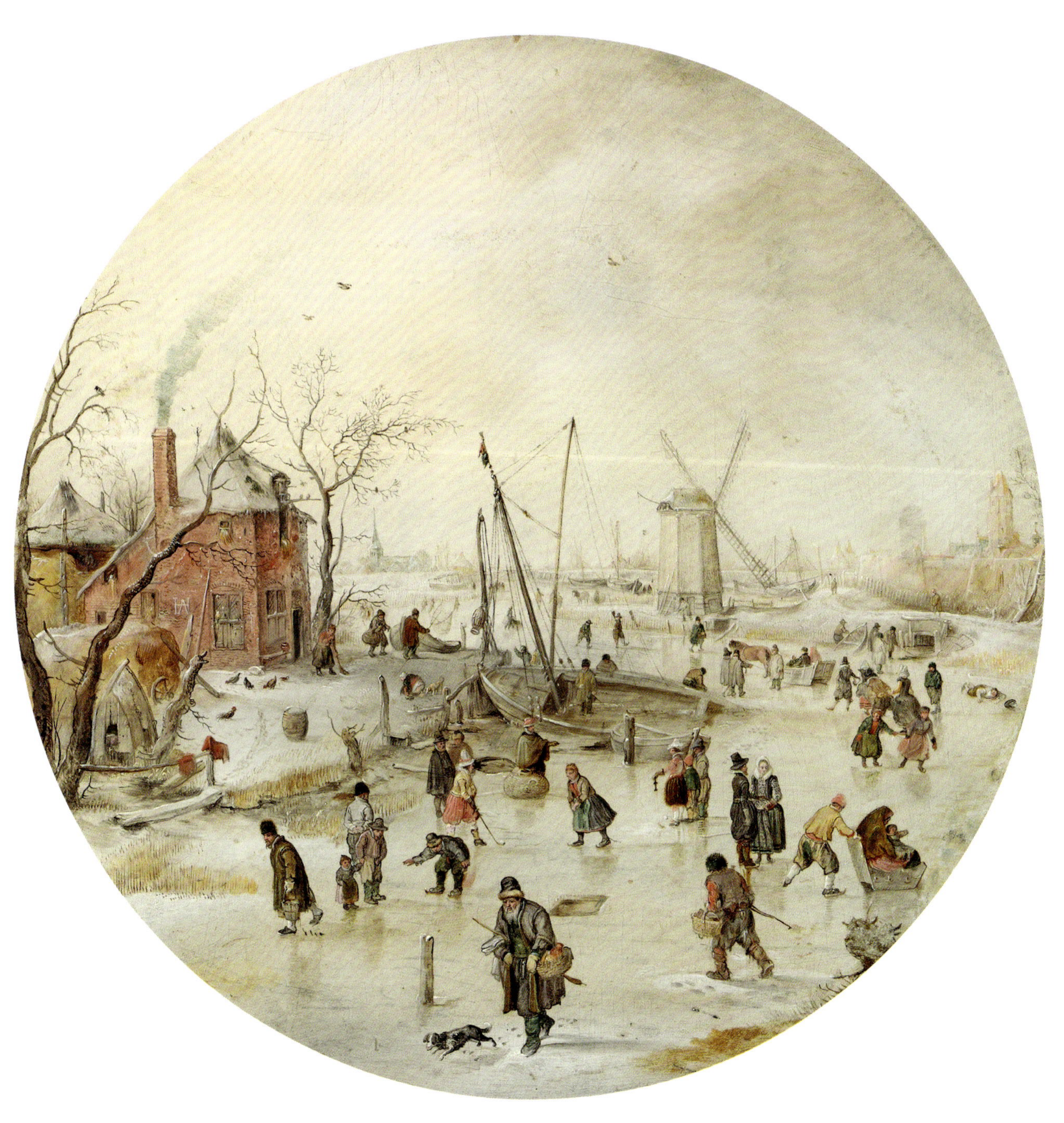

Leonhard Kern (1588–1662)

The Three Graces

ca. 1625–1650
Stained limewood, 63 × 44 × 19.5 cm
Purchased in Budapest, 1926
Inv. no. 6145

Like many of his fellow northern artists, Leonhard Kern travelled to Italy as a young man, where he spent no less than five years. The stations of his study tour were more unusual: as well as Rome he visited Naples, northern Africa, and Ljubljana. Later he settled in Schwäbisch Hall in southern Germany, where he ran a large workshop. His career was overshadowed by the Thirty-Year War (1618–1648), which almost completely prevented him receiving major commissions. Thus Kern was one of the first to start working for collectors and art dealers. His small-scale ivory, alabaster and wooden statues enjoyed particular popularity among his contemporaries.

More than half a metre tall and carved from several pieces of limewood, *The Three Graces* occupies a special place in the sculptor's oeuvre. Portrayals of the Three Graces grew popular in Renaissance Italy through the influence of classical art. The most favoured model was the Hellenistic marble *Three Graces* group, known through a Roman copy, which was installed in the Piccolomini Library in Siena in 1503. This may have inspired Kern's wooden sculpture, which somewhat differently to the prototype shows the female figure on the right not with her back, but frontally. Kern was fond of making nudes, which were inspired by both his experience in Italy and the female figures of Rubens. The three nudes in the Budapest group are linked by their arms with brilliant technical skill.

MIRIAM SZŐCS

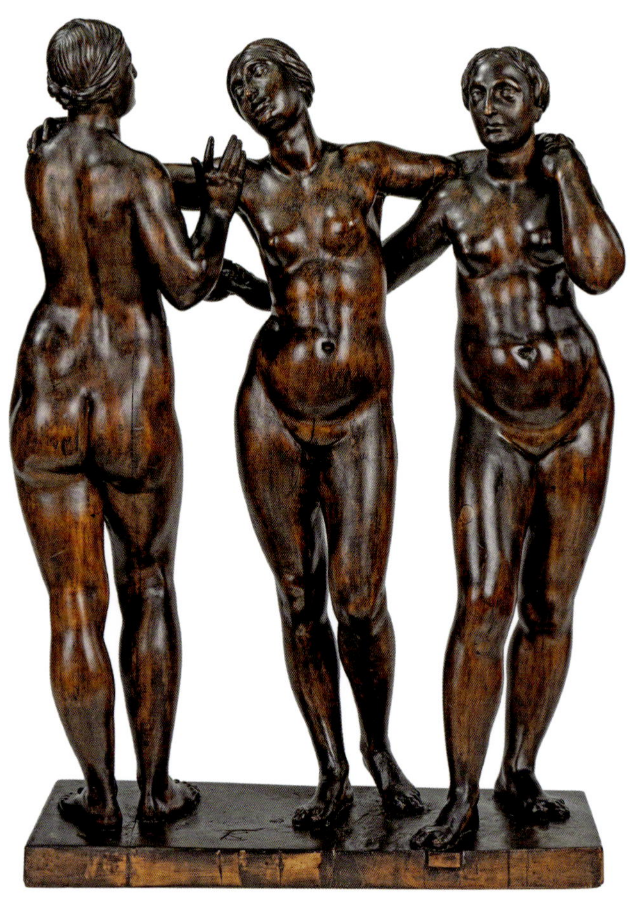

Peter Paul Rubens (1577–1640)

Profile Portrait of the Artist's Son, Albert Rubens

ca. 1618–1619
Black and red chalk, pen, ink and wash on paper,
246 × 202 mm
Esterházy collection, purchased in 1871
Inv. no. 1745

After several years in Italy Rubens returned to Antwerp, and soon became the most authoritative painter not just of his homeland, but of the whole of northern Europe. His reputation was further enhanced by his unique diplomatic career. While he commuted almost ceaselessly between the courts of Europe's monarchs, his many painting commissions were completed by a sizeable team in his well-organised workshop. Most often Rubens's work was restricted to the preparatory sketches and the final brushstrokes.

Like many of his contemporaries Rubens too was fond of depicting members of his family. Here he represented with special tenderness Albert, his son of about four from his first wife, Isabella Brant. The drawing was made in two clearly distinguishable phases. Rubens first sketched the main features in black and red chalk. Later he delicately reinforced the contours and more important details of the face in pen, and finally coloured the hair with brown ink, indeed so firmly that the original chalk lines can hardly be seen. In all likelihood this reworking is by Rubens himself, the reason for which may have been practical: he often used likenesses of his family for figures in his paintings. The portrait of Albert can be recognised almost unchanged as Saint John the Baptist in the *Madonna with Penitent Sinners and Saints* (Gemäldegalerie Alte Meister, Kassel), and as the putto in the lower right-hand corner of the *Madonna Surrounded by a Floral Wreath* (Alte Pinakothek, Munich).

ESZTER KARDOS

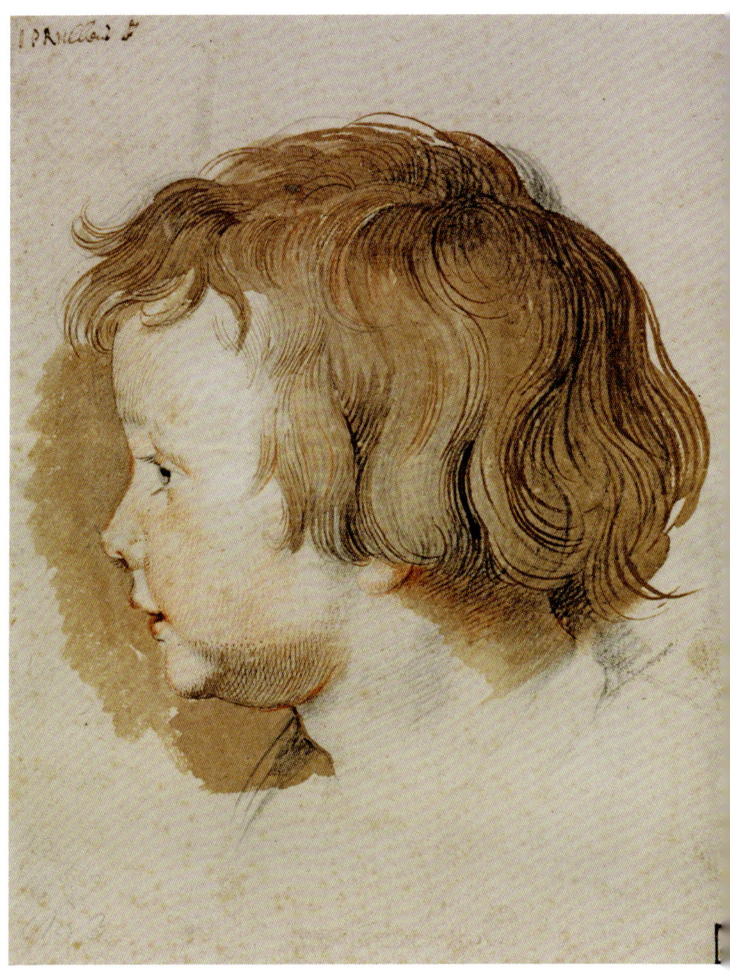

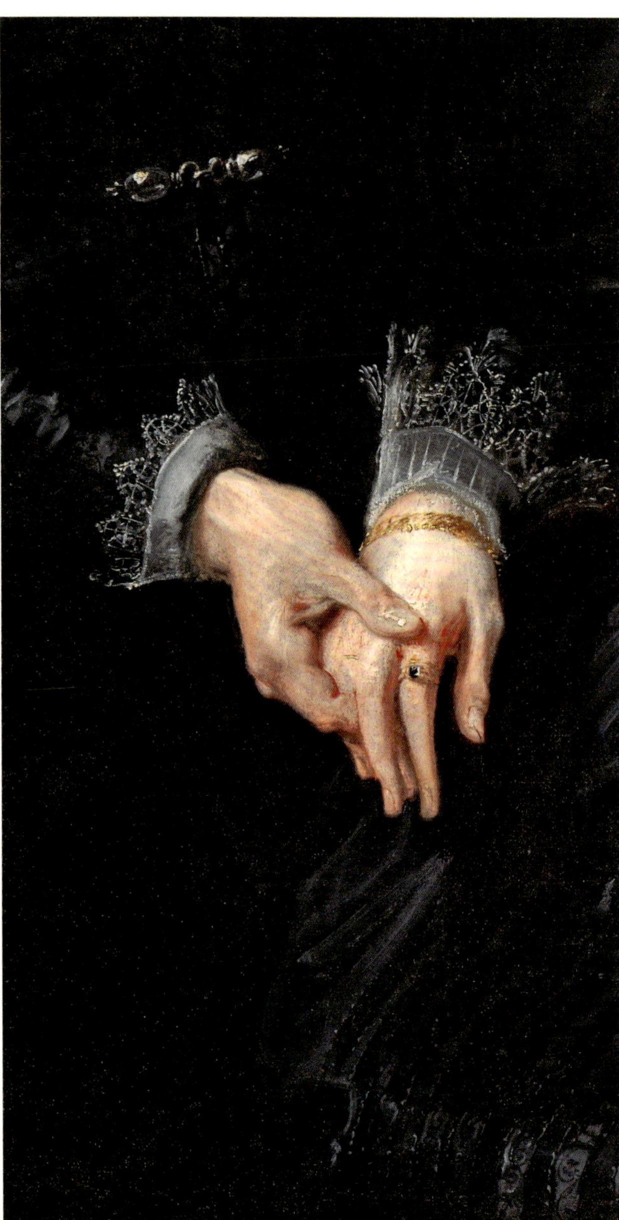

Anthony van Dyck (1599–1641)

Portrait of a Married Couple

ca. 1617–1618
Oil on canvas, 112 × 131 cm
Esterházy collection, purchased in 1871
Inv. no. 754

The "Mozart of painters", Van Dyck was barely more than a child when his fame spread. Like a firework he shot up into the heights, and turned out a host of brilliant masterpieces with ease, until finally he burnt out before his time, and the dazzling grand finale apparently never came. While still a teenager he produced celebrated works, and he was merely eighteen when he painted this *Married Couple,* a sure-handed masterpiece betraying superior technical skill and mature insight into human nature.

Another Mozartian trait in Van Dyck is that he shone even when his hands were tied by the wishes of clients. He resented almost all his commissions being for portraits, but it was in this genre, which leaves least space for creativity and is thus held in disdain by critics, that he created his greatest works. The focus of Van Dyck's portraits is not the face, which is always bathed in a haze of melancholy; that is a mask belonging to the role assigned on the stage of society, worn with obedience, rather than the true mirror of the soul. Far livelier and more revealing are the hands: they divulge the character, and tell tales about the heroes. The traditional symbol of marriage, two interlinked right hands are joined so as to display proudly the woman's valuable diamond engagement ring. Pride, tenderness, trust, and care are condensed in this single gesture. And although the sitters have passed the bloom of youth, it is possible that the picture commemorates a recently married couple.

AXEL VÉCSEY

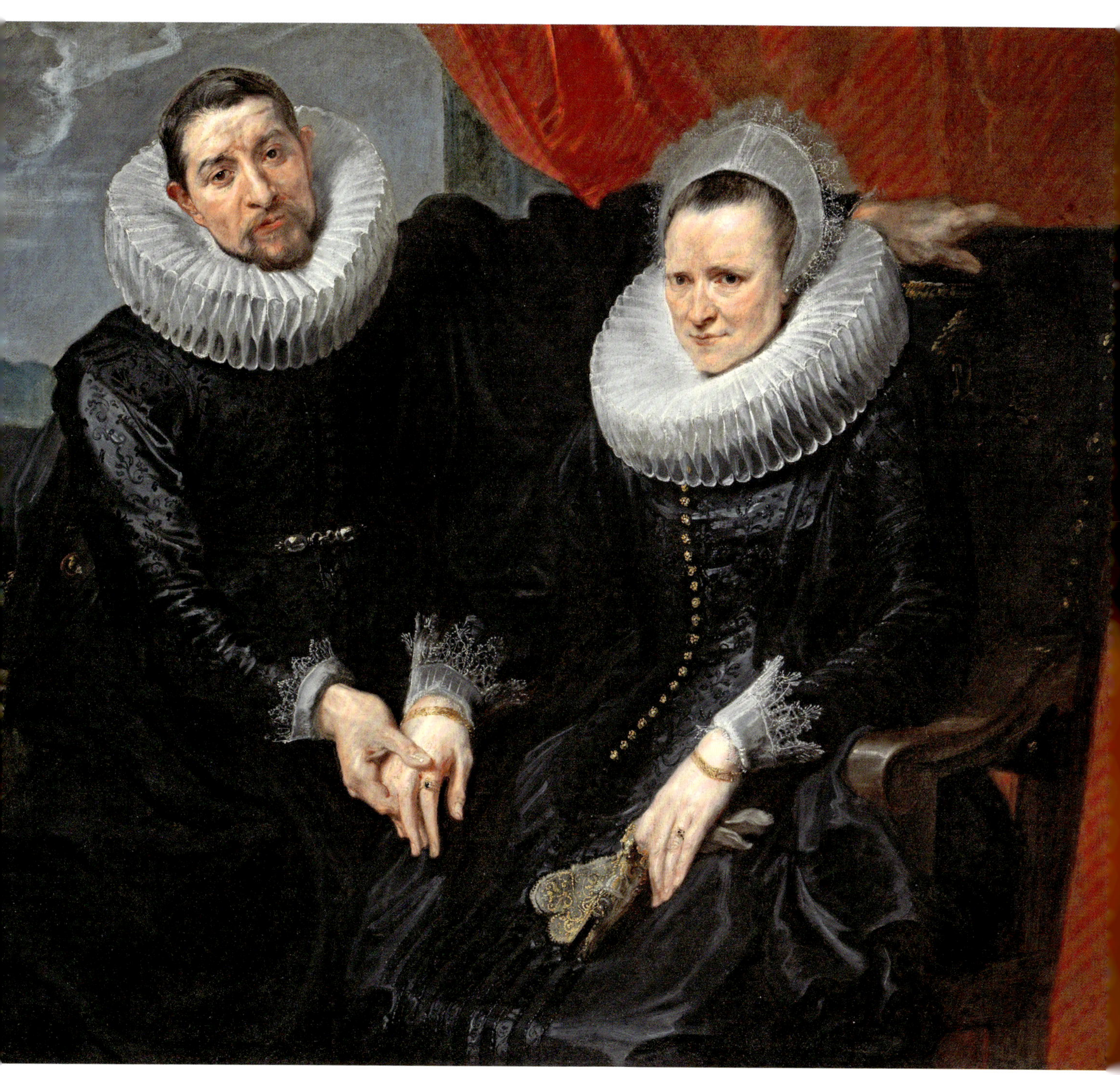

Nicolas Régnier (Niccolò Regnieri)

(ca. 1588–1667)

Tavern Scene (Card-Players)

ca. 1622–1623

Oil on canvas, 174 × 228 cm

Esterházy collection, purchased in 1871

Inv. no. 610

At the beginning of the seventeenth century, it was in Rome that the artistic heart of all Europe beat. Everyone thronged there from every corner of the continent to see the masterpieces of antiquity, and the modern classics , as Raphael and Michelangelo, who eventually surpassed the ancients. But on arriving there, quite a few pupils were more enchanted by radical contemporary movements, particularly the provocative art of Caravaggio, and quickly forgot the classical greats.

Perhaps it is no coincidence that the legacy of Caravaggio was first taken on by the young artists from the North (Holland, Flanders, France), whose home traditions laid closer to his naturalistic approach than those of the Italians, who pursued the celestial copy of reality. One of them was the French Nicolas Régnier, who grew up in Flanders. The monumental painting is the epitome of all that the northern youths did to transform what they inherited from Caravaggio. We rove through a decadent world, where ancient greatness has ebbed, and antique marbles are used as drinking benches. There are no upright heroes, only wily tricksters and foolish simpletons roam the ruins. All manner of parasites from nocturnal life – card tricksters, palm-readers, pickpockets, courtesans – have gathered here to rob the victims posing in fashionable clothes, their gaze all the emptier for that. The merrymakers mourn not the loss of the fortune squandered this night, but their entire, wasted, lives.

A X E L   V É C S E Y

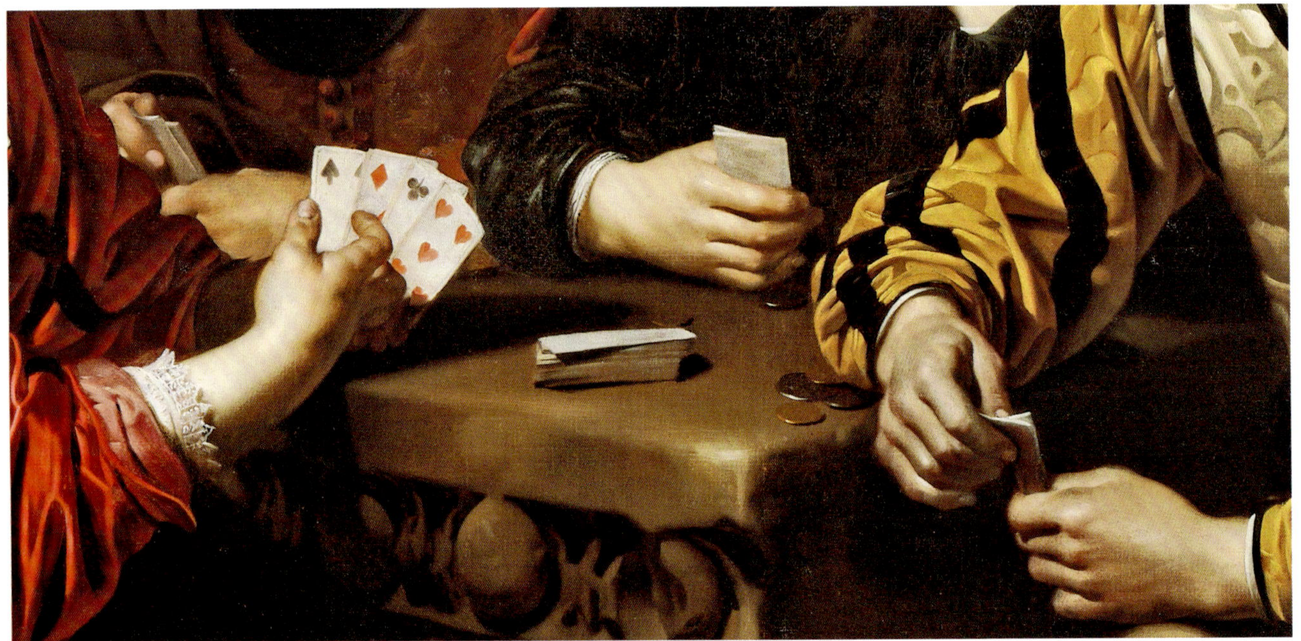

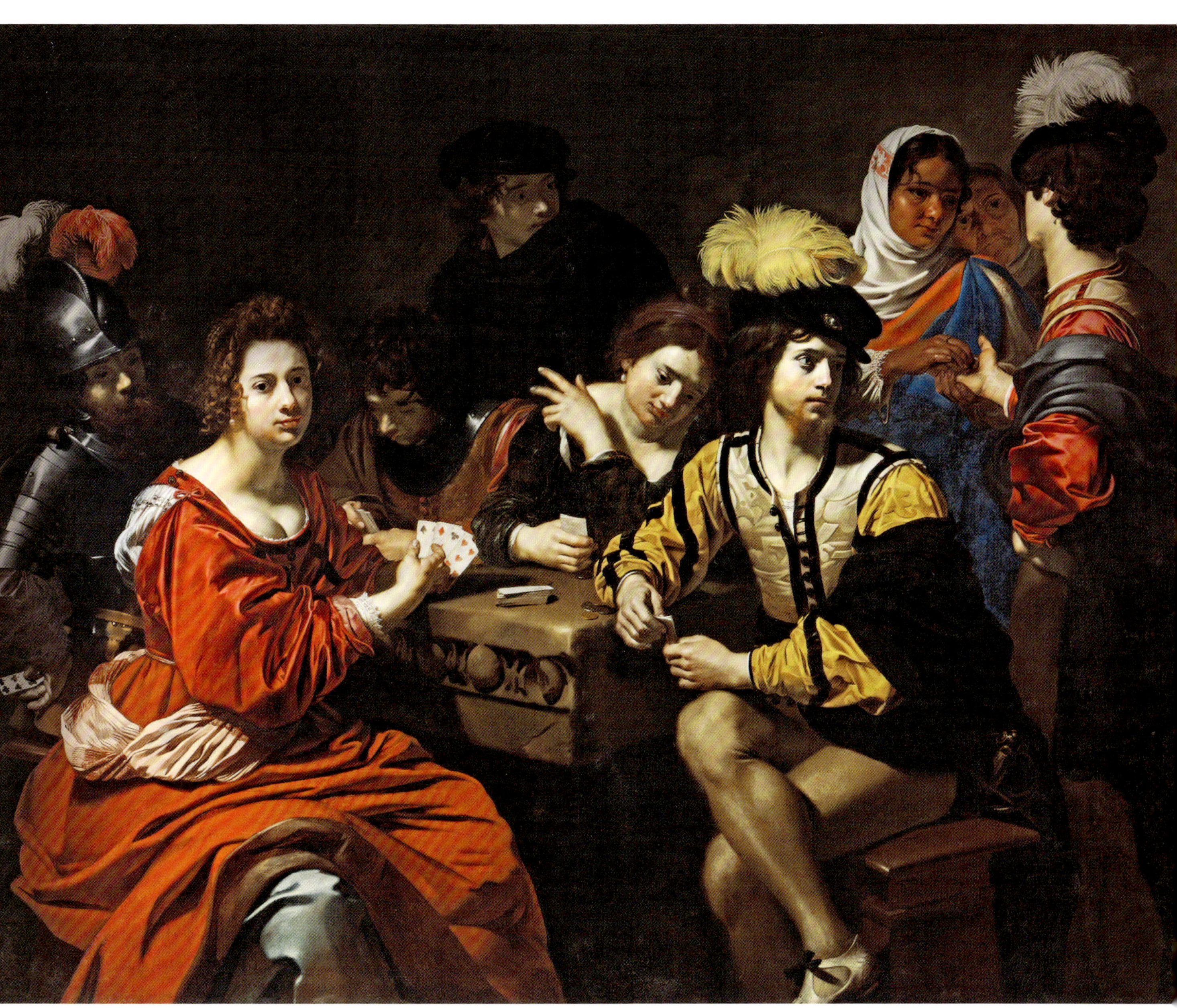

Diego Rodríquez de Silva y Velázquez (1599–1660)

Dining Scene

ca. 1618–1619
Oil on canvas, 96 × 112 cm
Purchased in London, 1908
Inv. no. 3820

There are many who are considered *one* of the greatest, but far fewer who are thought to be *the* greatest. In the history of western painting, besides Raphael, Titian and Rembrandt, only Velázquez belongs to this club. Manet called him the "painters' painter", and Picasso painted a host of paraphrases to uncover his secret. The essence of his magic was perhaps put most aptly by a contemporary writer, Francisco de Quevedo: Velázquez did not mimic reality, he created it.

In this *Dining Scene* and similar youthful *bodegons* (kitchen or tavern scenes named after the *bodega*, or inn) naturally the Spanish genius does not unfold in full maturity. Common folk populate the canvasses, in apparently banal situations, as if pages from the picaresque novels of Quevedo and his peers had come to life, where the larks of crafty servants and other villainous ruffians tickled the readers' fancy. This startling naturalism often invited claims of Caravaggio's influence, but at the time Velázquez had not even seen the pictures of the Italian vagabond. Even more importantly, in Velázquez there is no trace of Caravaggio's violent coarseness, however vulgar the subject may be, and a kind of calm, puritanical solemnity vibrates in the air. We can only guess at the exact story behind the image, but whether we see them as scheming gaol-birds or characters from an "exemplary story", the figures' presence has weight and significance – no less so than the kings who populated the works of his mature period.

A X E L   V É C S E Y

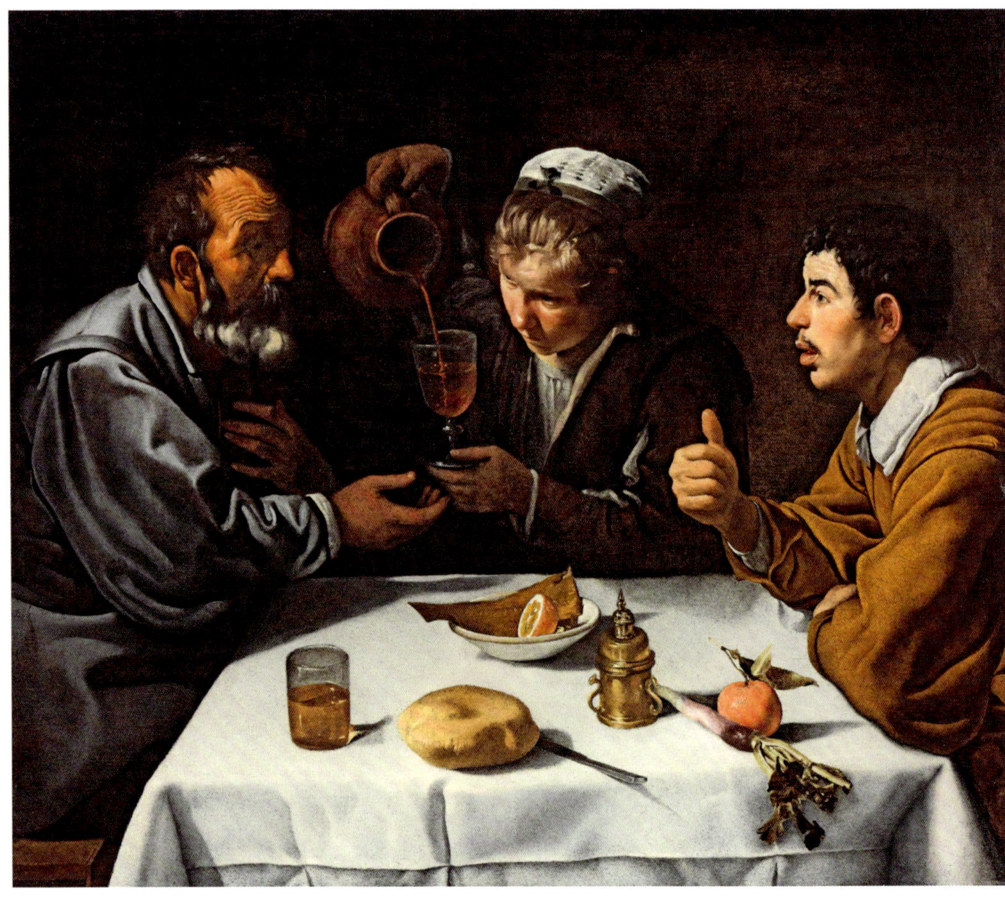

Pieter Claesz. (1597/1598–1661)

Still Life with Pie and Roemer

1647
Oil on oak, 63.6 × 88.3 cm
Purchased in Vienna, 1889
Inv. no. 1026

As if the table had been cut out of the previous Velázquez picture, the Dutch Pieter Claesz.'s still life adopts the same tricks of the trade: the knife protruding over the edge of the table (to create the illusion of space), the crisply ironed white tablecloth with a sharp crease, and the virtuoso contrast in the quality of matter – shiny against matt, greasy against dry, hard against soft. The similarity is by no means coincidental, since formally both pictures derive from the same tradition: that of portrayals of the Last Supper, Jesus's farewell to his disciples and the institution of the Eucharist. The still life is thus awash with religious connotations, and these associations are reinforced by various traditional Christian symbols (bread and wine, the vineshoot entwined around the wineglass, and the cruciform window frame reflected in the surface of the glass).

Though born in Antwerp, Pieter Claesz. was one of the "most Dutch" painters. No other images better epitomised the puritan, Protestant national character than his simple "Lenten still lifes". This ensemble of bread, wine, fruit and pie is not among his most ascetic compositions. The extravagance of the forsaken fruit pie signals the futility of earthly plenty, thus introducing a secondary layer of symbolic reference. Yet the overall mood is quiet and restrained, and this is mostly due to one indispensible component of Claesz.'s painting: he dulls the colours until he attains an almost monochrome palette.

AXEL VÉCSEY

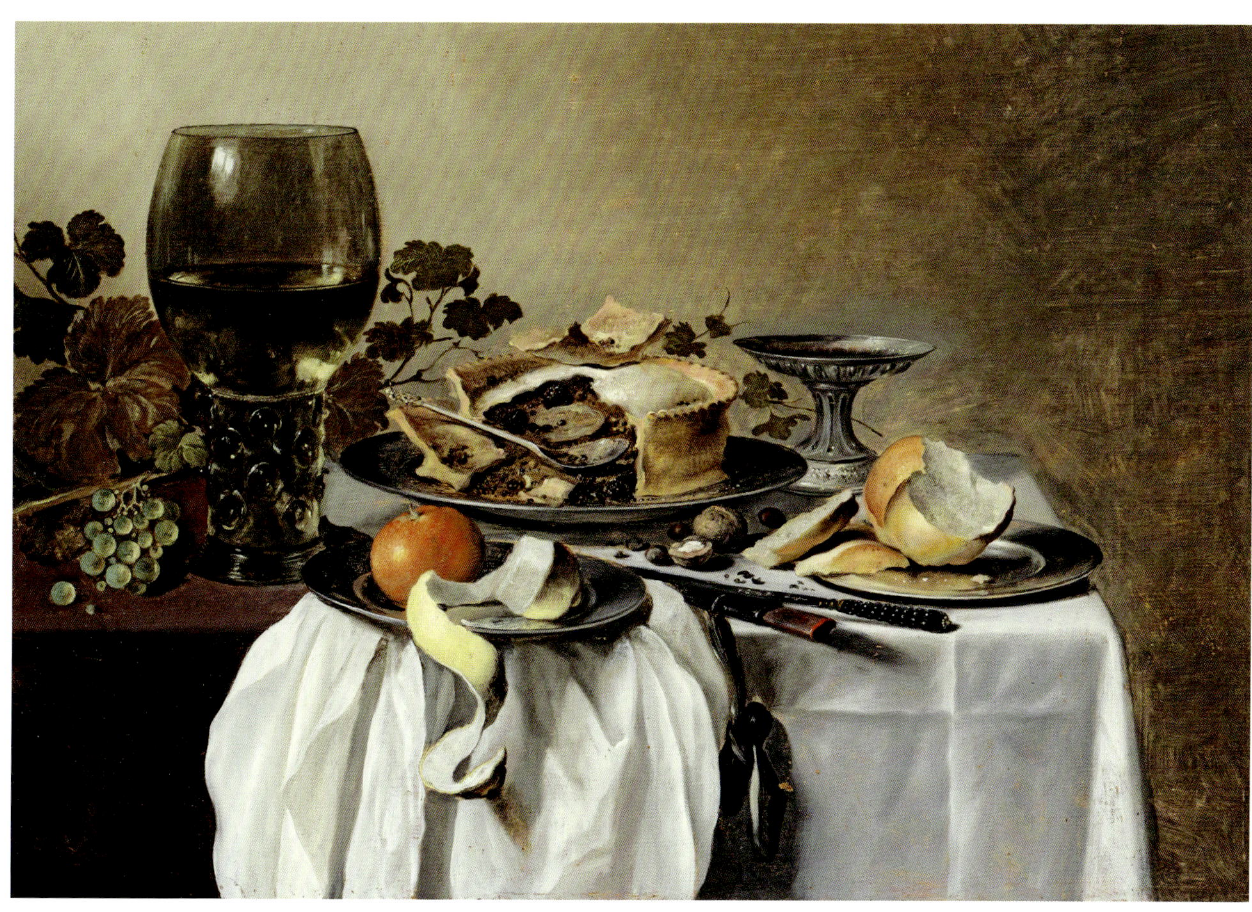

Jusepe de Ribera (1591–1652)

The Martyrdom of Saint Andrew

1628
Oil on canvas, 206.1 × 177.7 cm
Esterházy collection, purchased in 1871
Inv. no. 523

Seventeenth-century Naples was, according to many, hell upon earth. Impoverished by Spanish rule, the life of the people was embittered by continuous starvation, epidemics, earthquakes, and even the Vesuvius. The hovels of the poor were increasingly crowded, since the scant harvests had forced village folk into the city. Crime flourished in the stale air of the back streets. It was perhaps inevitable that Caravaggio's violent art, which grappled with the fear of death, came into its own in Naples, and for decades it set the way for the city's painters.

But the school of ruthless naturalism did not reach its peak until a generation later, with Ribera. This Spanish-born master was most in his element when portraying the tortuous deaths of Christian martyrs, with shocking verisimilitude, as in this masterpiece of his darkest period. The apostle Andrew preached the gospel in the East, until Roman governor of Achaea condemned him to follow the founder of his "superstitious sect" in death by crucifixion. If anybody, it is Ribera who manages to convince us that for Andrew martyrdom was redemption. His humiliated body is shrivelled by time, his withered skin hangs drily from his frame; and yet there emanates from him a metaphysical power of the soul. Over him tower shadows of a priest and the governor, presaging Goya's oppressive demons. They are not satisfied with destroying his body: to the very last moment they try to win over his soul, and persuade him to worship the idol of Jupiter.

AXEL VÉCSEY

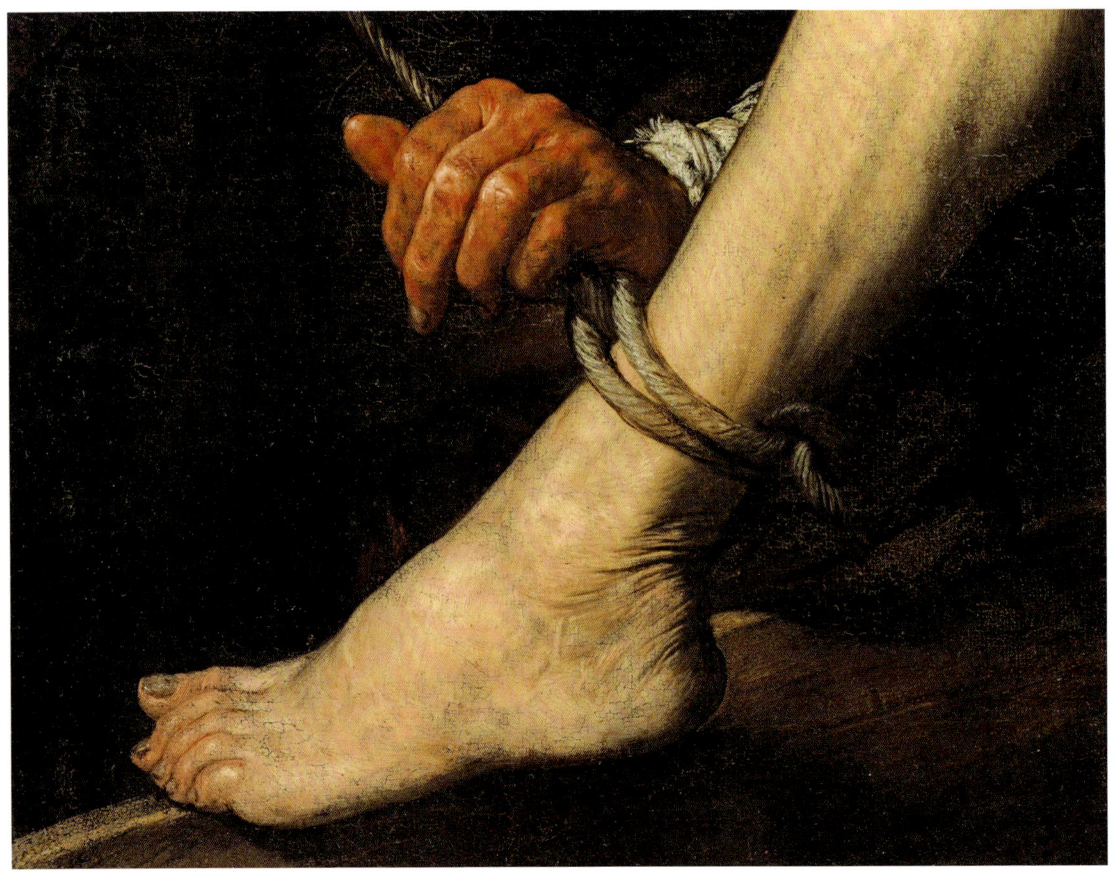

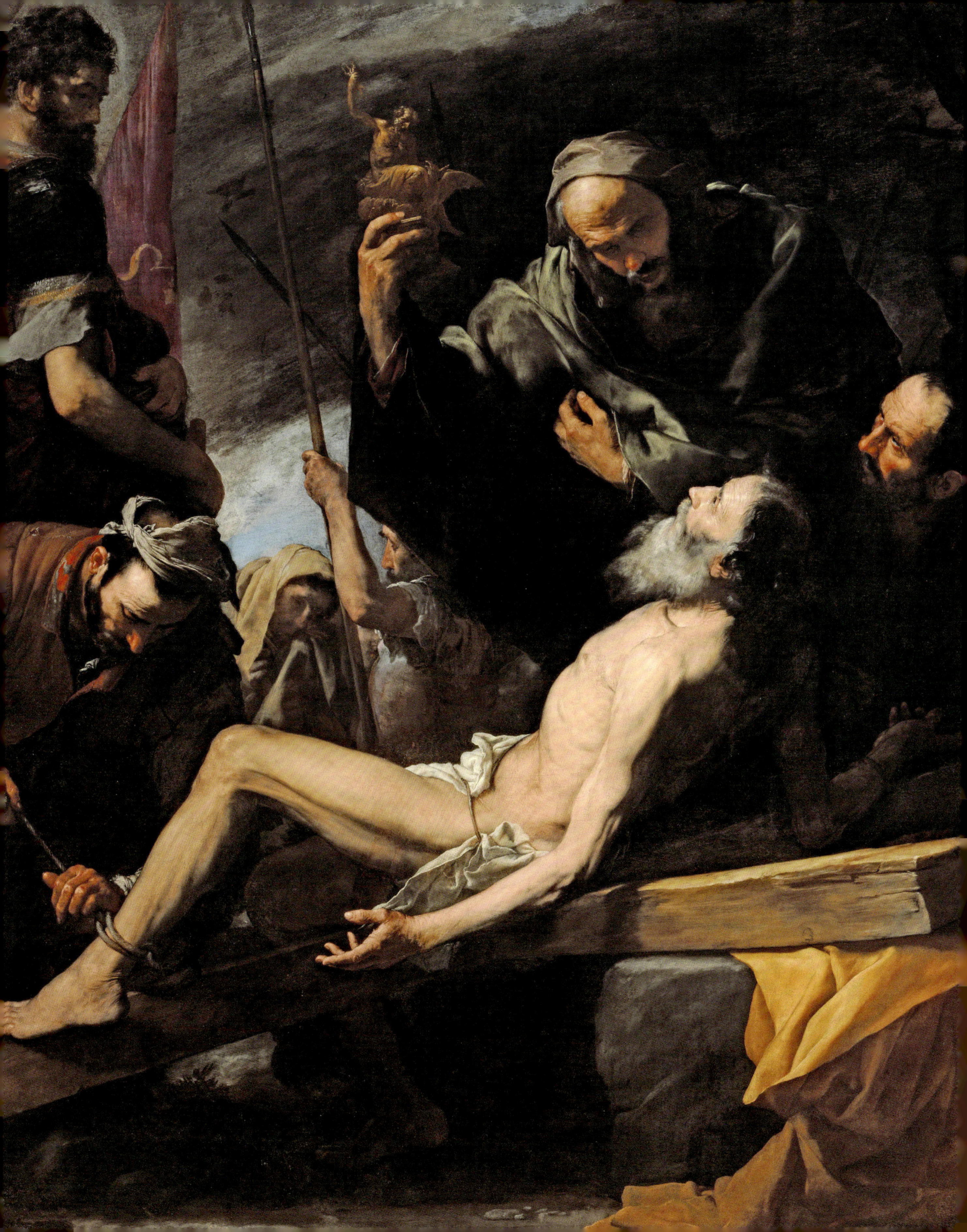

Daniele Crespi (1597/1600–1630)

Saint Cecilia at the Organ

1620s
Pen and brown ink over black chalk on paper,
276 × 378 mm
Esterházy collection, purchased in 1871
Inv. no. 2396

Daniele Crespi lived a mere thirty years, falling victim in 1630 to the plague raging in his native Milan. In spite of his brief career he left behind one of the most exciting oeuvres of the Lombard baroque. This was the period when art in Italy changed radically under the pressure of the Counter-Reformation movement. Crespi trained in the workshop of the mannerist Giulio Cesare Procaccini, famed for the idealised beauty of his works, but the pupil's brush soon turned out religious paintings conceived in the spirit of the Synod of Trent, full of dramatic realism and passionate emotions.

The *Saint Cecilia* is one of the most picturesque of his extant drawings. This saint died a martyr's death for her Christian faith in the third century. Since the Middle Ages she has been venerated as the patron saint of musicians, and she enjoyed special popularity in the century of the baroque. From the almost impenetrably dense vigorous, agitated penstrokes emerges a sketch whose expressive power is due mainly to the dynamic manner of drawing. Crespi achieved this through the highly inventive use of chalk and pen: flying in the face of contemporary technique he made not only the preparatory drawing in chalk, but also used it to reinforce the darker tones over the finished pen-and-ink drawing. The purpose of the work is not known. Not only the subject however, but the symmetrical scheme of the sheet suggests that perhaps it was made as a design for painted organ shutters.

ESZTER KARDOS

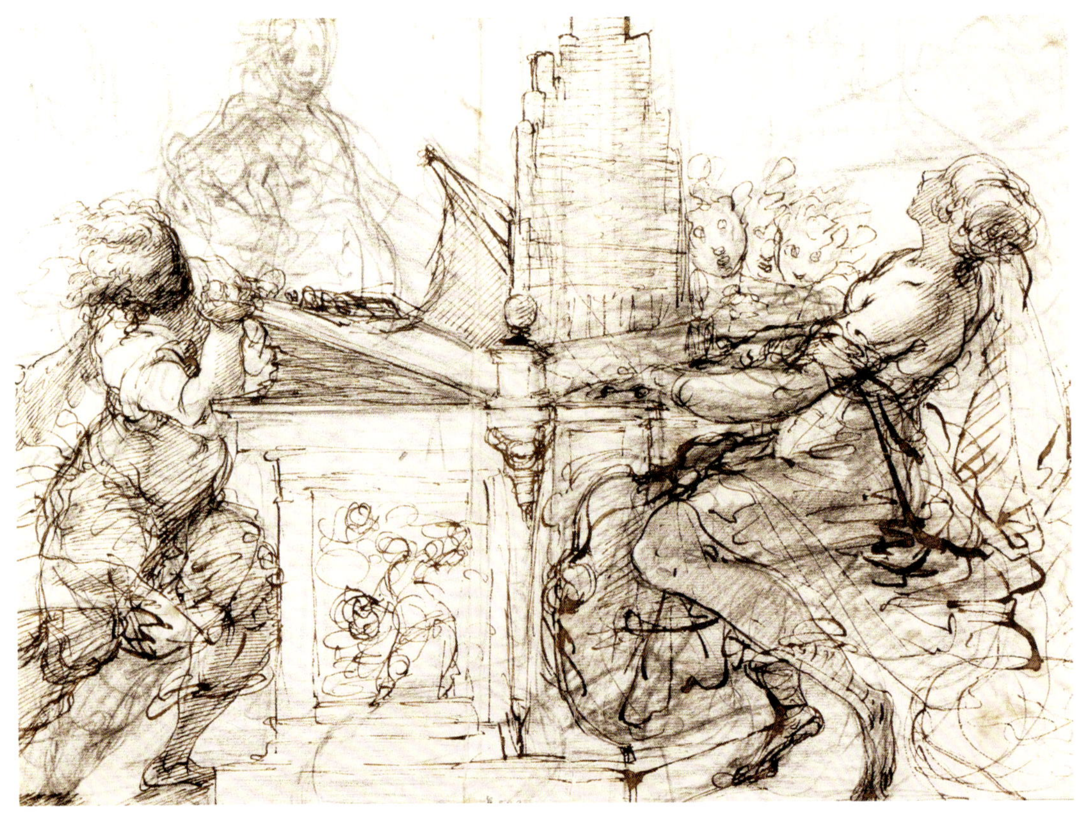

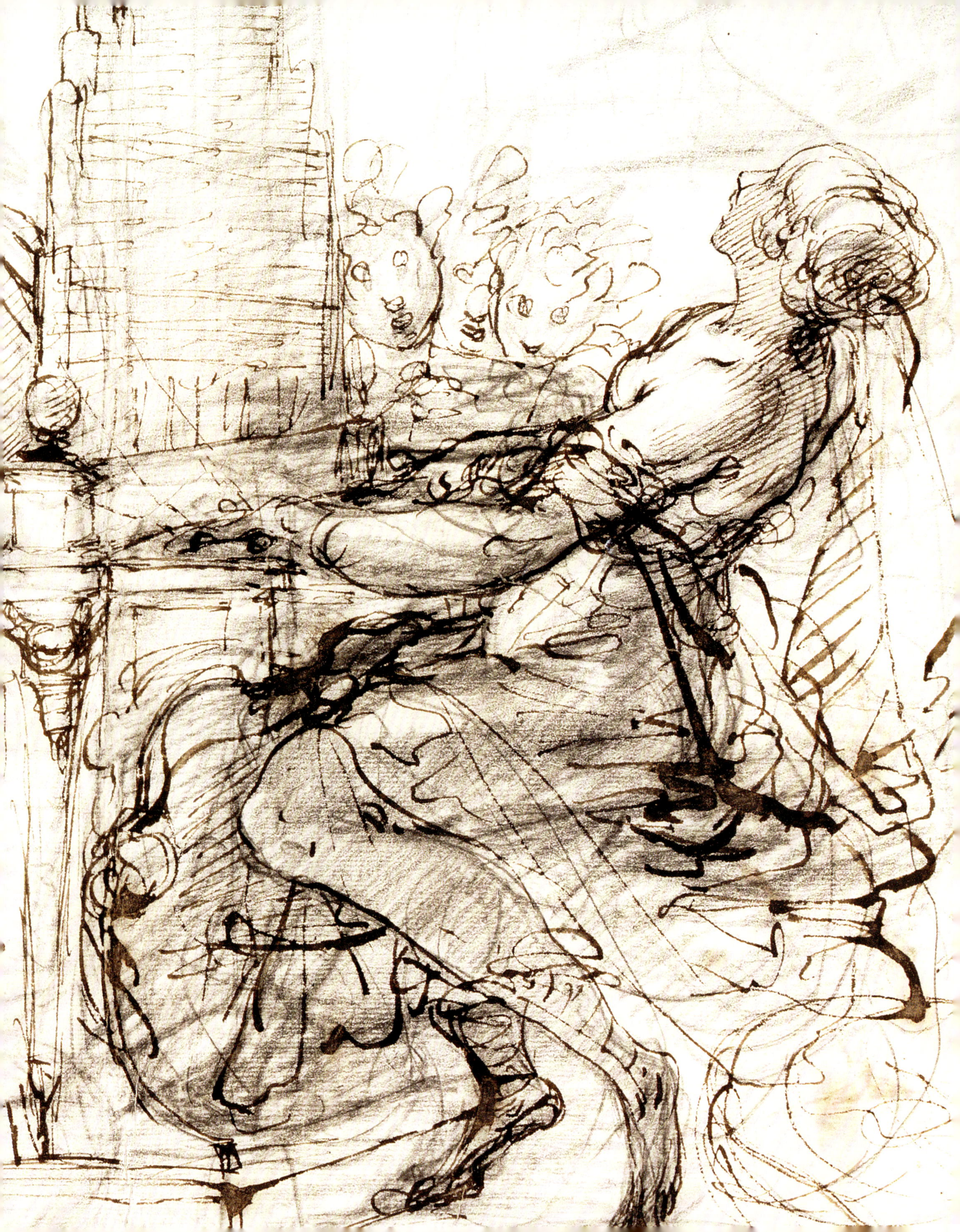

Nicolas Poussin (1594–1665)

The Holy Family Resting with Saint John the Baptist

ca. 1628
Oil on canvas, 57 × 74 cm
Purchased in Budapest, 1957
Inv. no. 57.18

Poussin is a painter at whom everyone marvels, but perhaps nobody likes. Nor was it his wish to be loved by the public: he declared that painting should address the mind, not the eye or the heart. Alongside Descartes he is the best known exponent of rationalism, the stony seventeenth-century French movement that stubbornly believed that perfection is attainable if we bend the world to the rules of reason. Poussin held the task of art to be that of staging the noble deeds of man in a logical system, as would happen in an ideal world.

However, this dogmatic rigour is barely discernible in the Budapest *Holy Family at Rest*. Of all Poussin's pictures it is perhaps the freshest, where we can even detect traces of tender emotions. But in this case the exception indeed proves the rule: this liberated mood is carefully calculated. Poussin consciously applied the theory of modes from the ancient aesthetics of music, in which the theme determines the particular emotional tone and the order of dramaturgy. But a refined, elevated melancholy is mixed into this serene idyll, as the child Saint John the Baptist proffers a palm cross to Jesus. This toy, prefiguring the child's horrific earthly fate, links the picture to one of the main themes of classical drama, the conflict between feelings and duty. The disciplined resignation of child and mother sets a model for the noble, wise handling of such conflicts.

AXEL VÉCSEY

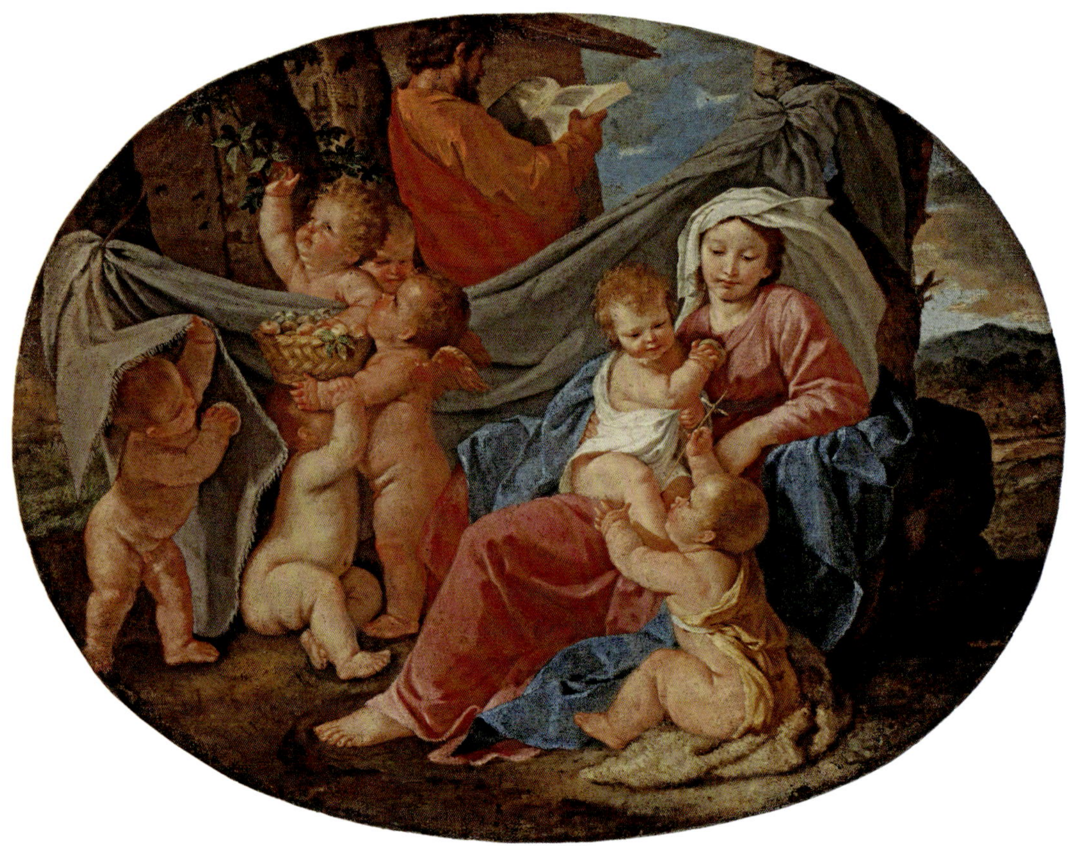

Bartolomé Esteban Murillo (1617–1682)

The Infant Jesus Distributing Bread to Pilgrims

1678

Oil on canvas, 219 × 182 cm

Esterházy collection, purchased in 1871

Inv. no. 777

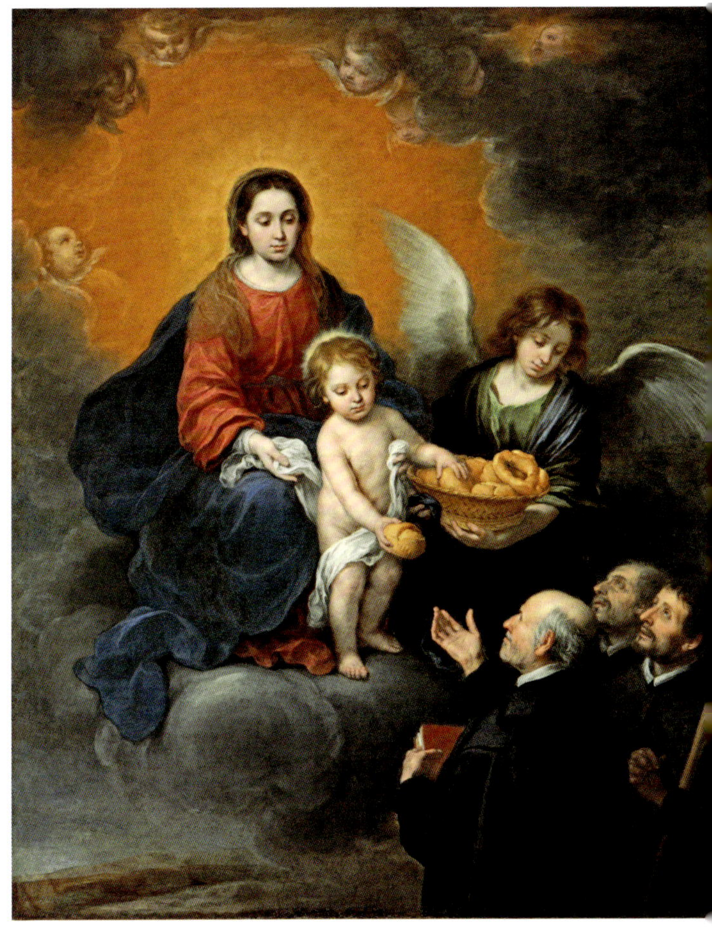

To this day there still hangs a copy of the *Jesus Distributing Bread* in its original location, a former rest-home for elderly priests in Seville. Murillo's masterpiece enjoys their admiration not merely for its captivating, gentle charm, but also because it would hardly be possible to express more perfectly the mission of the institution. The vision of Jesus distributing bread reminds us of the Christian duty to care for those who fall by the wayside, a duty that originates with Christ himself. Yet it affirms this with a self-evident naturalness free of any didactic overtones. The viewers thus experience the duty of mercy not as a chore, but as an inner spiritual compulsion which they willingly obey.

It was precisely this intimate immediacy and warm empathy which was the secret of Murillo's popularity, which in the eighteenth and nineteenth centuries rivalled Raphael's. Perhaps today the Spanish genius, sentimental mood seems too cloying, but it never errs into kitsch: the subject of its deep humanism is not some wistful ideal, but an ordinary man of flesh and blood. Though the mood is lofty, within the figures flickers the ghost of Caravaggio's plebeian characters. One former critic characterised his art as "noble naturalism". The dignity of the characters derives primarily from sincere humility, and it is this virtue that characterises the gesture of the donor of *Jesus Distributing Bread*, Canon Justino de Neve, who had his portrait placed among the needy pleading for charity.

AXEL VÉCSEY

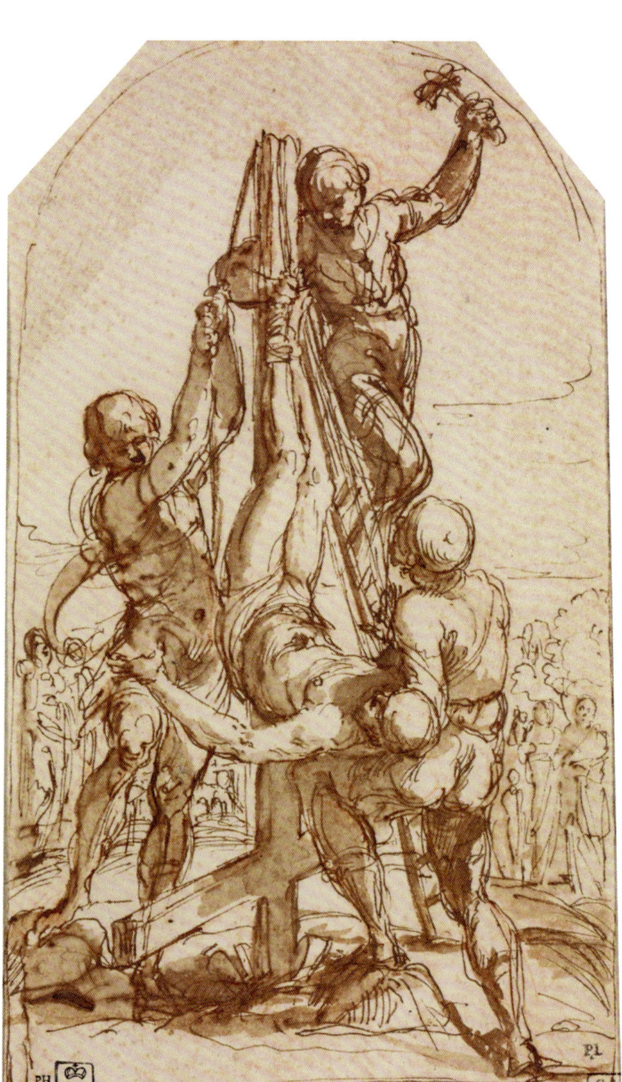

Guido Reni

(1575–1642)

The Crucifixion of Saint Peter

1604

Pen, brown ink, and brown wash on paper, 230 × 137 mm

Esterházy collection, purchased in 1871

Inv. no. 2366

In the final decades of the sixteenth century a bustling artistic life developed in Bologna. Denijs Calvaert was the first to open a workshop there, to be followed shortly by the academy of the Carracci brothers, goaded on by the Fleming's success. The Carracci school, where the training centred on drawing from live models, soon enjoyed unparalleled popularity, and won over even Calvaert's best pupils. Guido Reni was the most talented of them, and with time his fame exceeded even that of his masters.

Like many of his contemporaries, the young Reni also tried his fortune in Rome, where he was taken under the wing of Giuseppe Cesari, the favourite painter of Pope Clement VIII. It may have been Cesari's intercession that earned Reni the commission for the altarpiece of the church of San Paolo alle Tre Fontane in 1604. If contemporary gossip can be believed, Guido was a godsend to Cesari, enabling him to pluck the commission from the hand of his former apprentice and rival Caravaggio. The altarpiece representing the martyrdom of Saint Peter (now in the Pinacoteca Vaticana, Rome) reveals that Reni was truly at home in Caravaggio's "hunted and dark manner". Yet the raw naturalism based on sharp contrasts of light and shadow is counterbalanced by elegance, classical harmony and the accurate anatomy gleaned in the Carracci academy. The only surviving sketch for the altarpiece is our exceptionally vigorous sheet, which however faithfully evokes the dramatic power of its Caravaggiesque realism.

ZOLTÁN KÁRPÁTI

Guercino (Giovanni Francesco Barbieri)

(1591–1666)

The Flagellation of Christ

ca. 1641–1644

Oil on canvas, 351 × 176.5 cm

Bequest of Count János Pálffy, 1912

Inv. no. 4225

Giovanni Francesco Barbieri eked out his first fifty years in his native town, day after day waiting for the death of his hated rival Guido Reni. Barbieri's squint, which earned him the moniker Guercino, was not his only fault: his contemporaries found him vulgar, frustrated, and coarse. So in vain was his talent recognised, he gained far fewer clients than his handsome and pleasantly mannered adversary, and jealousy poisoned his soul. But when in 1642 news came of his enemy's death, he immediately moved to Bologna to stake his claim to the vacant throne of the preeminent painter. The move was successful, Guercino soon earned fame, stacked up quite a fortune, and by all accounts even his manners improved.

By the time the opportunity arose, Guercino's painting style had grown to resemble that of his rival. The dark tone, unbridled motion and aggressive naturalism of his youthful works had given way to the complete opposite. In their place were the Raphael-inspired sunshine, clarity and temperance, with which "the divine Guido" had endeared himself to the world. Nowhere is this as clear as in this enormous altarpiece, which was consecrated in August 1644, two years after Reni's death, in a private chapel of a family in Vicenza. Certain details copy slavishly one of Reni's last unfinished works with the same subject. But Guercino's Christ is more dignified, and rather than collapsing under the suffering, holds his head high to declare his triumph over those torturing him.

A X E L   V É C S E Y

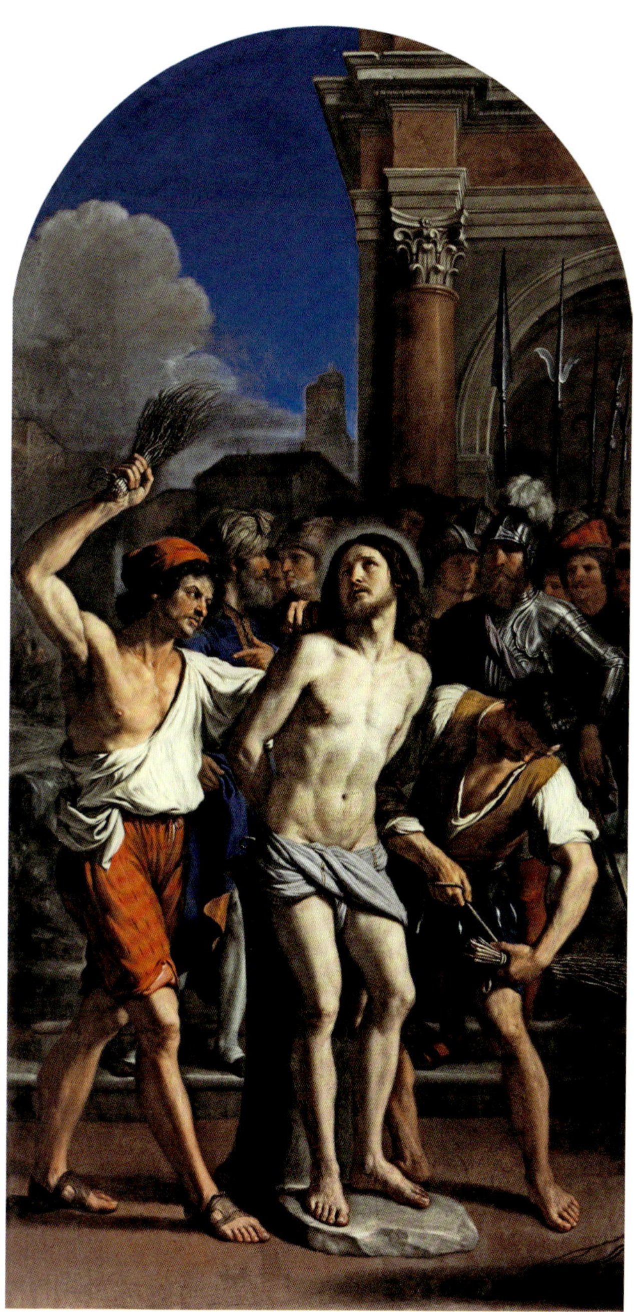

Salomon van Ruysdael (1600/1602–1670)

After the Rain

1631
Oil on oak, 56 × 86.4 cm
Esterházy collection, purchased in 1871
Inv. no. 260

When Hendrick Goltzius made a few drawings of the coastal dunes near Haarlem in 1603, perhaps even he did not suspect he was starting a revolution in European landscape painting. Instead of the Italianate golden-age idylls, to the Haarlem masters it was the here-and-now that mattered, and they painted everyday Dutch flatlands: dunes, canals, village streets, and the sea. These had hitherto been considered unworthy as subjects for a picture, but now seemed appropriate for conveying the new idea of the nation. And to make the new relationship clear, the viewpoint was brought down from on high to the ground. Now the sky dominated the picture, and the moist air cast a veil over the landscape.

The Haarlem landscapists are admired chiefly for their masterful suggestion of this humid atmosphere. Each artist was able to create a different mood. Of the two greatest masters it is said that in Jan van Goyen's works it always seems that rain is in the offing, while in Salomon van Ruysdael's we sense a fresh breeze has just dispersed the shower. In *After the Rain*, known by this title since the nineteenth century, one can almost smell the refreshing scent as the ground breathes after the storm. The crisp, crystal-clear outlines suggest that for a moment the mist has risen. The cool tones of colour create a chill mood, though a strip of the dune is bathed in golden radiance by the sun breaking through the clouds. In the house at the edge of the village the tired travellers find solace at last.

A X E L   V É C S E Y

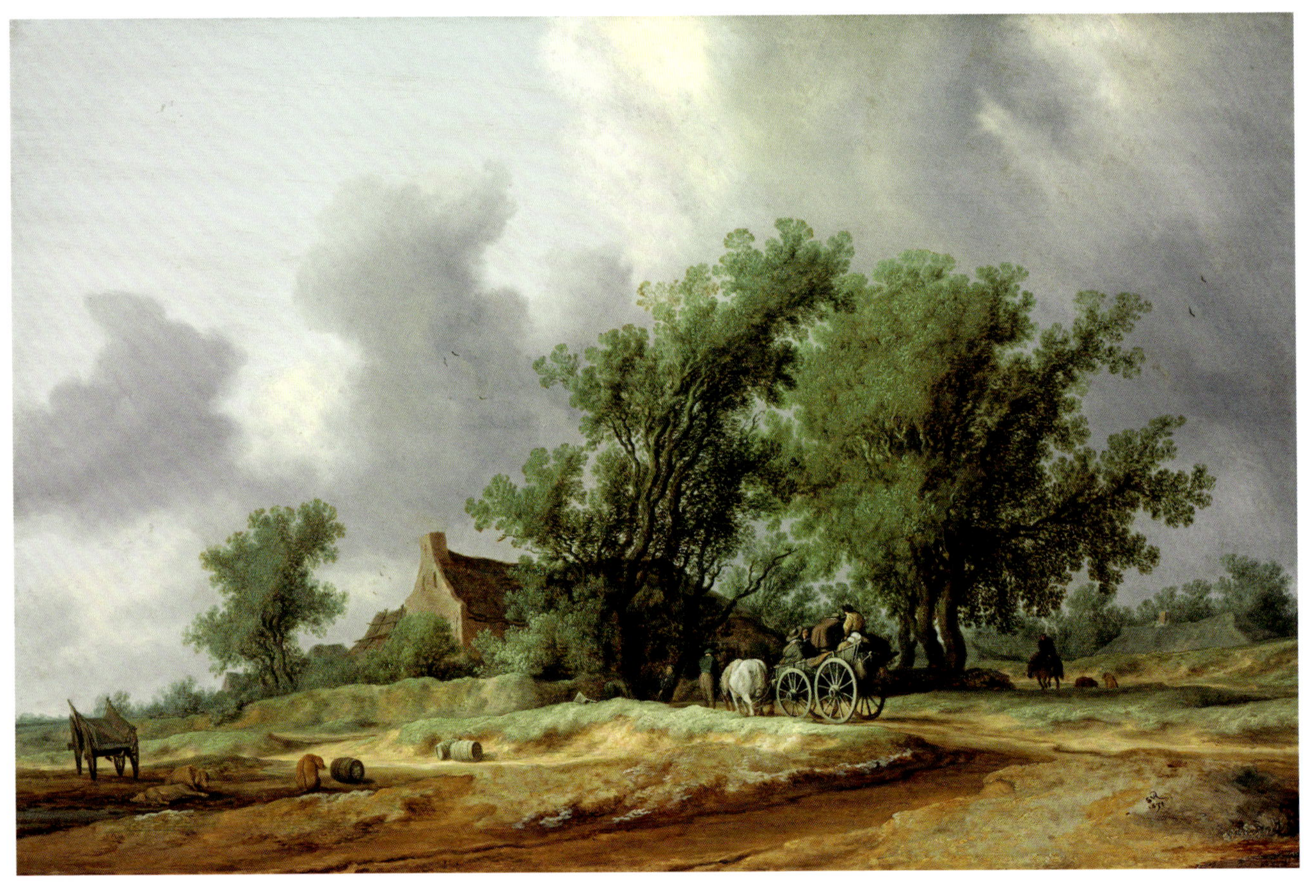

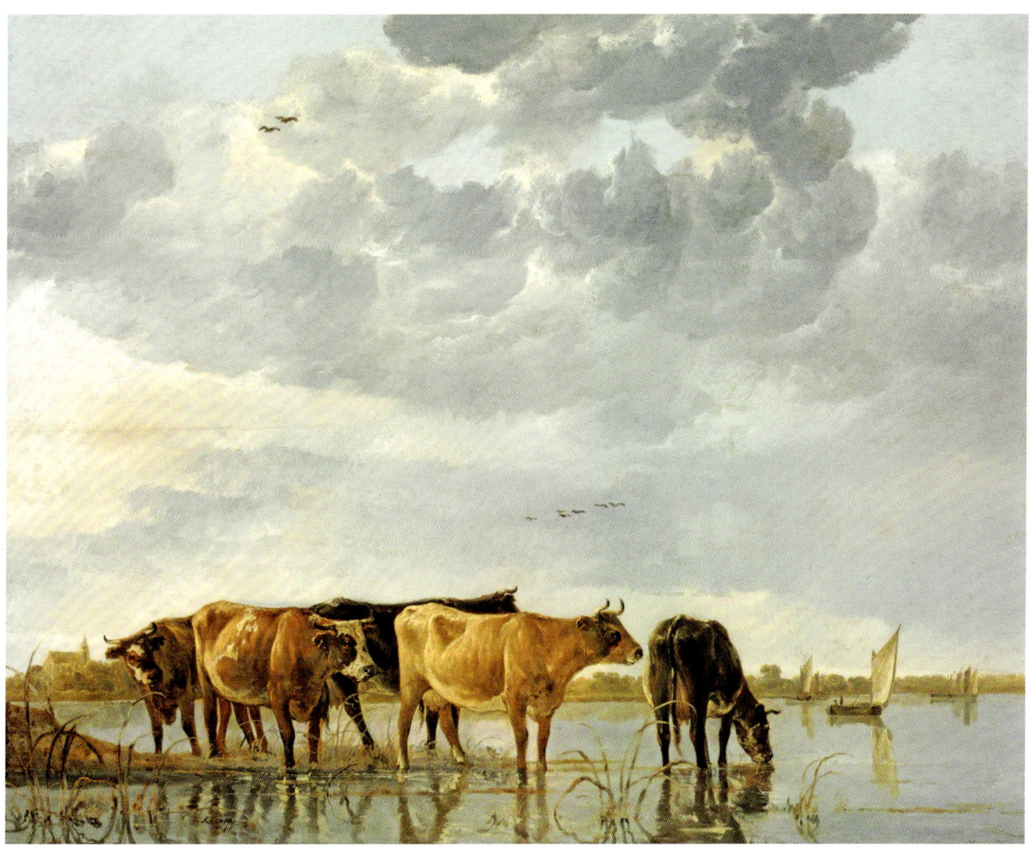

Aelbert Cuyp (1620–1691)

Cattle by the Riverside

ca. 1650

Oil on oak, 59 × 74 cm

Esterházy collection, purchased in 1871

Inv. no. 408

The tradition of landscape painting known as the Weltland-schaft (world landscape) played an enormous role in the development of the genre in the Low Countries from the early sixteenth century onwards. The two constants of the Weltlandschaft were the overhead perspective and the multitude of motifs that filled the spectacle. Each work of this kind presented us with an encyclopaedic and entertaining microcosmos. In this selection of works, the revolution that took place during the Golden Age of Dutch painting is represented by Salomon van Ruysdael's *After the Rain* (opposite page), which focuses on far fewer landscape and figural elements, seen not from overhead, but from eye level. Moreover, the unity of the vision not only depends on the well-structured composition, but also on the precision with which the effects of light and atmosphere are captured. Aelbert Cuyp's painting seems almost to flaunt its own stillness and simplicity. On a quiet afternoon somewhere near Dordrecht, five lumbering, leviathan cows have gathered on a narrow spit of land to quench their thirst in the shallow waters. That, in a nutshell, is the action. The rest of the picture is taken up by the reflection-filled expanse of water, some wilting reeds, the distant shore, some sailboats, a few birds on the wing, and above all, light, air and billowing clouds. The surface – or perhaps more accurately, the space – of the picture is three-quarters occupied by the cloudy sky. To do this with a pathos that is simultaneously intimate and pantheistic, and without merely padding out the canvas, is a feat that only Aelbert Cuyp and a handful of similarly talented painters could achieve.

VILMOS TÁTRAI

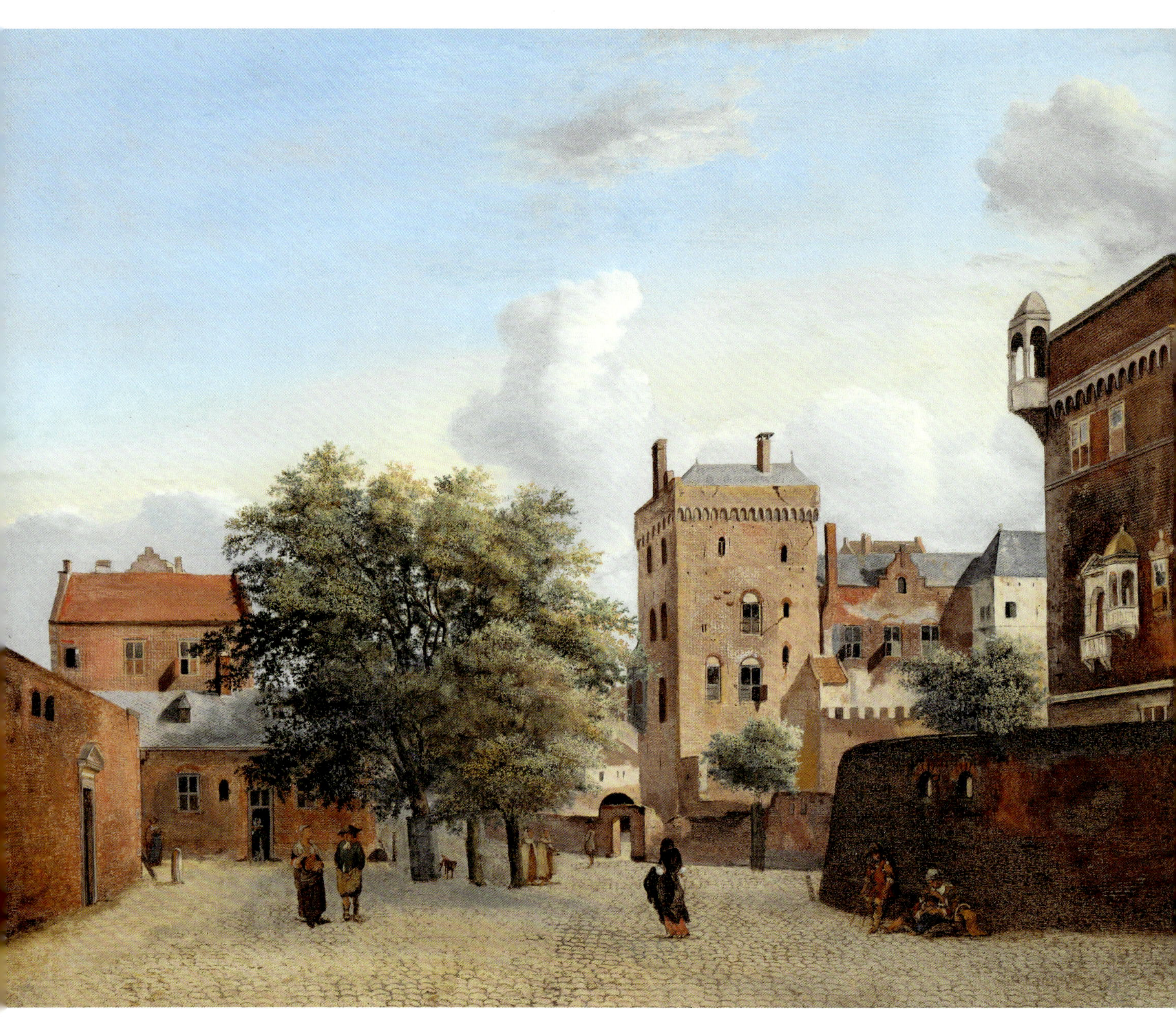

Jan van der Heyden (1637–1712)

Town Square with Figures Promenading

ca. 1684
Oil on panel, 31.7 × 40.5 cm
Deposit of the Hungarian National Bank
Inv. no. L.3.793

The most famous masters of the veduta (city view) were undoubtedly the eighteenth-century Venetians Canaletto and Bernardo Bellotto. Yet the genre was born not in Venice, but in seventeenth-century Holland, although it was the last of the genres to be formalised. The two greatest exponents in the second half of the seventeenth century were Jan van der Heyden and Gerrit Berckheyde. The longer history of the landscape is explained by the nostalgia among urban dwellers for a taste of nature, a feeling that arose in antiquity and which still lives on today. In both places where the veduta thrived, topographically accurate "city portraits" were produced, as well as imaginary capriccios. This painting probably belongs to the second category. One of the main characteristics of vedute, which sets them apart from the engraved illustrations found in chronicles, is that they do not show the entire city from above, but focus on a detail, whose attraction stems either from featuring a well-known landmark, or from evoking a sense of homeliness. In this diminutive painting, executed in great detail but without pedantry, Van der Heyden shows a square that is open only from the viewer's side, fringed with picturesque buildings whose identity and location cannot be ascertained. Beneath the even light, conjuring up the atmosphere of a sleepy Sunday, are an assortment of figures, walking, sitting or standing around.

Jan van der Heyden was more than just an artist. In his adopted home of Amsterdam he held several official positions, earning the respect of his contemporaries not only for his paintings, but also for introducing street lighting and for designing a water-pumping mechanism for fighting fires.

VILMOS TÁTRAI

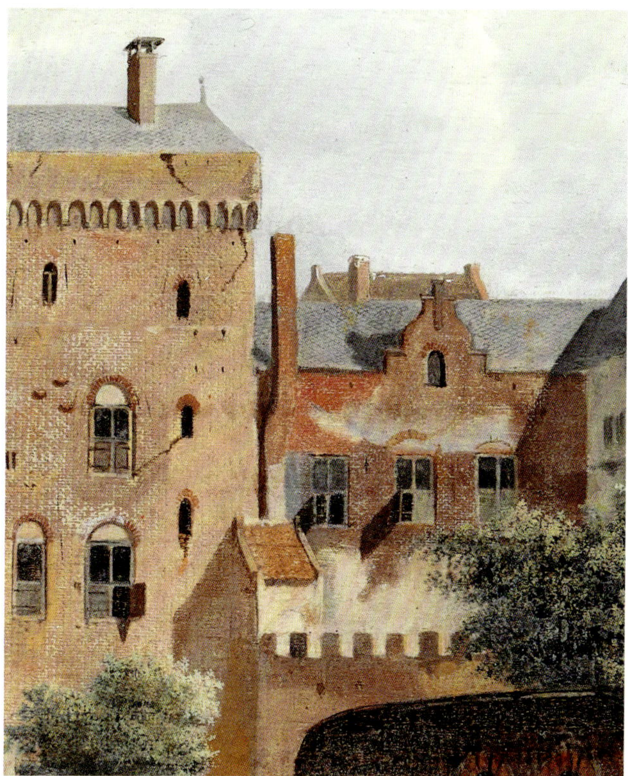

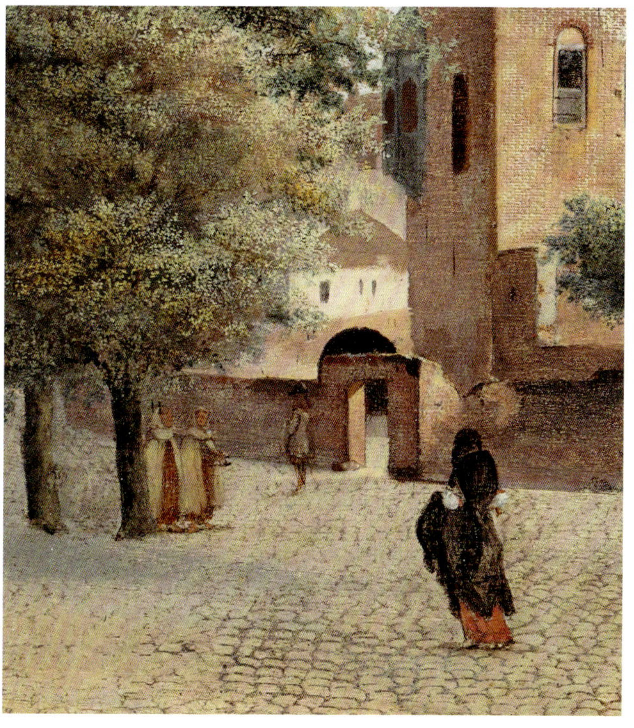

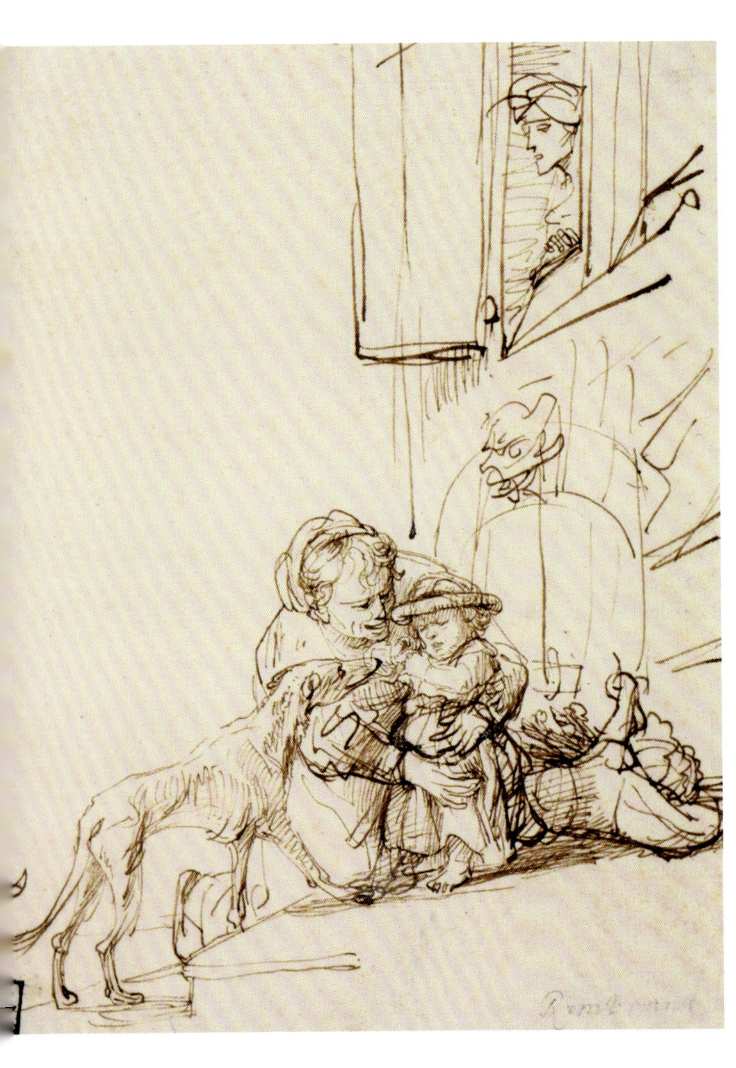

Rembrandt van Rijn (1606–1669)

Woman with a Child Frightened by a Dog

1635–1636

Pen and ink on paper, 182 × 145 mm

Esterházy collection, purchased in 1871

Inv. no. 1589

Rembrandt is the key figure of seventeenth-century Dutch art, and one of the greatest engravers and drawers of all time. He had four children from his wife, Saskia van Uylenburgh, who met an early death; only the youngest of them, Titus, lived to adulthood. In the first years of his marriage Rembrandt was keenly preoccupied with the depiction of women and children: one extant inventory of his goods lists one hundred and thirty-five such drawings. As well as his household, he liked to portray others too, and captured scenes from every-day life in lightning sketches, which did not necessarily serve any other purpose beyond the artist's observation.

In this drawing he brings a charming street scene to life. On the way home from the market a mother comforts her child, frightened by a dog: she kneels by him, embraces him protectively and smiles as she pacifies him. In the Frits Lugt collection in Paris there is a drawing in which the artist (probably still at the scene) put the three figures on paper. In the Budapest sheet Rembrandt elaborated the spontaneous sketch into a genre drawing: the group of figures is tighter-knit, their movements more clarified, and as he conjured up the surroundings, with a few brisk pen-strokes he sketched the steps and the house, with the caricature-like woman looking with curiosity from the window. This version was presumably made in the studio, and yet preserves the nimbleness of the sketches made from life.

ESZTER KARDOS

Pieter Jansz. Saenredam (1597–1665)

The Interior of Nieuwe Kerk in Haarlem

1653
Oil on oak, 86 × 103 cm
Esterházy collection, purchased in 1871
Inv. no. 311

A few decades ago the art history world was buzzing with a provocative theory put forward by an American scholar. According to this still hotly disputed thesis, Dutch art, unlike the Italian tradition, which always told stories, basically strove to observe and describe objects, and ultimately to know the world through experience; one might say this approach was of scientific nature, rather than literary. Whatever one's view of such a generalisation, one thing is certain: a memorial statue to such an artistic attitude could be modelled on Saenredam. He developed a complex working method based on mechanical calculations so that he could depict with documentary fidelity the Protestant churches and town-hall chambers which symbolised the ideals of the young Dutch nation. His paintings were created through long months of painstaking work, and thus are extremely rare and precious, with no more than sixty of them known. But art is never purely documentation, and sure enough not even Saenredam was always perfectly faithful to what he saw. Due to the carefully chosen viewpoints and light conditions, the spaces often appear (as in the present painting) lighter, airier, and more grandiose than the impression from a visit to the location itself. More surprising however is that this image of the Nieuwe Kerk includes several architectural elements which featured only in the plan, but for financial reasons were eventually not executed in the building.

AXEL VÉCSEY

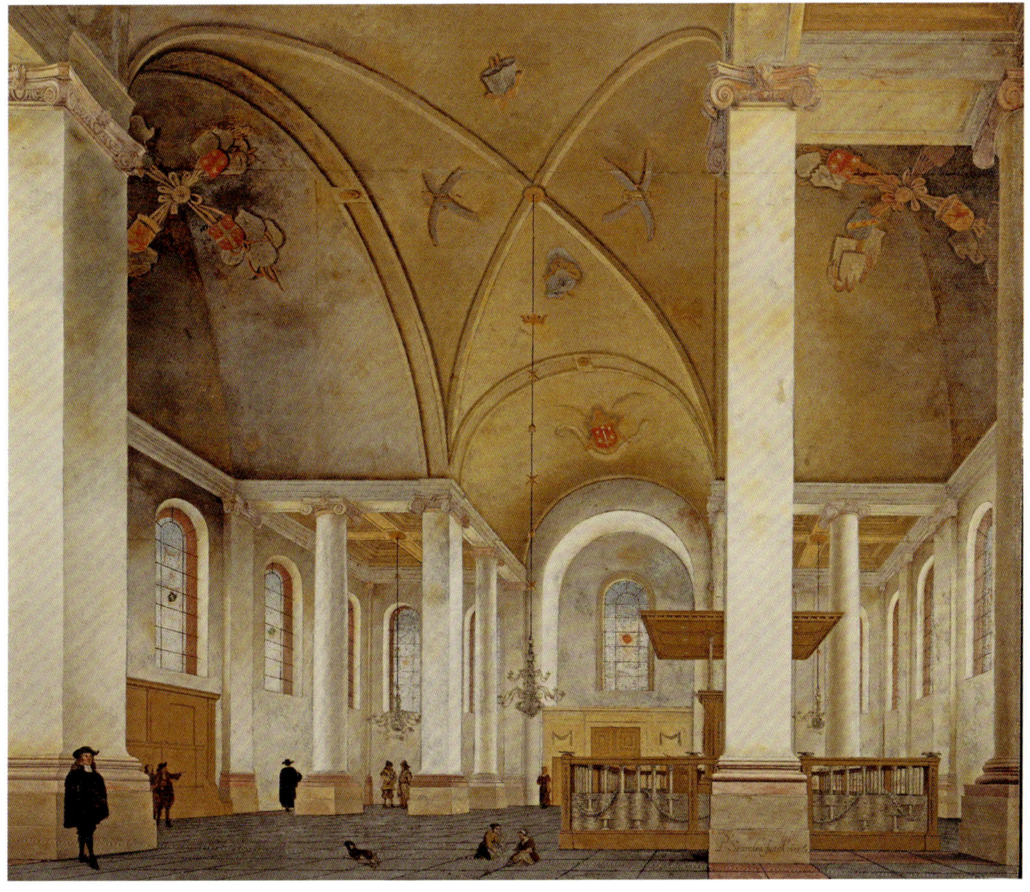

Jan Fyt (1611–1661)

Still Life with Hare and Game Birds

ca. 1640s

Oil on canvas, 62.5 × 86 cm

Esterházy collection, purchased in 1871

Inv. no. 729

Hunting has long been entertainment for the privileged. No wonder then that the genre of painted hunting trophies flourished most in Flanders in Rubens's time, which more than any other era was in the sway of the cult of heaving plenty and worldly extravagance. Surprisingly, though obviously not coincidentally, in the other half of the Netherlands, newly seceded Protestant Holland, an art of the most puritan approach sprang up simultaneously. One might think there would be no exchange between these two worlds, even though their watchful eyes were always fixed on the other – but there, indeed, was.

The prince of game pieces, Jan Fyt visited Holland in 1642, after which the tone of his painting changed considerably. Into the triumphant uproar of brazen baroque there crept more muted, melancholy chords. The magnificent spread of the kill of game here is more a lament to mortality, than an invitation to a vain banquet. The message is completed with a symbol aptly Dutch in its directness: thorns referring to the passion of Christ. But Fijt could not change his spots, and even with its serious content, in this picture the sound of triumph dominates – that of the painter, ostentatiously flaunting his truly compelling skill. And that of his virtuoso brush, which like Proust's famous madeleine, through the eye awakens the other senses too, so that the softness of the splendid hare's fur becomes almost palpable, or we strain to hear the dying warbles of these brilliantly coloured songbirds.

A X E L   V É C S E Y

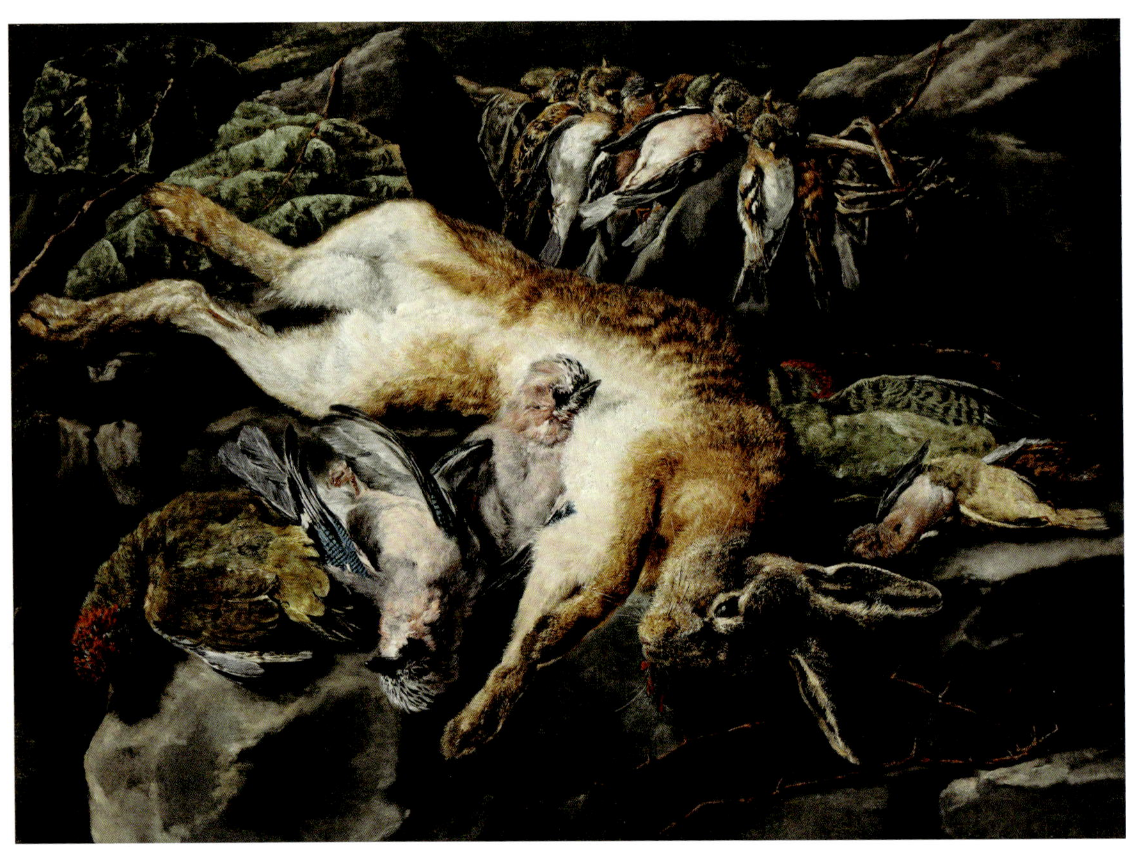

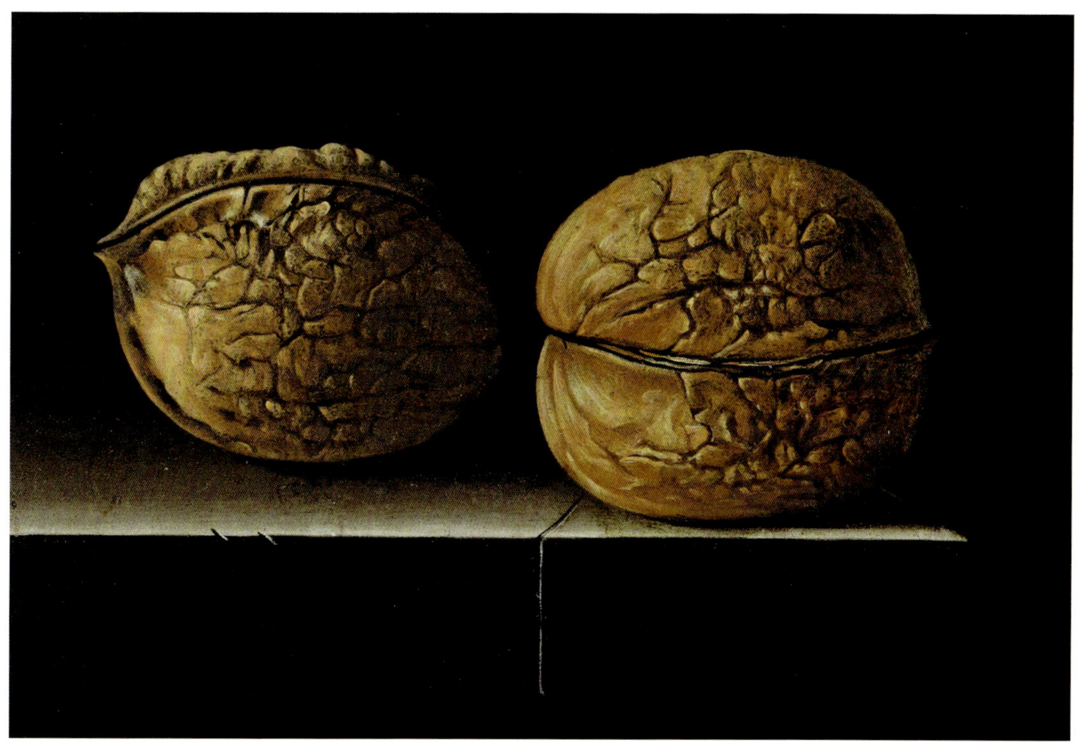

Adriaen Coorte (ca. 1665–1707/1770)

Two Walnuts

1702
Oil on paper, mounted on cardboard, 10.2 × 15.2 cm
Purchased in Budapest, 1975
Inv. no. 75.9

In the bottom left of the painting, on the side of the stone tablet that faces us, the painter's signature and the year 1702 can be read in carefully formed letters and numbers. The master of Middelburg must have been proud of this little painting, which shows two life-size walnuts bathed in glowing light against a dark background, showing all the wrinkles on the hard shells and the lines where the two halves join. In all his still lifes, most of which depicted fruits or sometimes shells, Coorte used very few motifs, but never fewer than in this work. According to the great English researcher of still-life painting, Sam Segal, the painter gives the impression of having observed these walnuts from the perspective of a mouse, which for all its absurdity is an apt idea, generating empathy in the viewer. One of the eternal problems of interpreting art is that, when faced with reductions of this kind, we tend to make judgements from the point of view of minimal art or some other contemporary trend. However, unlike the movements of the twentieth century, there was no ideology of any kind underlying the creation of the Two Walnuts or similar still lifes. Coorte's intent was probably merely to raise his own profile in the competitive world of Dutch still-life painting by producing something extraordinary to catch the eye of potential buyers. Unique achievements of technical prowess and inventiveness, associated with an artist of repute, became highly sought-after among connoisseurs from the sixteenth century onwards, when the golden age of collecting art began. Coorte's innovation was likely regarded as an achievement of this kind.

VILMOS TÁTRAI

Claude Lorrain (Claude Gellée)
(ca. 1604/1605–1682)

Villa in the Roman Campagna

ca. 1646–1647
Oil on canvas, 68.8 × 91 cm
Esterházy collection, purchased in 1871
Inv. no. 708

The life of Claude Lorrain was like a fairytale. He was just twelve when after he set off from his native village in France all the way to Rome. With no experience but a brief apprenticeship in a pastry-cook's at home, there were gaps in his education, to say the least, and he never learnt Italian properly; yet the fashionable, urbane aristocracy adored him, and his pictures were so admired that there was a considerable business forging them. In spite of being a reserved dreamer he attained unparalleled success in the capital of intrigue and envy. He tamed even the archfoe of glory, time: the greatest landscapists of the nineteenth century – the British William Turner, or the Hungarian Károly Markó, still chased Claude's mellow sunlight.

For this is the secret of Claude's art: sunlight which permeates all and gives life. Whether he paints imaginary antique harbours, or the Campagna, the plains surrounding Rome, it is the light which clothes the view in the radiance of the Golden Age, and lends a cosmic dimension to modest settings. It seems as though Virgil's ancient idylls have come to life, though the Renaissance castles dominating the area are much more recent. The castle in this drawing is the famous La Crescenza, which often features in Claude's pictures, and following his example later artists (such as Corot) were also fond of painting it. Some believe the painting shows the same castle too, but this building, though assembled from familiar elements, is a product of the imagination.

AXEL VÉCSEY

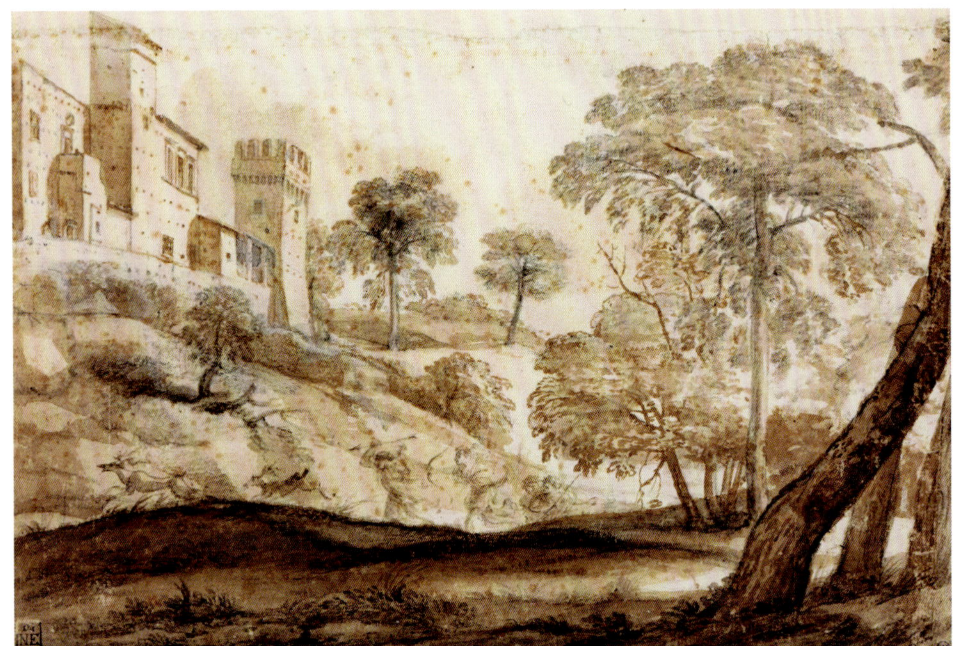

Deerhunting

ca. 1645
Black chalk, brown ink
and wash on paper,
233 × 329 mm
Esterházy collection,
purchased in 1871
Inv. no. 2849

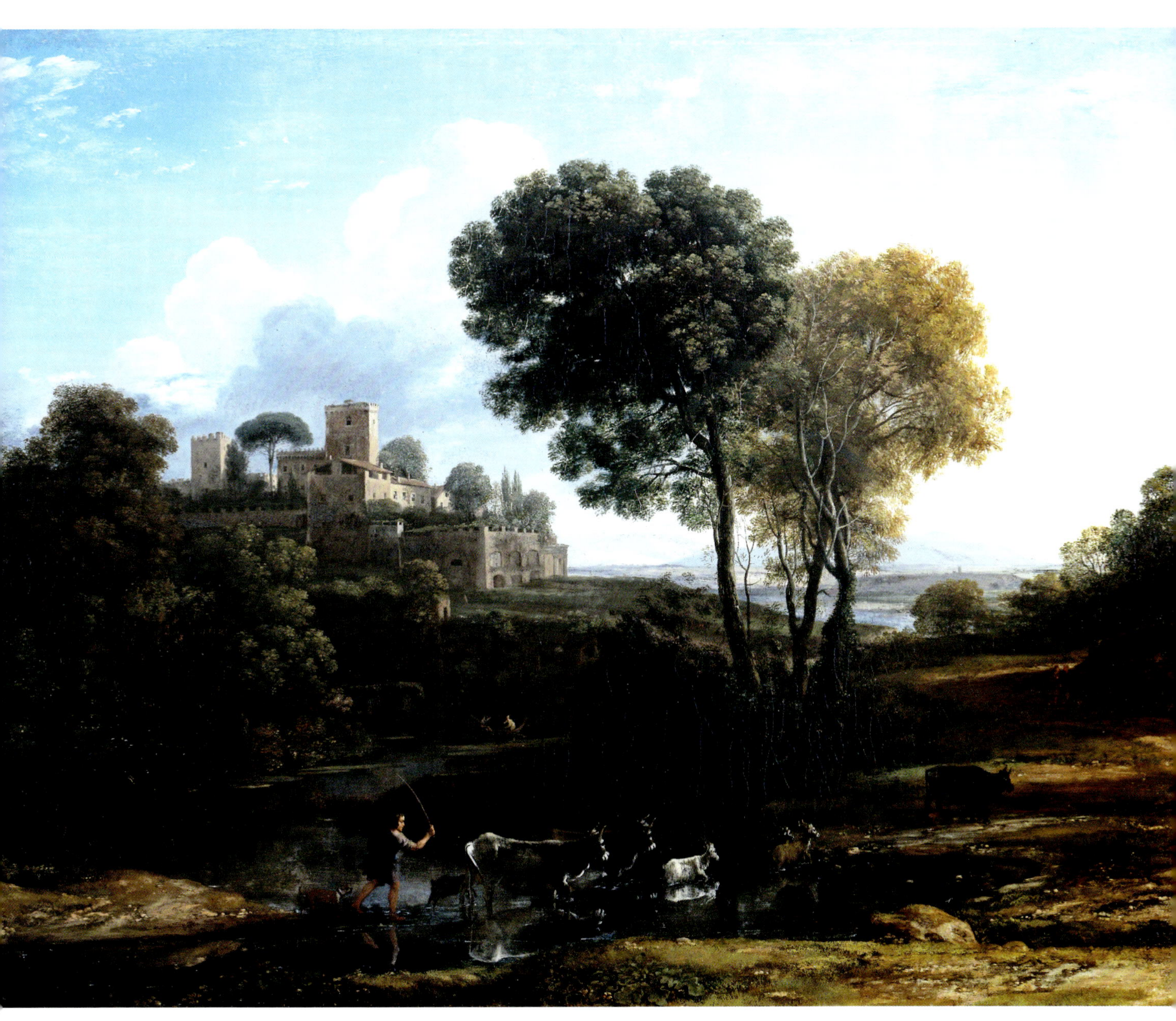

Jacob Bogdani (before 1660–1724)

Fruit Still Life with Parrots and a White Cockatoo

1710s

Oil on canvas, 98 × 128.5 cm

Purchased from an English private collection, 1907

Inv. no. 3681

Jacob Bogdani specialised in still lifes and animal paintings, both popular genres during his lifetime. Born in Hungary to a Protestant family, the painter learnt his trade in Amsterdam, one of the main centres of still-life painting at the time. In 1688, fully trained and experienced, he moved to England, where he soon amassed a wealth of commissions from members of the aristocracy and even the royal family, maturing into a successful and highly esteemed artist. He was considered a Hungarian painter, and for a long time he signed his paintings with the epithet "Hungarus". He also maintained contact with his compatriots, exchanging letters with, among others, the outstanding typographer and printer, Miklós Misztótfalusi Kis.

In England, Bogdani initially painted still lifes with flowers and fruits, and then from the 1700s he achieved popularity with his bird paintings, which followed the Dutch fashion. He would combine familiar wild ducks, geese, magpies or pigeons with more exotic, brightly feathered birds, such as cockatoos and other parrots, set in landscape surroundings, often with aesthetically arranged fruits. Collecting exotic wildfowl was a hobby among wealthy aristocrats in those days; one of Bogdani's clients, Admiral George Churchill, kept a collection of birds in Windsor, where the artist could paint directly "from nature". This painting is an example of some interesting birds and an array of different fruits composed in an elegant English country garden. With their colourful plumage, the birds appear as elegant characters in a genre painting, engaging in polite conversation.

ZSUZSANNA BODA

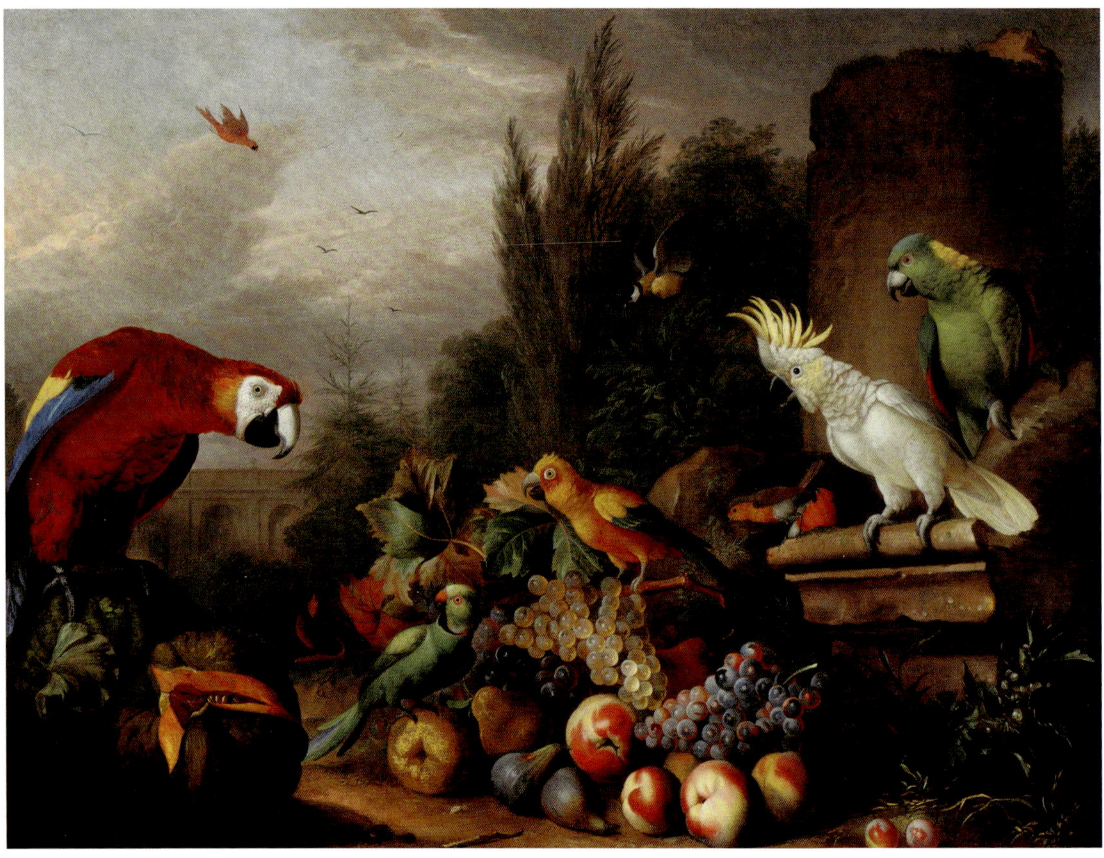

Ádám Mányoki (1673–1757)

Portrait
of Prince Francis II Rákóczi

1712
Oil on canvas, 75.5 × 67.5 cm
Gift from Marcell Nemes, 1925
Inv. no. 6001

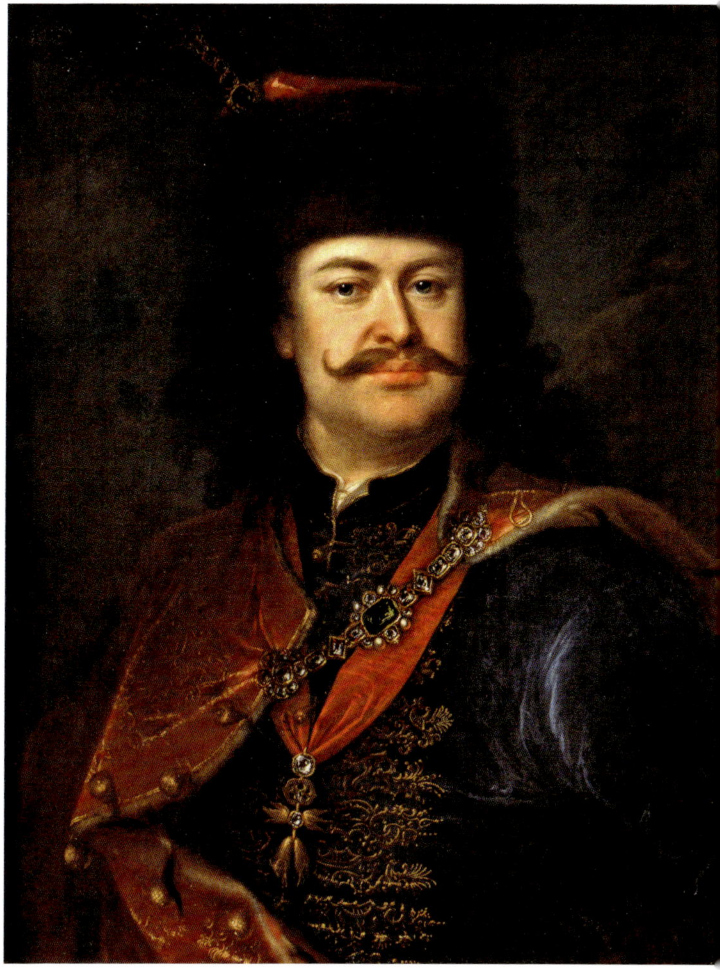

In the modern public consciousness, the name of Ádám Mányoki is closely associated with Prince Francis II Rákóczi, although in his own time the artist, who was born in Hungary and raised in German lands, was better known as court painter to Augustus II the Strong, King of Poland and Elector of Saxony. Mányoki's oeuvre consisted mostly of German court portraiture, and much of his output can still be found in German collections, in the places where the artist was once active.

Mányoki met Rákóczi in autumn 1707, and the prince engaged the services of the painter for a substantial annual salary. The high esteem in which Mányoki was held is demonstrated by the fact that, as a member of the prince's circle of aristocrats and intellectuals, the artist also performed diplomatic tasks for the cause of independence. One mission took him to Holland in 1709, where he served as a courier and printed and distributed pamphlets. This portrait is a summary, as it were, of the knowledge of Dutch painting that Mányoki acquired at the time, which, besides numerous artistic innovations, can be seen above all in the refinement of his technique, his use of glazing as a means for creating form, and a handling of light as a compositional tool that was completely new for this artist.

This is an iconic work of Hungarian baroque portrait painting, not only because of who the prince was, but also because of the intensive combined effect of natural dignity and an exceptional personality, which cannot be found elsewhere in Mányoki's works. The portrait was executed in Gdansk, Rákóczi's first home during his exile, where Mányoki painted the prince as a private citizen, living incognito, surrounded by a modest court and withdrawn from politics.

ENIKŐ BUZÁSI

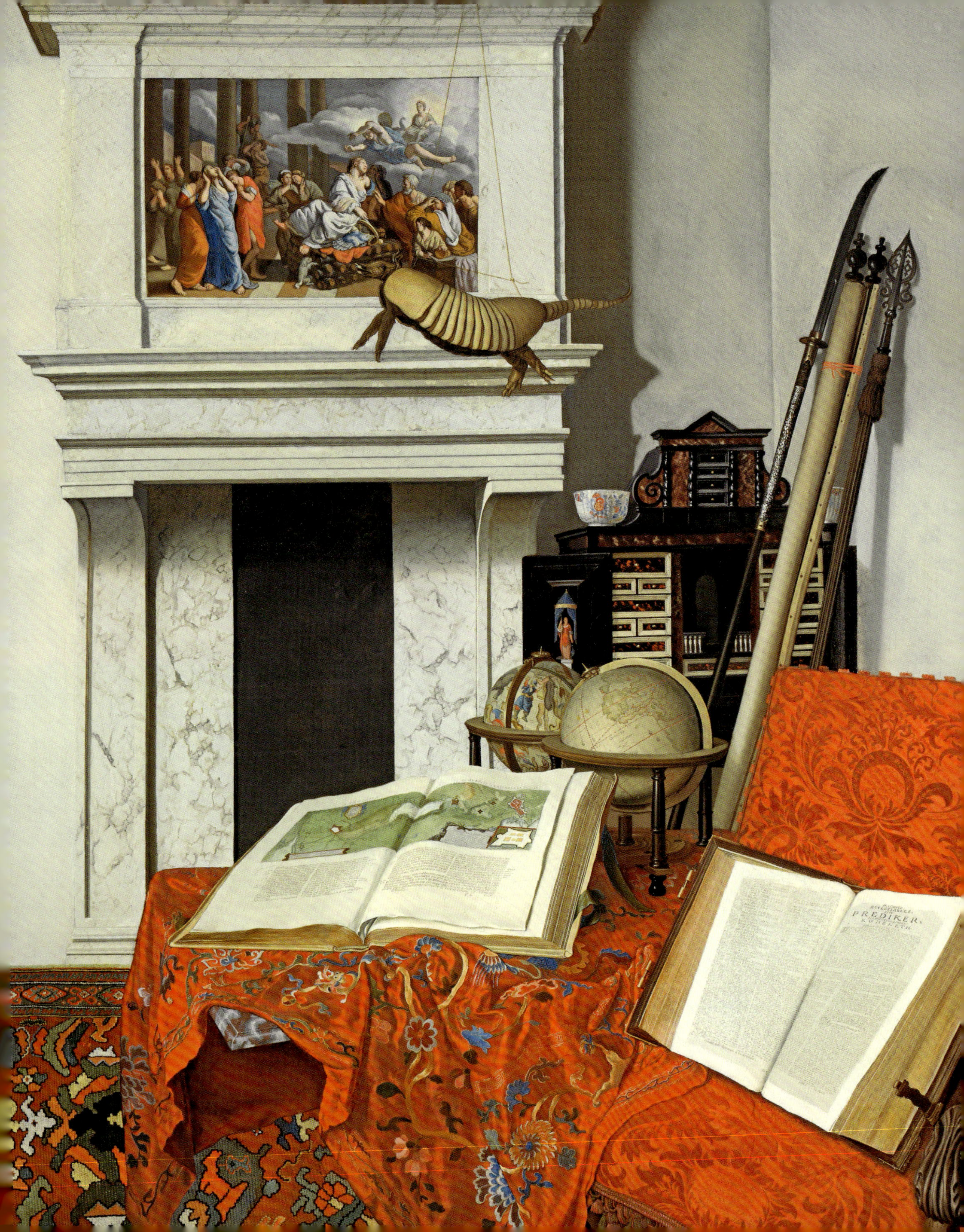

PREDIKER

Jan van der Heyden (1637–1712)

Corner of a Room with Curiosities

1712
Oil on canvas, 43 × 35.8 cm
Esterházy collection, purchased in 1871
Inv. no. 201

The Bible in the foreground is open at the famous line from Ecclesiastes: "Vanity of vanities, all is vanity". As if a stern lecturer were explaining with a cane in his hand, the book seems to force the message upon us: all earthly knowledge and beauty are futile, for in the end comes death, and all that man has accumulated vanishes.

Such "vanitas still lifes" have a long tradition, though initially they condemned only revelry. Here however the objects represent the entire worldly culture, not just the opulent but also the noble. We set out from Willem Blaeu's atlas, the origin of every Dutch expedition, which lies open where the country was "born": the first victory of the war of independence was won at Bergen. Then we are taken on a journey over all the routes of the glorious Dutch merchant fleets, with a Turkish carpet, Chinese silk and porcelain, Japanese weapons and a stuffed armadillo from South America. Nor is classical culture, the cradle of European civilization, absent: above the fireplace is the tragedy of Dido, and the German cabinet is decorated with an image of Minerva. Finally, terrestrial and celestial globes raise the ensemble to the universal dimension. Van der Heyden painted this summative masterpiece at the age of seventy-five, the year he died, and the concept is obviously linked to the sense of the end drawing near. Though he may have felt it vanity, he did after all make a final display of the virtuoso skill which has protected his name from oblivion ever since.

AXEL VÉCSEY

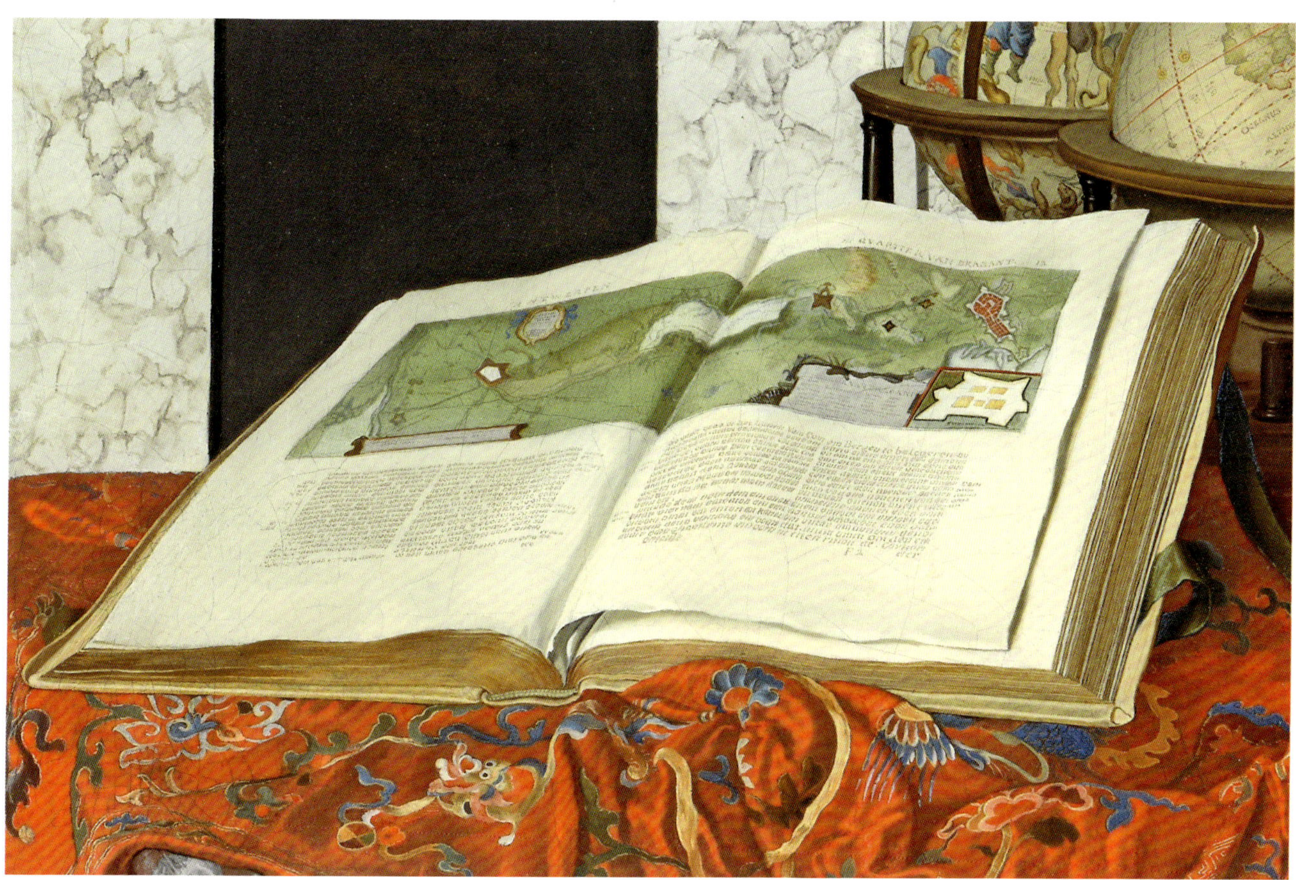

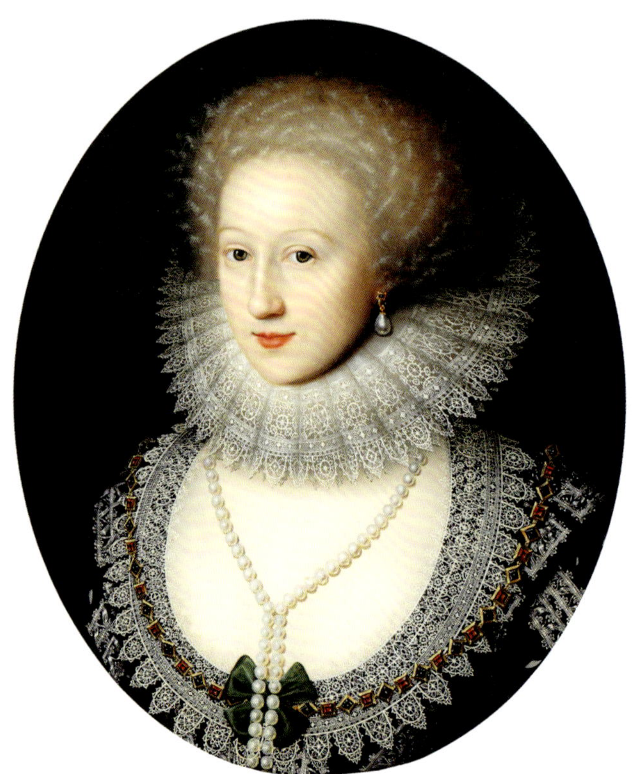

William Larkin (ca. 1585–1619)

Portrait of a Lady

ca. 1613–1616
Oil on oak, 57.5 × 44.1 cm
Purchased in London, 2016
Inv. no. 2017.1

The demand for portraits among the ruling and aristocratic classes of England was enormous. It is not by chance that one of the three national galleries in London specialises in portraits. The golden age of English portraiture was the eighteenth century, with Gainsborough at its forefront. Whenever demand could not be met by home-grown artists, the sitters turned to foreign painters. The features of King Henry VIII were immortalised by Holbein, for example, while Charles I and his family and courtiers were painted by Van Dyck. Between these two reigns, during the Elizabethan and Jacobean periods, a number of English portraitists were active, and William Larkin was the last of these, chronologically but not in terms of quality. The recent acquisition by the Collection of Old Master Paintings is a bust by Larkin of an aristocratic lady. We would be wrong to interpret the model's smile as a reflection of her character. It was important, to both the artist and the client, for the subject of the portrait to be recognisable, but no effort was made to convey her spirit or personality. A member of a blue-blooded family turns to us with her inexpressive gaze, wearing the mask of protocol as she prepares to take her place in the ancestors' gallery. Her head, crowned with her hair in curls, is given just as much emphasis as her dress, which is befitting of someone of such high social stature, with her lace décolletage adorned not only with a ribbon, but with priceless gemstones. The string of pearls around her neck and her pearl earring also grab our attention. Her face is framed with a splendid lace collar, which had fallen out of fashion by the second half of the 1610s. This is one of the details that enables us to estimate the date when the painting was made.

VILMOS TÁTRAI

Anthony van Dyck (1599–1641)

Wedding Portrait
of Mary Henrietta Stuart

1641
Oil on canvas, 158.2 × 108.6 cm
Purchased in London, 2019
Inv. no. 2019.2

Van Dyck deployed a rich repertory of artistic tools to convey the innate superiority of his aristocratic models. With a supremely assured hand, he adjusted every pose and gesture, every facial expression, every garment and curtain, architecture, colour and light, to win the delighted approval of his clients. Never before had any artist so convincingly captured the appearance of relaxed elegance, and even after him, only Gainsborough had the ability to match his accomplishment. But what to do when the model is both from royal stock and still a child? Van Dyck took up the challenge undauntedly. What do children enjoy more than imitating adults? Isn't dressing up and role-playing one of their favourite games? Looking out at us from the canvas, the nine-year-old princess in this portrait is a true child. The ladylike way she holds her hands, the ringlets in her hair, her pearl necklace, the coral-pink dress with silver embroidery and lace collar and cuffs, as well as the green curtain drawn to the side, are all accessories to the role she is playing, even if we know that this game will soon turn serious. The girl is not particularly pretty, but for all her politesse and her adherence to the rules of court etiquette, her childish charm and innocence shine through. It must be added that, when it comes to shaping our overall impression, the role of the ethereal, poetic colouring of the work cannot be overestimated.

This portrait of the daughter of King Charles I of England, one of Van Dyck's last completed works, was made to commemorate her dynastic marriage to the fourteen-year-old William II, future Prince of Orange, son of the stadtholder of the Netherlands.

VILMOS TÁTRAI

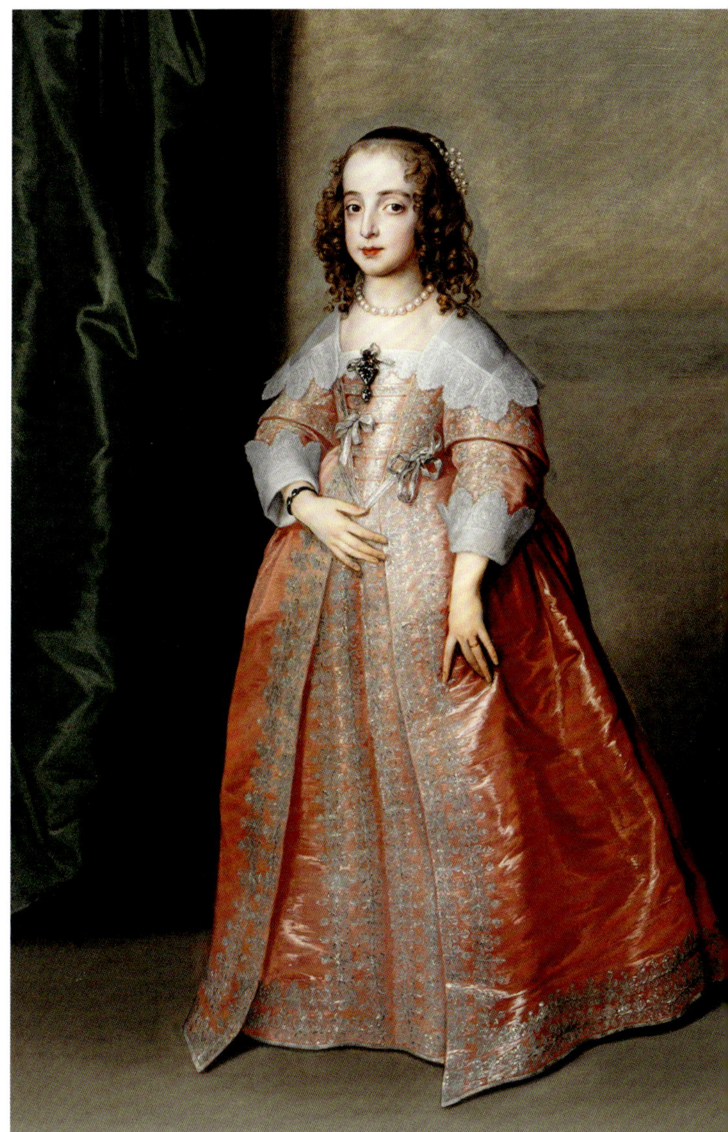

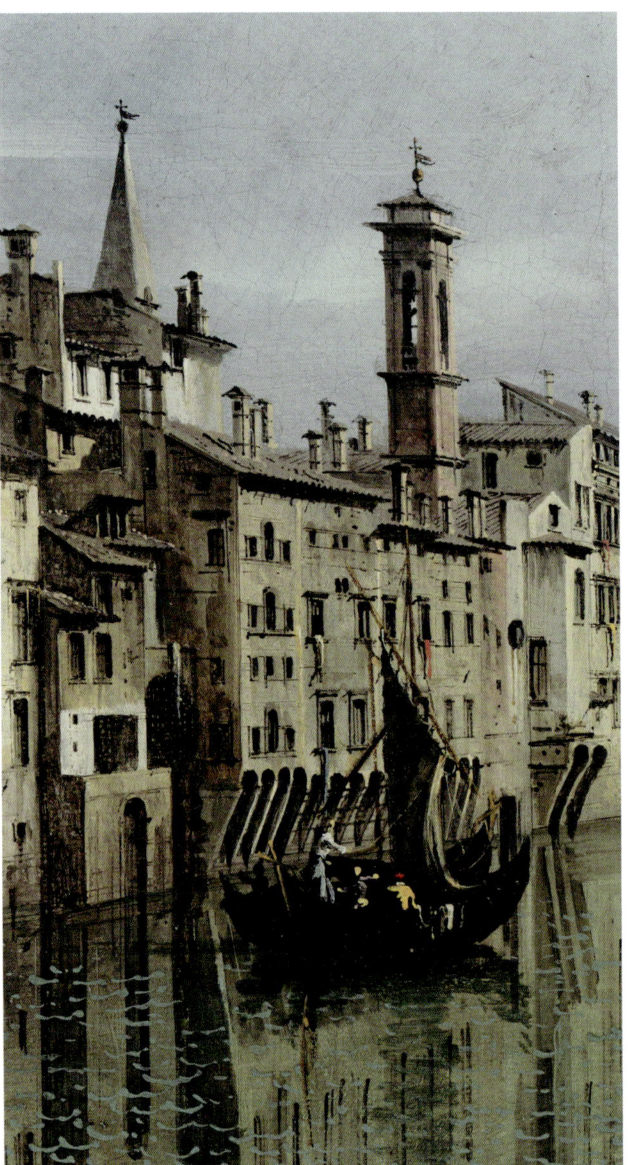

Bernardo Bellotto (1721–1780)

The Arno in Florence

1740
Oil on canvas, 62 × 90 cm
Esterházy collection, purchased in 1871
Inv. no. 647

By the end of the eighteenth century Venice was living from its past glories. The main source of income in the city had become tourism, and where two centuries ago the crews of victorious fleets of ships had marched, now adventurers, courtesans and cardsharps teemed around the British, German, and Hungarian gallants. Tourism gave birth to a new genre of painting: the cityscape, which the visitor could take home as a souvenir, there to conjure up the world of Casanova and Vivaldi.

The master who created the genre was Antonio Canale, known as Canaletto, though his nephew Bernardo Bellotto, by no means fell short of him in quality. Yet while the uncle incessantly painted the familiar corners of Venice (a decade in London aside), Bellotto became a chronicler of the whole of Europe, from Rome to Vienna, from Dresden to Warsaw. Yet, albeit made in Florence, this enthralling youthful masterpiece cannot help but reveal where the artist learnt to look and to see. The precisely constructed lines of the buildings claim that we have here a document of photographic fidelity, yet the River Arno seems to don the mask of the Grand Canal in Venice. The more thickset forms of Florentine architecture are delicately, almost imperceptibly elongated, and the boats seem to wilfully imitate gondolas. By far the most noticeable give-away is the magical light sparkling on the surface of the water: perhaps it does indeed sparkle this way in Florence too, but only in Venice can it be observed so closely.

AXEL VÉCSEY

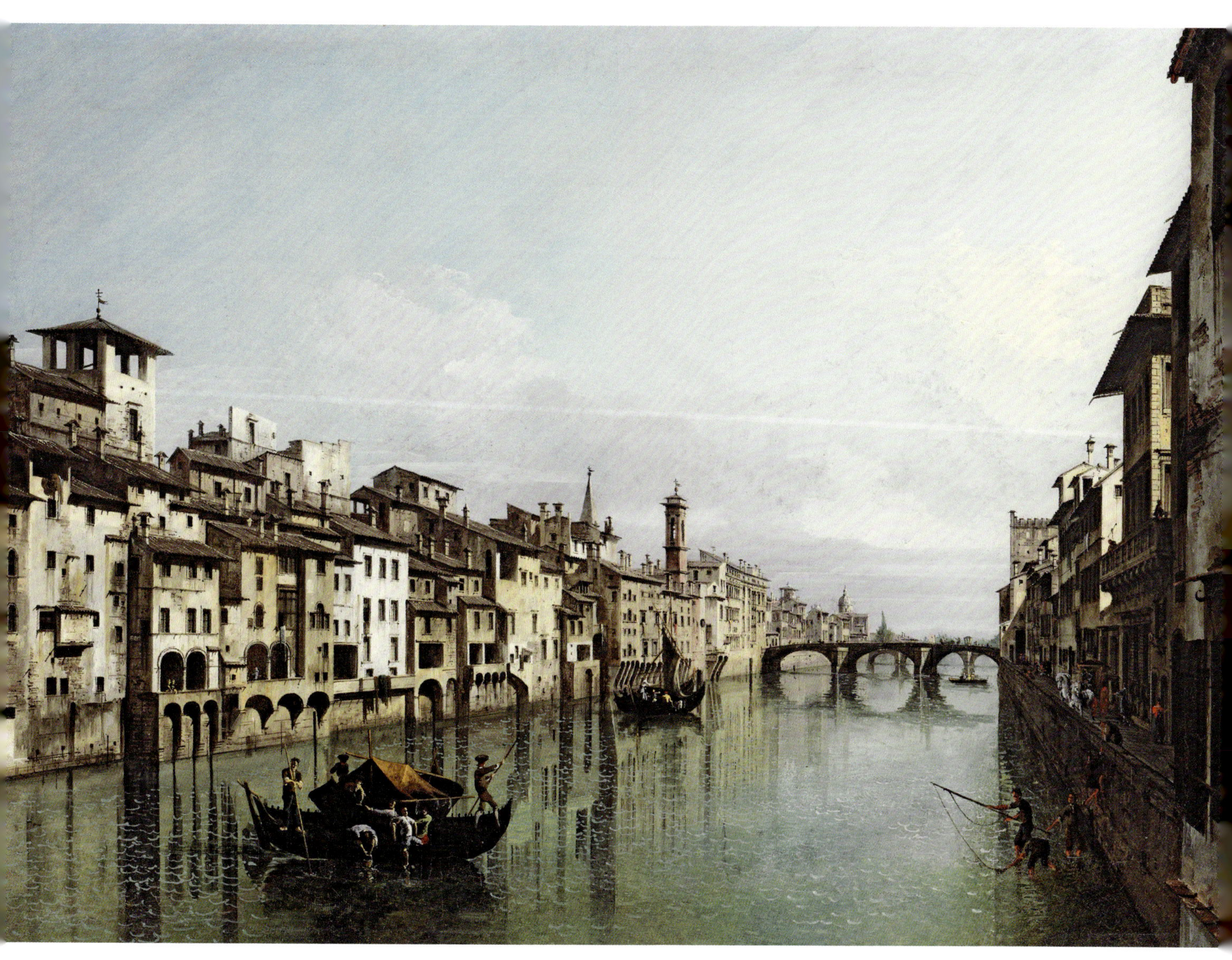

Giovanni Battista Tiepolo (1696–1770)

Saint James the Great Conquering the Moors

ca. 1749
Oil on canvas, 317 × 163 cm
Esterházy collection, purchased in 1871
Inv. no. 649

Giovanni Domenico Tiepolo (1727–1804)

Saint James

1749–1750
Red and white pastel on paper, 322 × 253 mm
Gift of Simon Meller, 1929
Inv. no. 1929–2164

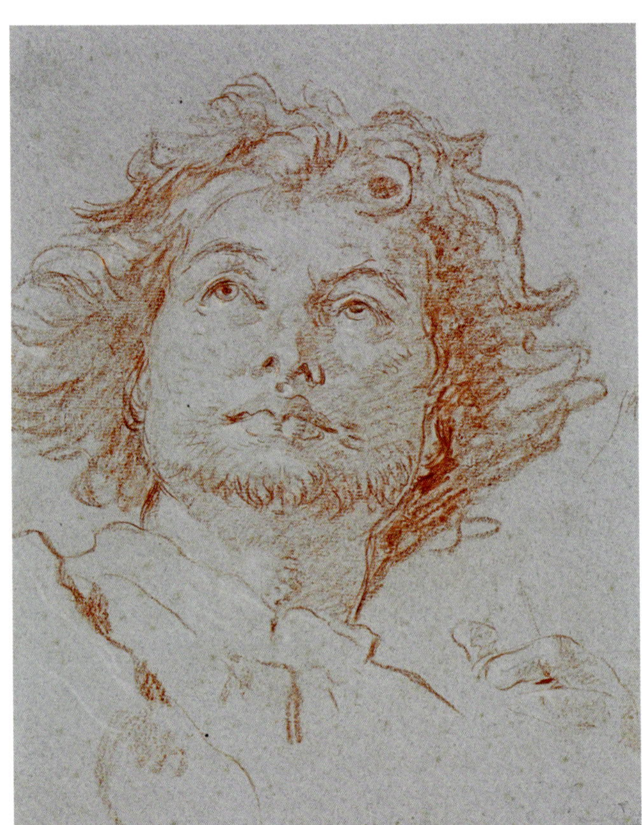

"It is as if God created Tiepolo for us. He follows in Veronese's path, all spirit, fire ablaze, his colours are marvellous, his speed astonishing", gushed the Swedish ambassador from Venice. Although the Stockholm job came to naught, Tiepolo was sought after by every court in Europe, and he produced legions of masterpieces from Madrid to Würzburg. His monumental picture of Saint James of Compostela was also made for an international commission. Ricardo Wall, Spanish ambassador to London (who later, despite being Irish, became prime minister), intended it for the altar of the embassy chapel. In the capital of Protestant England the Roman rite could be practised only in chapels of Catholic embassies, which thus became public spaces, displays of the power of these nations.

The metaphor for Hispania's historic mission, the triumphant Battle of Clavijo in 844, seemed the perfect choice of subject for the location: the nation's patron saint appears as a vision to lead the Christians to victory against the pagans. Once finished, the painting was celebrated at a public exhibition in San Marco in Venice, and Tiepolo's son reproduced prints of it. (The head study was made for the engraving.) Yet it was not, finally, installed in its intended place: the Spanish turned shy at the sight of the enormous battlehorse dominating most of the picture, which when placed on an altar would, they opined, provide fodder for the Protestants' accusations of idolatry in the Catholic veneration of images.

A X E L   V É C S E Y

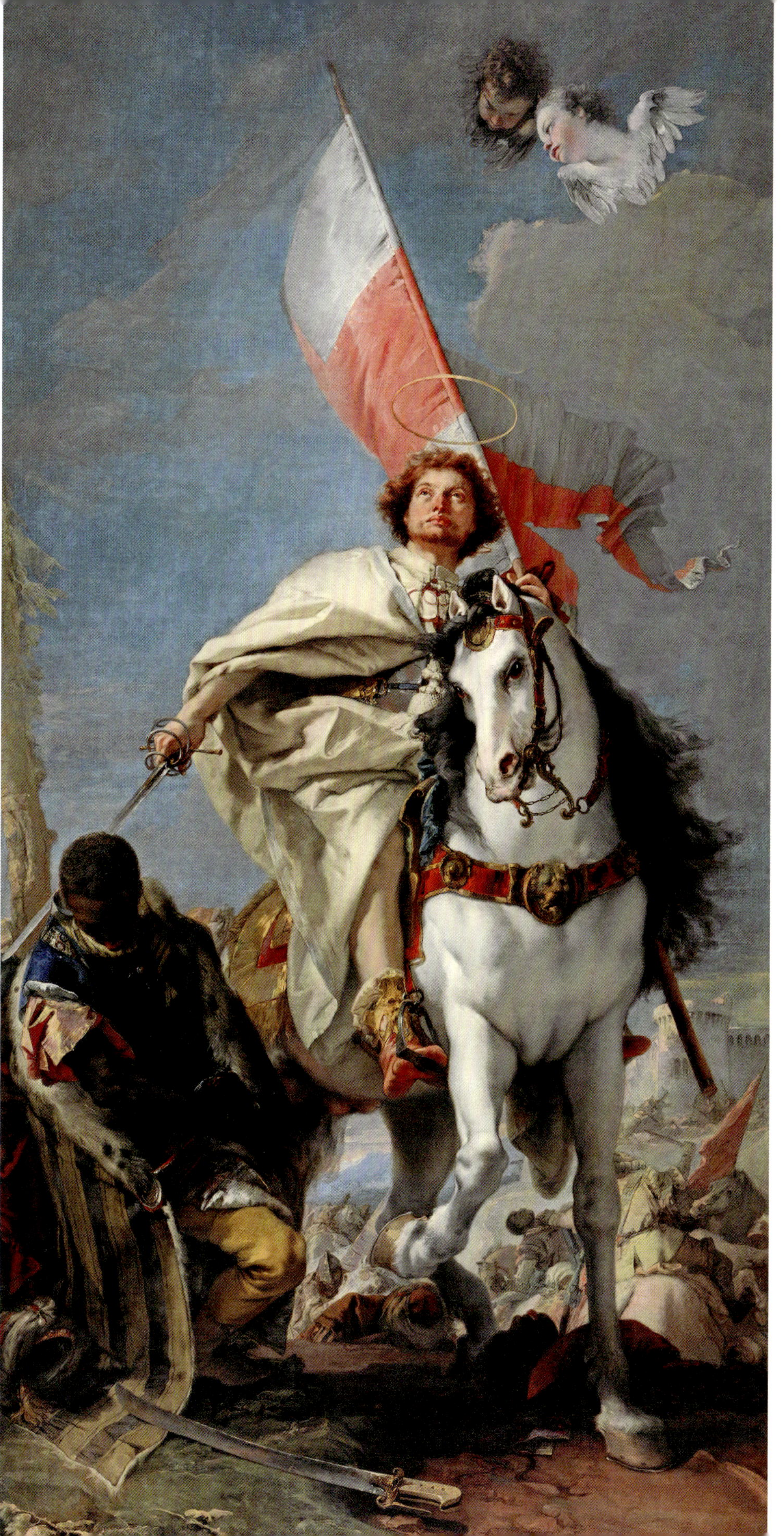

Franz Xaver Messerschmidt (1736–1783)

Character Head: The Gentle, Quiet Sleep

1777–1783
Tin, 43 × 22.5 × 24 cm
Bequest of Jenő Zichy, 1906
Inv. no. 53.656

Character Head: Childish Weeping

1771–1775
Tin and lead alloy, 45 × 22 × 25 cm
Purchased in Vienna, 1894
Inv. no. 51.936

Character Head: The Yawner

1777–1781
Tin, 42 × 21.5 × 26 cm
Bequest of Jenő Zichy, 1906
Inv. no. 53.655

The upward path of Messerschmidt's career was brought to a halt by a mysterious illness. He was tipped to be professor of sculpture in the Academy of Arts in Vienna, and was a favourite sculptor in the imperial court, when he was suddenly pensioned off on account of his mental illness. Upset, he took leave of Vienna for good and settled in Pozsony (today Bratislava, Slovakia). It was here that most of his *Character Heads* were made, a unique series of about fifty busts. Much headscratching has gone on over the interpretation of the busts, which after the sculptor's death were displayed as a raree-show in the Prater in Vienna. Initially they were associated with the artist's presumed schizophrenia, and in a Freudian vein they were seen as a reflection of the subconscious. Others suggested that the heads were inspired by the peculiar methods of the doctor Franz Anton Mesmer, a close friend of the artist's, which are held to be the forerunner of psychotherapy. Mesmer believed the root of psychological and even indirectly physical diseases was the disorder of the magnetic field of the nervous system. During the sessions Messerschmidt would have seen such extreme emotions on the patients' faces. It is true, however, that in Messerschmidt's time the representation of human emotions was a central issue of art. As a teacher at the academy he certainly knew contemporary studies of expressions, thus in spite of their traditional titles the heads explore various, sometimes extreme grimaces rather than human characters.

MIRIAM SZŐCS

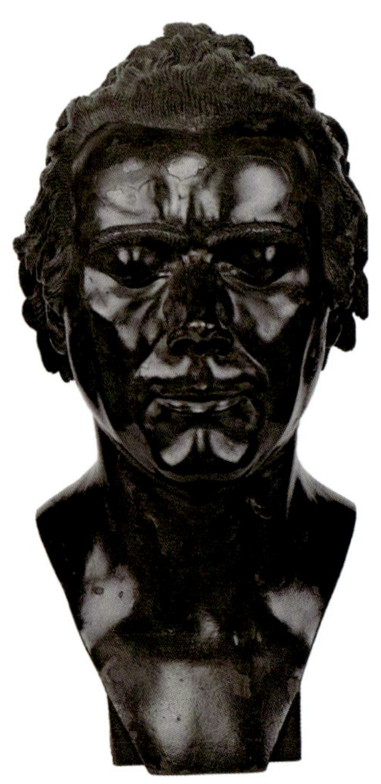
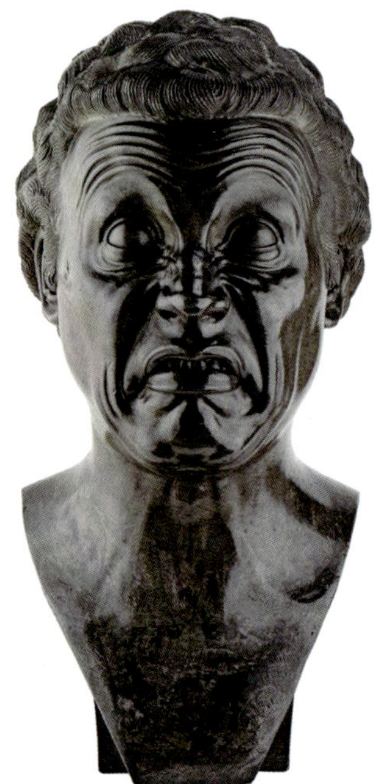
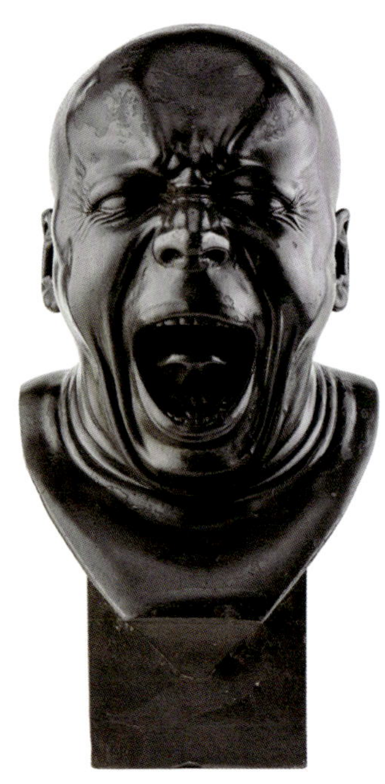

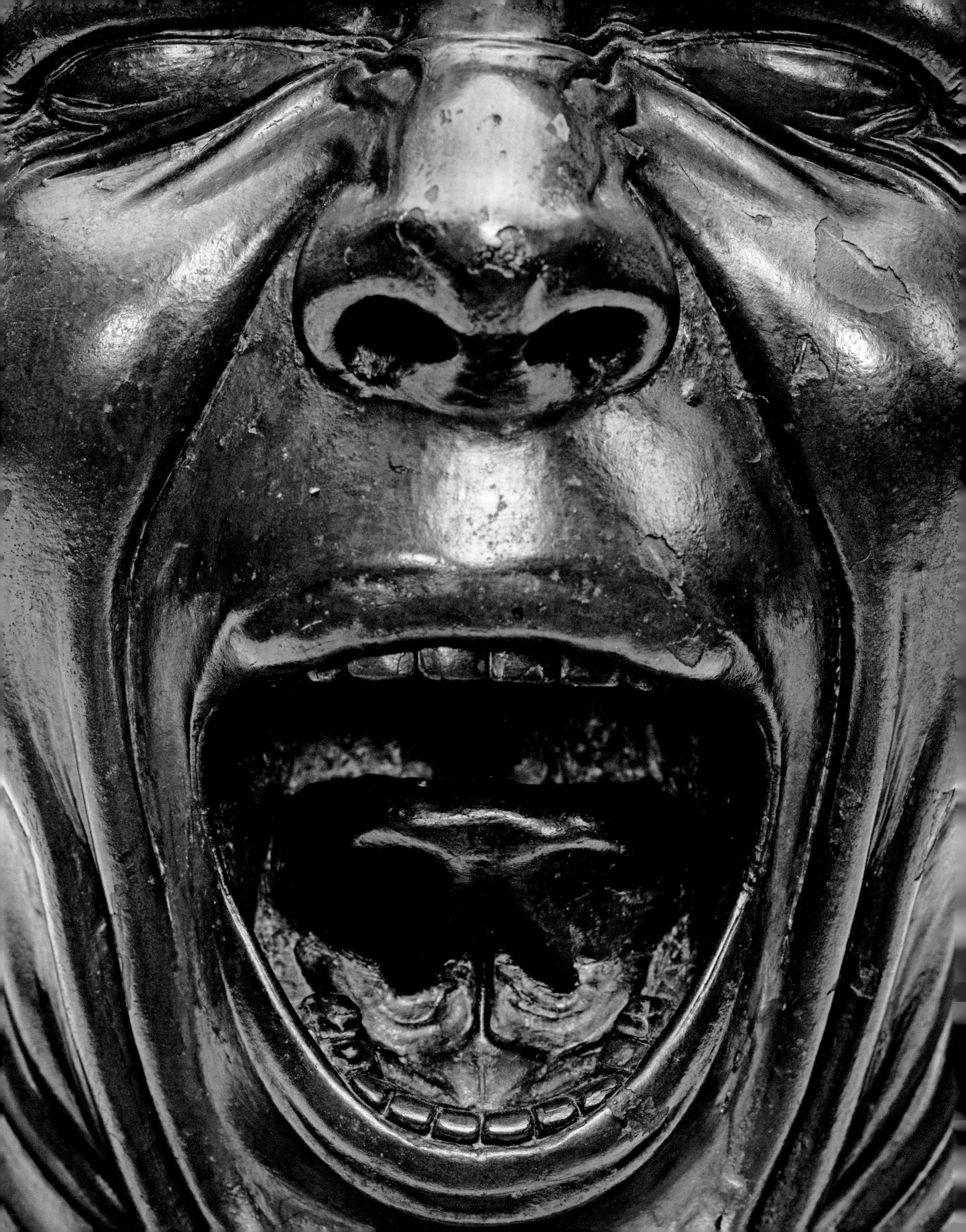

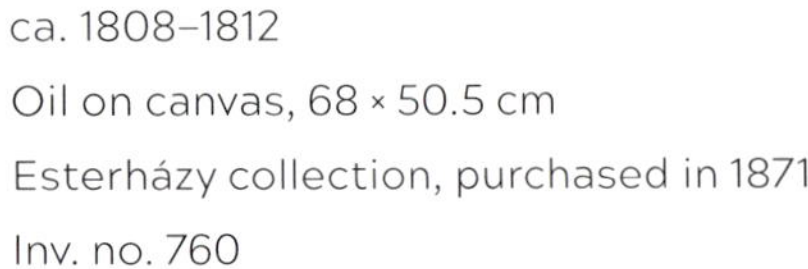

The Water Carrier

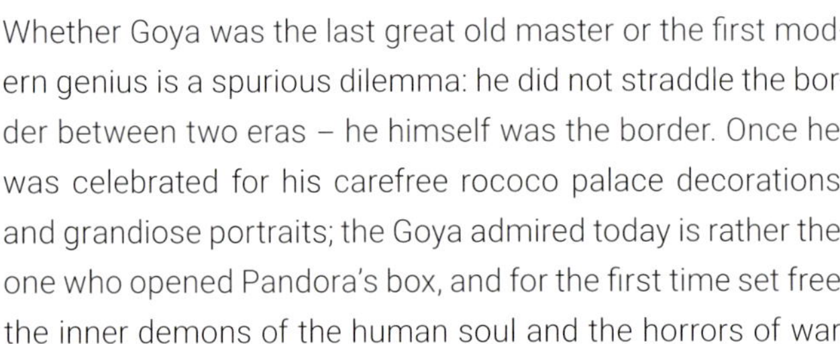

ca. 1808–1812

Oil on canvas, 68 × 50.5 cm

Esterházy collection, purchased in 1871

Inv. no. 760

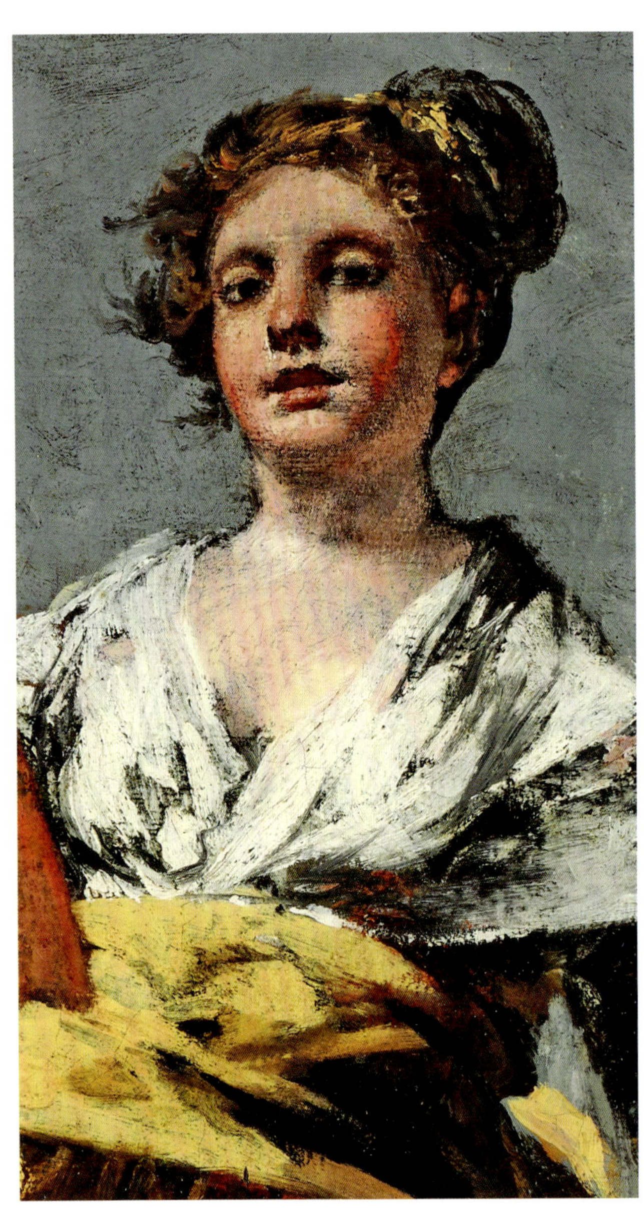

Whether Goya was the last great old master or the first modern genius is a spurious dilemma: he did not straddle the border between two eras – he himself was the border. Once he was celebrated for his carefree rococo palace decorations and grandiose portraits; the Goya admired today is rather the one who opened Pandora's box, and for the first time set free the inner demons of the human soul and the horrors of war.

The Water Carrier bears the imprint of both Goyas. At first glance it seems a simple rustic genre picture: a somewhat rough-hewn, yet ethereally charming young girl carries water and food to someone. A forerunner to this figure can be found on tapestry designs twenty years earlier, which Goya made for the Madrid court, at a moment of European optimism, when it seemed that the Enlightenment would bring general welfare. But then all hell was breaking loose and by the time the picture was made Spain had been sacked by Napoleon's troops. The idyllic world of the tapestries had gone, and the air is charged with a surly restlessness instead. Indeed, it is war we see here: the water is needed by the nameless heroes of Zaragoza, who held up the invaders practically with their bare hands. It is not suffering that dominates here, as in the famous *Disasters of War* prints. With a pathos unusual for Goya, the figure of the girl is ennobled almost to the status of a memorial: a statue to the stubborn, ordinary heroism of a people seeking to set the world back on the right track.

AXEL VÉCSEY

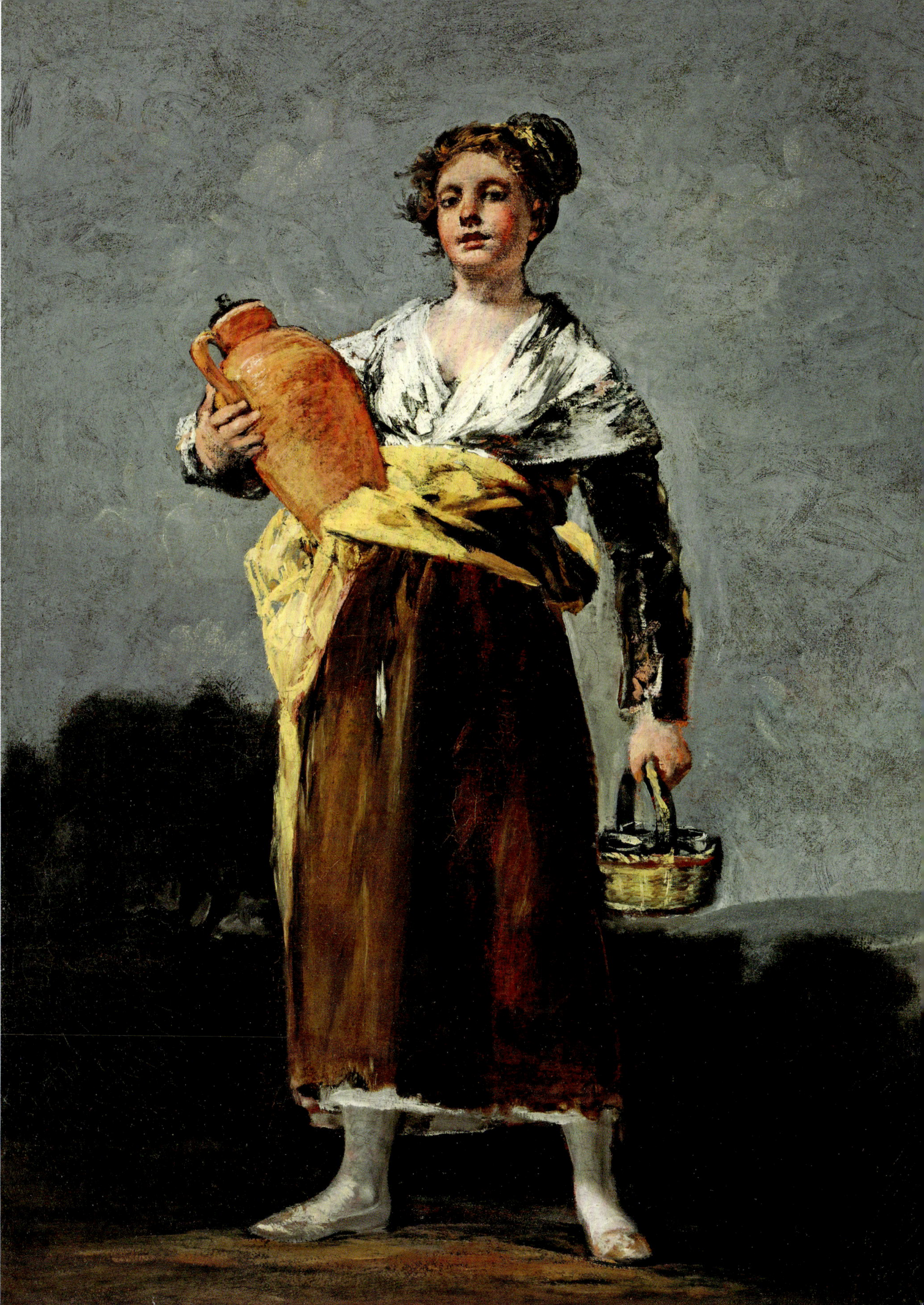

INDEX